REGIONALISM IN EAST ASIA

Why has it flourished since 2000
and how far will it go?

REGIONALISM IN EAST ASIA

Why has it flourished since 2000 and how far will it go?

Richard Pomfret

University of Adelaide, Australia

 **World Scientific**

NEW JERSEY · LONDON · SINGAPORE · BEIJING · SHANGHAI · HONG KONG · TAIPEI · CHENNAI

Published by

World Scientific Publishing Co. Pte. Ltd.

5 Toh Tuck Link, Singapore 596224

USA office: 27 Warren Street, Suite 401-402, Hackensack, NJ 07601

UK office: 57 Shelton Street, Covent Garden, London WC2H 9HE

British Library Cataloguing-in-Publication Data
A catalogue record for this book is available from the British Library.

REGIONALISM IN EAST ASIA
Why Has It Flourished Since 2000 and How Far Will It Go?

ISBN-13 978-981-4304-32-0
ISBN-10 981-4304-32-8

Typeset by Stallion Press
Email: enquiries@stallionpress.com

Printed in Singapore.

Table of Contents

List of Figures

List of Tables

Abbreviations and Acronyms

AANZFTA	ASEAN–Australia–New Zealand Free Trade Agreement
ABMI	Asian Bond Market Initiative
ADB	Asian Development Bank
AEC	ASEAN Economic Community
AFTA	ASEAN Free Trade Area
AIA	ASEAN Investment Area
AIP	ASEAN Industrial Project
AMF	(proposed) Asian Monetary Fund
APEC	Asia–Pacific Economic Cooperation
APTA	Asia–Pacific Trade Agreement
ARF	ASEAN Regional Forum
ASA	Association of Southeast Asia
ASEAN	Association of Southeast Asian Nations
ASEAN5	The original ASEAN members (Indonesia, Malaysia, Philippines, Singapore and Thailand)
ASEAN+3	ASEAN, China, Japan and South Korea
ASEAN+6	ASEAN, China, Japan, South Korea, Australia, India and New Zealand
ASEM	Asia–Europe Meeting
AUSFTA	Australia–US Free Trade Agreement
BIMP-EAGA	Brunei, Indonesia, Malaysia, Philippines East ASEAN Growth Area
BIMSTEC	Bangladesh, India, Myanmar, Sri Lanka and Thailand Economic Cooperation
BIS	Bank of International Settlements
CACM	Central American Common Market

CAREC	Central Asian Regional Economic Cooperation
CENTO	Central Treaty Organization
CEPEA	Comprehensive Economic Partnership in East Asia
CER	Closer Economic Relations (between Australia and New Zealand)
CGE model	computable general equilibrium model
cif	value of an imported good including cost, insurance and freight
CLMV	the four newest and poorest ASEAN members: Cambodia, Laos, Myanmar and Vietnam
CMEA	Committee for Mutual Economic Assistance (Comecon)
CMI	Chiang Mai Initiative (CMIM = CMI Multilateralization in 2009)
EAC	East African Community
EAEC	East Asia Economic Caucus
EAS	East Asia Summit (of the ASEAN+6 countries)
EBRD	European Bank for Reconstruction and Development
ECAFE	UN Economic Commission for Asia and the Far East (renamed ESCAP in 1974)
ECO	Economic Cooperation Organization
EFTA	European Free Trade Association
EMEAP	Executives' Meeting of East Asia–Pacific Central Banks
ERIA	Economic Research Institute for ASEAN and East Asia
ESCAP	UN Economic and Social Commission for Asia and the Pacific
EU	European Union
EurAsEc	Eurasian Economic Community
EVSL	Early Voluntary Sectoral Liberalisation initiative (APEC)
FDI	foreign direct investment
fob	free-on-board value of a traded good at the point of export
FTA	free trade area

G7	Canada, France, Germany, Italy, Japan, UK and USA
G8	G7 plus Russia
G20	Argentina, Australia, Brazil, Canada, China, France, Germany, India, Indonesia, Italy, Japan, Mexico, Russia, Saudi Arabia, South Africa, South Korea, Turkey, UK, USA and EU.
GATT	General Agreement on Tariffs and Trade
GDP	gross domestic product
GETI	Global Enabling Trade Index (of the World Economic Forum)
GMS	Greater Mekong Sub-region
GSP	Generalized System of Preferences
GTI	Greater Tumen Initiative
IAI	Initiative for ASEAN Integration
IIT	intra-industry trade
ILO	International Labour Organization
IMF	International Monetary Fund
IMT-GT	Indonesia–Malaysia–Thailand Growth Triangle
IOR-ARC	The Indian Ocean Rim — Association for Regional Cooperation
ITA	WTO Information Technology Agreement
MFN	most-favoured nation
NAFTA	North American Free Trade Agreement (between Canada, Mexico and USA)
NATO	North Atlantic Treaty Organization
NTBs	non-tariff barriers to trade
OECD	Organization for Economic Cooperation and Development
P4	Brunei, Chile, New Zealand and Singapore (trade agreement signed in 2005)
P5	Australia, Chile, New Zealand, Singapore and the USA (proposal in 1998)
PAFTAD	Pacific Trade and Development Conference
PBEC	Pacific Basin Economic Council
PECC	Pacific Economic Cooperation Council

PIF	Pacific Islands Forum
PPP	purchasing power parity
PRD	Pearl River Delta
RAMSI	Regional Assistance Mission to Solomon Islands
RCD	Regional Cooperation for Development (Iran, Pakistan and Turkey)
RTA	regional trading arrangement
SAARC	South Asia Association for Regional Cooperation
SARS	severe acute respiratory syndrome
SCO	Shanghai Cooperation Organization
SDR	special drawing rights (with IMF)
SEATO	Southeast Asia Treaty Organization
Sijori	Singapore–Johor–Riau
SMEs	small and medium-sized enterprises
SPARTECA	South Pacific Regional Trade and Economic Co-operation Agreement
SPS	sanitary and phytosanitary measures
SRZ	sub-regional economic zone
TBT	technical barriers to trade
TF	trade facilitation
TFAP	Trade Facilitation Action Plan (of APEC) — TFAP-1 2001–6; TFAP-2 2007–10.
TPP	Trans-Pacific Partnership trade agreement
TVE	township and village enterprise (in China)
UK	United Kingdom of Great Britain and Northern Ireland
UN	United Nations
UNCTAD	United Nations Conference on Trade and Development
UNDP	United Nations Development Programme
USA	United States of America
USSR	Union of Soviet Socialist Republics (also known as the Soviet Union)
WTO	World Trade Organization

$ refers to United States dollar unless otherwise stated.
Billion = thousand million.

Preface

The focus of this book is on economic regionalism, because this has been the dominant driver of regionalism since the 1950s. This was clearly the case for European integration (the European Economic Community and European Free Trade Association), at least until after the name European Union was adopted in 1992, and for regional integration elsewhere (e.g. NAFTA and Mercosur in the Americas). In Asia, the primary regional institutions, such as ASEAN or the CMI or ESCAP and the ADB have been economic in focus. There have been and still are regional institutions with a non-economic focus (e.g. SEATO and ARF); they will be mentioned in this book, but they have not been drivers of Asian regionalism. Although I argue that the basis for regionalism in East Asia in the early twenty-first century differs from earlier drivers of regionalism elsewhere in the world in the second half of the twentieth century, it is still primarily economic.

An important definitional distinction will be made between regionalism and regionalization.[1] Regionalism is policy-driven, involving agreements among national governments. Regionalization describes an increase in regional ties measured, say, by the share of intra-regional trade in total trade or by the direction of investment flows. Somewhere in between these two concepts are sub-regional zones (SRZs), which are integrated regions consisting of parts of larger economies and may be market-driven (as in the Pearl River Delta SRZ

---

[1] The distinction, emphasized by Detlef Lorenz (1991), is often made in the literature, but not always carefully used. In the recent literature on East Asia, Dent (2008) emphasizes the distinction between regionalism and regionalization and his arguments, from the perspective of international relations or international political economy, are often complementary to those in my book which takes a more narrowly economic perspective.

involving Hong Kong, Macau and Guangdong Province of China) or policy-driven (as in the Tumen River SRZ covering parts of North Korea, Jilin Province of China and Primorski Krai in the Russian Far East). Among this last category, SRZs that have been primarily policy-driven, such as the Tumen River SRZ, have been far less significant than those such as the Pearl River Delta which have been primarily market-driven. On a larger scale, regionalism in East Asia has become significant when it has followed regionalization rather than when it has been policy-driven.

The book is based on my research on evolving East Asian regionalism since I attended a 1987 conference in Kuala Lumpur on *ASEAN at the Crossroads*; there have been many crossroads since then! The book draws most heavily on a plenary lecture that I was invited to give at the Korea and World Economy Conference held at Hong Kong Baptist University in July 2009 (Pomfret, 2009) and on my contribution to the Bijit Bora memorial volume (Pomfret, 2010); I am grateful to the organizers of both for encouraging me to think about the big questions of East Asian regionalism. The book also draws on the work of hundreds of researchers. The lengthy bibliography acknowledges some of these debts, but to the many other authors and speakers whose ideas I have absorbed and reused without acknowledgment I apologize with gratitude. One positive element of the rise of East Asian regionalism has been the active debates among scholars of the region and, certainly among economists, the creation of a scholarly community.

Chapter 1

Introduction

Until 1995, when the World Trade Organization (WTO) was established, regionalism was conspicuously absent from East Asia. During the previous half century, it became common to contrast the situation in East Asia with the waves of regional trading arrangements (RTAs) occurring in Europe, the Americas and Africa. Japan, Korea and Hong Kong were the only charter members of the WTO not party to any RTAs. China was busy negotiating accession to the WTO and pursued a multilateral trade policy before its 2001 WTO accession. Mongolia, which joined the WTO in 1997, and Taiwan, which joined in 2002, also had non-discriminatory trade policies. The only RTA in East Asia was the Association of Southeast Asian Nations (ASEAN), and by common consent ASEAN had little impact on trade flows since its inception in 1967.

In sharp contrast, the twenty-first century has seen East Asia in the vanguard of a new wave of regional and bilateral trade agreements. What explains this dramatic change of direction? If East Asian regionalism is thriving, this raises two further questions: how wide is the region that it covers and what is the content of, or how deep is, the regional integration?

This book traces the emergence of Asian regionalism, analysing why it was so limited before 2000 and why it flourished after 2000. The book takes a mixture of chronological and topical approaches. Chapters 2–4 deal with the half century before 2000, or more specifically the decade after 1989 in Chapters 3–4. Chapter 5 focuses on the transitional years 1997–2000 dominated by the Asian financial crisis. The last four chapters concern the decade after 2000.

1

Chronology is important not just because any policy towards regionalism is influenced by what has happened before and by the current state of affairs, but also because the global and Asian background has changed dramatically over the period covered by this book. In the 1950s, 1960s and 1970s, East Asia hosted major hot wars along the fault lines of the global Cold War. Even more strikingly, Asia's economic position in the world was transformed from backwater to dynamo. The dynamism spread from Japan and Hong Kong to South Korea, Taiwan and Singapore, and then to Malaysia, Thailand, China and Indonesia by the 1980s. The sources of Asian "economic miracles" will not be analysed in any detail, although it is clear that the development path was outward-oriented, involving specialization in labour-intensive manufactured exports. By 2007, the nine high-performing Asian economies produced over a third of the world's manufactured exports (Table 1.1).

This book is not an economic history of Asia. Nevertheless, it is important for understanding regionalism in East Asia to recognize the broader economic developments in this dynamic part of the world. Table 1.1 provides data on population and economic size in 1989 and 2007, highlighting the rapid increase in output in many countries in the region and also the large range of size and economic performance. The speed of change is important both for living standards and for relative economic power.

Rapid economic growth in China in the three decades after 1979 was the source of the biggest reduction in poverty in human history; China's GDP per capita at purchasing power parity, which takes into account differences in price levels across time and across countries and is the best single measure of material well-being, increased from $747 in 1989 to $5,383 in 2007. Living standards more than tripled in Malaysia, Singapore, South Korea, Taiwan, Thailand and Vietnam over these two decades, despite the severe short-term shock of the 1997–1998 Asian Crisis. The rate of increase was slower in the countries that already had high per capita incomes in 1989, but it is still noteworthy that Japanese GDP per capita at purchasing power parity doubled during these decades when media reports focused on Japan's economic malaise.

Table 1.1 Population, Output and Trade, Selected Economies, 1989–2007.

	Population (million)		GDP ($ billion)		GDP per capita ($)		GDP per capita (PPP)		Exports ($ billion)		Imports ($ billion)		Share of manufs	
	1989	2007	1989	2007	1989	2007	1989	2007	1989	2007	1989	2007	1992	2007
Australia	16.8	21.0	295	821	17,545	39,066	15,784	34,923	37	142	45	174	0.4	0.4
Brunei	0.2	0.4	3	12	11,950	30,032	34,973	50,199	2	7	1	4	0	0
China	1,118.7	1,318.3	344	3,206	307	2,432	747	5,383	53	1,219	59	956	2.5	11.9
Hong Kong	5.7	6.9	69	207	12,091	29,912	15,906	42,306	73	345	72	368	4.1	3.5
Indonesia	175.1	225.6	102	433	580	1,918	1,349	3,712	22	114	17	75	0.6	0.5
Japan	123.1	127.8	2,940	4,384	23,882	34,313	17,293	33,632	275	715	210	622	12.2	6.8
Korea	42.4	48.5	231	970	5,438	20,014	7,318	24,801	61	374	60	357	2.7	3.5
Malaysia	17.6	26.5	39	187	2,207	7,033	4,358	13,518	25	176	23	147	1.0	1.3
New Zealand	3.4	4.2	43	136	12,514	32,086	13,783	27,336	9	27	9	31	0.1	0.1
PNG	4.0	6.3	4	6	881	990	1,259	2,084	1	7	2	3	0	0
Philippines	59.8	87.9	43	144	712	1,639	1,680	3,406	8	51	11	55	0.2	0.3
Singapore	2.9	4.6	30	161	10,275	35,163	15,718	49,704	45	300	50	263	1.8	2.4
Taiwan	20.1	22.9	153	383	7,596	16,764	8,832	30,443	66	247	52	219	3.0	3.0
Thailand	53.6	63.8	72	245	1,347	3,844	2,621	8,135	20	153	25	141	0.8	1.2
Vietnam	64.8	85.2	6	69	97	806	610	2,600	3	49	3	63	–	0.7

Sources: based on tables reported by APEC Policy Support Unit (2009); original datasources are population and GDP from World Bank *World Development Indicators*; exports and imports from International Monetary Fund *Direction of Trade Statistics*; Taiwan *Taiwan Statistical Data Book 2008* and Chinese Taipei Bureau of ForeignTrade; share of manufactured goods from UN Comtrade database.

Note: Share of manufs = exports of manufactured goods as a share of world trade in manufactured goods.

With high growth rates and large variations, not only relative living standards but also relative economic power shifts substantially. At the height of Japan's economic primacy in 1987, when the post-1985 yen appreciation had peaked and before this impacted negatively on economic growth, Japan's GDP at current prices in 1987 was $2,470 billion. India's GDP was $273 billion. The next largest East Asian economies' GDP in billion US dollars were China 268, Australia 224, South Korea 140, Indonesia 76, Thailand 51, and Hong Kong 50; Taiwan should be in this group, but is not included in the source. No other East Asian economy had a 1987 GDP over $40 billion.[1] Two decades later, in 2007, Japan's GDP at current prices was $4,384 billion and China's was $3,206 billion; the output gap between Japan and China had shrunk from 9.2:1 to 1.3:1, and given the two countries' relative growth rates, Japan would soon be inevitably overtaken by China as the world's second-largest economy. The two countries' roles in world trade also switched during these two decades, as Japan's share of world trade in manufactures fell from 12% in 1992 to 7% in 2007 and China's share increased from under 3% to 12%.

Regionalism did not flourish in the second half of the twentieth century because Asian countries pursued inward-oriented development strategies or, when they pursued outward-oriented strategies, their trade was, overwhelmingly with countries outside the region.

---

[1] Current price data are a better measure of economic power because they capture a country's purchasing power in world markets, although large exchange rate fluctuations can introduce 'noise' into the data. These data, like those in Table 1.1, are from the World Bank's *World Development Indicators*. World Bank, IMF, ADB, UN and other multilateral institutions are useful data sources because their statisticians make national data conceptually consistent. However, they have to rely on national statistical offices for data collection, which can vary substantially either due to poor local capacity or for political reasons. Data on North Korea, Laos and Cambodia for 1989, for example, are of lower quality than the data for the economies reported in Table 1.1. In all cases, economic data are approximations. Population figures are usually the most accurate, especially if the enumeration is the basis for the electoral roll in a democracy, but even these figures include some estimation because full censuses are not conducted every year and some groups are under-reported, e.g. the homeless or slum-dwellers. Output data are usually better reported than income data, which is why we rely on GDP rather than on national income measures, and estimates at market prices are more reliable than PPP measures, which require an additional step using imperfect data (for relative prices). Imports are typically better counted than exports because they are monitored for customs duties, but if the duties are high then there may be under-reporting due to smuggling.

Intra-Asian preferential trading arrangements held no attraction, and when countries liberalized trade policies it was on a non-discriminatory basis (Chapter 2). When regionalism was actively debated in the late 1980s in the context of lagging multilateral trade negotiations and of developments in Europe (completion of the EU internal market) and in North America (NAFTA), a discriminatory or exclusive grouping was rejected in favour of the open regionalism of APEC (Chapter 3). At the same time, however, the East Asian economy was becoming increasingly regionalized in the 1990s with the emergence of regional value chains, and one response was the emergence of sub-regional economic zones (Chapter 4).

The 1990s saw a major change in the nature of Asian participation in global manufacturing as East Asian countries shifted from bilateral sales to the high-income countries of the Americas, Western Europe and Australasia to forming a more integrated regional economy based on increasingly complex supply chains. This was accompanied by substantial reduction of tariffs on a non-discriminatory basis. During the first half of the decade, APEC provided a forum for coordinated unilateral trade liberalization by several Asian countries, and this liberalization was reinforced and consolidated by the completion of the Uruguay Round of multilateral trade negotiations and establishment of the World Trade Organization in 1995. Additionally, the economic dynamism of regional neighbours became apparent, following reforms in the 1980s in Australia and New Zealand and in the 1990s by India.

Several catalysts encouraged monetary integration after 1997 (Chapter 5). Despite talk of an Asian sequence of monetary integration preceding trade integration, actual steps in the monetary sphere have been small. In contrast, since 2000, there has been an explosion of bilateral and plurilateral trade agreements, targeting non-tariff or regulatory impediments to trade (Chapter 6). The proliferation of agreements has raised concerns about how to simplify the noodle bowl and consolidate regional arrangements, which in turn raises questions about which countries would be included in consolidated Asian regional arrangements (Chapter 7). The driving force behind East Asian regionalism is identified, in Chapter 8, as the rapid growth of intra-regional trade centred on regional value chains; in a region of low most-favoured nation tariffs, the functioning of regional value chains can be facilitated by bilateral or plurilateral agreements to remove trade barriers and reduce trade costs.[2] The concluding chapter argues that East Asian regionalism will continue to deepen because trade facilitation addresses "beyond trade" issues of harmonization, mutual recognition of regulations and so forth, and its width will be related to the geographical reach of the regional value chains.

The recurring theme is that East Asian regionalism has its unique historical roots and is driven by bottom-up pressures generated by the market-driven regionalization that gathered force in the 1990s. The preferential tariffs of a classical free trade area are of little relevance because tariffs have been unilaterally cut, apart from on sensitive goods, for which protection is non-negotiable even in bilateral or plurilateral negotiations. The supranational institutions inherent in a customs union or common market are unwelcome in Asia, where all countries jealously guard their sovereignty; no regional institution, apart from the UN regional commission (ESCAP) and the regional development bank (the ADB), has a large presence — even the ASEAN Secretariat has little influence. The Great Power dynamics are quite different to those in post-1945 Europe or in North America, especially in the fraught relations between China and Japan and those countries' competition for regional hegemony.

Against all of these negatives for regionalism, East Asia has been for several decades the most dynamic part of the world economy and, combined with the accelerating regionalization, this puts pressure on governments to provide the institutional framework for an integrated regional economy set in the global multilateral trading

---

[2] By trade costs I mean the costs of international trade excluding trade taxes. As tariffs have fallen, the relative importance of trade costs has risen. In Australia, which has the best documented measures of aggregate trade cost in the eastern hemisphere, trade costs fell from 8% of the free-on-board value of imports in 1990 to 5% in 2007. Tariffs fell faster, so that whereas in the 1970s and 1980s tariffs were the main trade barrier, by the 2000s trade costs were larger than tariffs; in 2007, Australia's average tariff was 4%. As more attention has been paid to trade costs, they have also fallen. However, trade costs are difficult to define precisely and more difficult to measure than tariffs. Because the concept of trade costs and the pace of their reduction (i.e. trade facilitation) has been a major topic in East Asian regionalism, these measurement issues are addressed in some detail in the Appendix.

system. National governments which do not respond to such pressures will see their economies excluded from the regional value chains and their people's living standards falling behind those of their neighbours' population. Competitive and coordinated trade facilitation in Asia will raise incomes just like any other improvement which reduces the costs of trade and increases the benefits from specialization and trade, and, because trade is a positive-sum game, it will also benefit Asian countries' trading partners around the world.

Chapter 2

Before 2000: The Case of the Missing Regionalism

The concept of Asia or East Asia as a region is relatively modern. In various historical epochs, Chinese cultural influence has been widespread in East Asia and Indian culture has influenced much of Southeast Asia, but none of this was seen as integrating "Asia." Following the Portuguese voyages of discovery from Europe in the 1500s and the establishment of Manila in 1571 as the Asian capital of Spain's New World colonies, European powers and, later, the USA built up empires in Asia.[1] Although the outside trading nations sometimes collaborated or acquiesced, these were competing rather than unifying.[2] Within the global economy established in the nineteenth century, Chinese, Indian and other diasporas increased in importance, but they created informal

---

[1] The Spanish Governor General in Manila reported to the Viceroy of New Spain in Mexico. The Manila-Acapulco galleon route provided the main economic link between Asia and the Americas from 1571 until 1815. Several unsuccessful uprisings by segments of the large Chinese community against Spanish rule (in 1574, 1602, 1662 and 1684) emphasised the widening gulf in military and economic power between European and Asian forces.

[2] In the 1800s, Siam (Thailand) was able to maintain its independence as a buffer state between the British and French Southeast Asian empires because neither European power wanted to see the other in control. In Shanghai, the foreign powers cooperated in administering the International Settlement, whose autonomous status contributed to making Shanghai, with perhaps four million inhabitants, the most important commercial centre in Asia before it was occupied by Japanese forces in 1937. The second-class status of Chinese nationals in this enclave, as in the French Concession in Shanghai, clearly revealed that it was not operated for Asians, and the "unequal treaties" underlying extraterritoriality in Shanghai were abrogated by China's allies in 1943.

networks which might cover part of Asia or extend to East Africa rather than a formal Asian community.

A first explicit pan-Asian enterprise was the Japanese reference to the areas brought under its control in the 1937–1945 war as a Greater East Asia Co-Prosperity Sphere. The high point was the Greater East Asia Conference in Tokyo on 5–6 November 1943, at which Japan hosted the heads of state of various component members of the Greater East Asia Co-Prosperity Sphere: Hideki Tojo, Prime Minister of Japan; Zhang Jinghui, Prime Minister of Manchukuo; Wang Jingwei, President of the Reformed Government of the Republic of China; Ba Maw, Head of State, State of Burma; Subhas Chandra Bose, Head of State of Provisional Government of Free India; José P. Laurel, President of the Second Philippine Republic; and Prince Wan Waithayakon, envoy from the Kingdom of Thailand. The conference was intended to illustrate the Japanese Empire's commitment to a pan-Asian ideal and to emphasize its role as the liberator of Asia from western colonialism, and it issued a Joint Declaration promoting economic and political cooperation. Opponents of the Greater East Asia Co-Prosperity Sphere linked it to Japanese militarism rather than a genuine concern for the people of Asia.

Following the end of the war in 1945, Asia went through a period of economic disintegration as new countries appeared and often sub-divided. Global trends in forming regional trading arrangements (RTAs) passed Asia by. During the 1960s, many observers saw the global trading system caught in a headlong rush to regionalism (Pomfret, 2001). Following the example of Western Europe, an alphabet soup of regional trading arrangements was created in Latin America, the Caribbean and Africa. The non-European RTAs had little economic impact and the wave ebbed. In the 1980s and early 1990s, a second wave of RTAs included the deepening of the European Union, formation of the North American Free Trade Area (NAFTA) and discussion of a Free Trade Area of the Americas, leading commentators to fear a collapse of the global system into three blocs centred on Europe, the Western Hemisphere and Asia. In both waves, Asia was the missing link, with no serious RTA formation or creation of a regional bloc. The only significant regional arrangement in East Asia was ASEAN, and its economic impact was minor.

From 1945 to 1967

In the second half of the 1940s, Asia was characterized by regional disintegration. The areas unified under Japanese control in the Greater East Asia Co-Prosperity Sphere were again set apart. China regained its northeast provinces and Taiwan from Japan, but with the end of the civil war in 1949, Taiwan again came under separate administration. Korea regained independence, but its territorial integrity was split by Cold War politics and then by civil war.[3] The major European empires — Britain in South Asia and Malaysia, France in Indochina, and the Netherlands in the Dutch East Indies[4] — were briefly restored, but would disappear within a decade. Moreover, the successors to British India and French Indochina themselves fragmented; the bitter division between India and Pakistan created a militarized border in what had been a unified economy,[5] while the division between North and South Vietnam

---

[3]In August 1945, the former Japanese colony of Korea was occupied by Soviet and US troops with a demarcation line on the 38th parallel. The 1948 UN elections were opposed and then boycotted by the Soviet Union. In the South, a national constitution was promulgated on 17 July 1948, US-educated Syngman Rhee was elected president, and the Republic of Korea was established. In the Russian Zone of Occupation, the North Korean Government was led by Kim Il-sung. In 1950, troops from the North invaded the South in an attempt to reunify the country by force. After intervention by the USA and allies in support of the South and by China in support of the North, an armistice restoring the original demarcation line was signed in July 1953.

[4]During World War II, the Dutch East Indies were occupied by Japan and the Netherlands by Germany. Two days after Japan's surrender in 1945, nationalist leaders Sukarno and Hatta declared Indonesian independence, but this was not recognized by the Netherlands until December 1949. Western New Guinea remained under Dutch rule as Netherlands New Guinea until 1962 and was formally annexed by Indonesia in 1969. After Portuguese decolonization in 1975, Indonesia invaded and annexed East Timor in 1976, but in 1999 Indonesia relinquished control of the territory and Timor-Leste joined the United Nations as a sovereign state in 2002.

[5]In June 1947, the British Governor-General of India announced the partitioning of the British Indian Empire into a secular India and a Muslim Pakistan. In August 1947, Pakistan was declared a separate nation and India became an independent dominion. In 1950, India became a republic, and subsequently absorbed Pondicherry (ceded by France in 1953–1954), Goa (from Portuguese control in 1961), and Sikkim (after a referendum in 1975). Violent clashes between Hindus and Muslims accompanied partition, and India and Pakistan fought over the border in Kashmir until a UN ceasefire was brokered in 1948. A Second Kashmir War was fought in 1965. Following a third war between India and Pakistan, Bangladesh, formerly East Pakistan, became independent in 1971. The 1999 Kargil Conflict, initially ascribed by Pakistan to local Kashmiri independence fighters, also involved the two states, both, by then, nuclear powers, and was resolved under international pressure by return to the original Line of Control. Following an attack on the Indian Parliament in December 2001, both countries mobilized until the build-up of troops on both sides of the border was the largest ever; the situation was defused, and a ceasefire agreed in 2003.

became a critical fault line between Communist and non-Communist Asia.[6]

Independent countries became members of the United Nations. The UN created a system of regional commissions which included the Economic Commission for Asia and the Far East (ECAFE), founded in 1947 and based in Bangkok. In the early 1960s, ECAFE promoted the establishment of a regional development bank; after several years of negotiation, the Asian Development Bank (ADB) was established in 1966 and based in Manila. As regional institutions, these initiatives did not go beyond meetings or loose consultations, in contrast to the active promotion of regional integration by the UN Economic Commission for Latin America. Nevertheless, in the 1950s and 1960s, the two institutions represented the first conceptualization of the region, which included East and South Asia and the Pacific islands, but not Southwest Asia, which in the Eurocentric language of the time was part of the Middle East. However, the membership of ECAFE (rebadged in 1974 as the Economic and Social Commission for Asia and the Pacific, ESCAP) and the ADB is not identical; notably Iran is part of ESCAP but not the ADB.[7]

In the 1950s, the region was split by the Cold War contest between Communism and capitalism. After the creation of the Peoples Republic of China in 1949, China aligned with the Soviet Union and supported

---

[6]During World War II, French Indochina was administered by Vichy France under Japanese occupation, until after the fall of Vichy France when Japan briefly assumed full control. After 1945, the Vietminh, led by Ho Chi Minh, began a revolt against French rule. In 1949, the anti-Communist state of Vietnam was granted independence with its capital in Saigon. In 1954, following military defeat at Diên Biên Phu, France accepted Vietnamese independence, and Cambodia and Laos also became independent. The 1954 Geneva Accord called for the withdrawal of troops behind a demarcation line on the 17th parallel; the Vietminh became the government of North Vietnam, with Hanoi as the capital, and the central region was divided between the North and South. The Geneva Conference was not attended by the South Vietnamese government, which rejected the call for national elections to restore the territorial integrity of Vietnam on the grounds that a fair election would not be permitted in the North. After 1959, internal opposition to the regime in the South by the National Liberation Front (or Vietcong) was supported by the North, while the South received military support from the USA and other anti-Communist foreign powers. After military victory by the Communist forces, Vietnam was unified in 1975.

[7]The ADB also had 12 charter non-regional members (Canada, the USA and ten European countries), since joined by Turkey and six other European countries. The only non-regional members of ECAFE/ESCAP are countries with permanent seats on the UN Security Council (France, the USSR/Russia, the UK and USA).

the Democratic People's Republic of Korea. Japan, South Korea and Taiwan became heavily dependent on a security umbrella provided by the USA. Although China split with the Soviet Union in 1961, relations with the USA remained confrontational until the early 1970s and with Taiwan and South Korea for even longer. North Vietnam joined the Soviet-led Committee for Mutual Economic Assistance (CMEA, also known as Comecon). The anti-Communist countries (Thailand, the Philippines and Pakistan, plus non-regional countries) formed the Southeast Asia Treaty Organization (SEATO) in 1954, with its headquarters in Bangkok.[8] Indonesia and India were leading members of the Non-aligned Movement which sought to stay outside the Cold War, but which were viewed by the USA with suspicion for this reason.

Within Southeast Asia, there were other regional conflicts and institutional responses, primarily driven by proposals for the formation of Malaysia, which led to tensions with Indonesia. Malaya had become independent and Singapore self-governing in 1957, and in the early 1960s, Britain proposed a federation of these two ex-colonies with its colonial territories on the island of Borneo (Sarawak, Brunei and North Borneo). The plan was opposed by the Philippines, which claimed Sabah, and by Indonesia, which perceived an imperialist plot to destabilize the non-British part of the island, the Indonesian province of Kalimantan.[9] After a counter-proposal to create a larger union of these territories and Indonesia and the Philippines (MAPHILINDO) failed, the former British colonies in Malaya, Singapore, North Borneo (Sabah) and Sarawak were brought together in 1963 as the Malaysian Federation.[10] Brunei Darussalam opted to

---

[8]SEATO had eight members: Australia, France, New Zealand, Pakistan, the Philippines, Thailand, the United Kingdom and the USA. The Southeast Asia Collective Defence Treaty, which created SEATO, only committed signatories to consult on ways to meet a common danger. Unlike, say, NATO, it did not consider an attack on one member as an attack on all, and it had no standing forces. Pakistan left SEATO in 1973 and France left in 1974. The organization was formally terminated in 1977, although it remains the basis for the alliance between Thailand and the USA.

[9]Indonesia denied any territorial claims to the British colonies on Borneo, but the takeover of East Timor in 1975, when the Portuguese Empire imploded, casts doubt on the long-term value of such a commitment.

[10]In July 1963, Philippine President Diosdado Macapagal convened a summit meeting in Manila, at which MAPHILINDO was proposed as an association bringing together the Malay peoples

remain self-governing, and eventually became an independent state in 1984.[11] The MAPHILINDO plan became moot when Indonesian President Sukarno's policy of *konfrontasi*, an undeclared war between Malaysia and Indonesia over the future of the island of Borneo, led to active fighting between Indonesian and Malaysian forces, supported by British Commonwealth troops. After a failed military coup in Indonesia in September 1965, power shifted from President Sukarno to General Suharto; Indonesia began to signal an end to the *konfrontasi* policy, and in 1966, with the signing of Bangkok Accord, Indonesia and Malaysia finally agreed to end the hostilities between them.[12] In the Philippines, the election of President Ferdinand Marcos in December 1965 marked the softening of Philippines' claim over Sabah.

In 1961, Malaya, Thailand and the Philippines formed the Association of Southeast Asia (ASA). From the beginning, ASA was handicapped by its limited membership and by the charge that it was a Western-influenced anti-communist group with largely political motives. During the latter part of 1963, ASA was further disrupted by deteriorating diplomatic relations between Malaya and the Philippines over Manila's claim to North Borneo (Sabah), which became part of the Malaysian Federation in September 1963. After Singapore seceded from the Malaysian Federation in 1965, and tensions between Indonesia and Malaysia and between the Philippines and Malaysia cooled in 1966, the way was opened for the five non-Communist countries to create a regional institution. In 1967, they formed the Association of Southeast Asian Nations (ASEAN), an organization for non-security cooperation.

---

who had been artificially divided by colonial frontiers. Although MAPHILINDO was described as a regional association that would approach issues of common concern in the spirit of consensus, it was also perceived as a tactic by Indonesia and the Philippines to delay, or even prevent, the formation of the Federation of Malaysia.

[11] The Sultan of Brunei resisted pressures to join Malaysia. Under a 1959 constitution, Brunei was declared a self-governing state, while its foreign affairs, security, and defence remained under the responsibility of the United Kingdom. In 1979, Brunei and the United Kingdom signed a new treaty of friendship and cooperation, and on 1st January 1984, Brunei Darussalam became a fully independent state.

[12] After the September 30 coup, Suharto's faction controlled the army, using its power to eliminate the Communist Party as an effective force and undermining Sukarno's position. Sukarno was formally replaced by Suharto as President in February 1967.

The Association of Southeast Asian Nations (ASEAN)

In the last third of the twentieth century, the only significant regional arrangement in East Asia was ASEAN, whose political origins lay in links between the anti-Communist regimes of the region and in confidence-building between Malaysia and Indonesia (Severino, 2009). ASEAN had a low profile in the 1970s and 1980s. Until 1975, politics in southeast Asia were dominated by the war in Vietnam. After the end of the wars in Indochina in 1975, geopolitical concerns shifted to Vietnamese expansionism and, in the 1990s, to worries about Chinese expansionism.

At the first ASEAN summit, held in Bali in 1976, the leaders signed the Treaty of Amity and Cooperation, committing members to mutual respect for independence, sovereignty, equality, territorial integrity and national identity and stipulating that they would not resort to violence against other signatories. An ASEAN secretariat was established, based in Jakarta. At the second summit in 1977, ASEAN introduced the dialogue partners framework to bring together foreign ministers from ASEAN member countries, the European Communities, the USA, Japan, Australia, New Zealand and South Korea to discuss security matters. ASEAN had no economic content until the 1976 Bali summit, when members agreed to consider preferential tariffs and co-ordinated industrial policies.[13]

The economic strategies of the ASEAN members, except Singapore, were focused on a mild form of import-substituting industrialization, while their largely primary product exports were sold outside the region. The main activity after 1976, intended to provide an economic impetus to ASEAN, was the ASEAN Industrial Projects (AIPs) program, which aimed to identify areas of specialization which would be reserved for one ASEAN member with an implicit understanding that the project would supply the entire ASEAN market. The host country was expected to take up three fifths of the AIP's equity and the other

---

[13]The idea of coordinated projects had been floated in a 1974 United Nations study "Economic Cooperation among Member Countries of the Association of Southeast Asian Nations" (published in the *Journal of Development Planning, 7*), and was adopted in principle by the ASEAN governments in 1976.

four ASEAN members 10 percent each. Despite the early assignment of one AIP to each ASEAN member and Japanese financial aid for the program, the first project did not come on stream until 1984; of all the proposed AIPs, only those in Indonesia and Malaysia really prospered, and their relative success owed little or nothing to their AIP status.

Each country wanted to have a good AIP, but became jealous if one of their partners' AIP appeared to have better economic prospects. The diesel engine debacles illustrated the scope for conflict over which country should be the ASEAN producer of a good perceived as having good prospects. Singapore was allocated a diesel engine project. This was subsequently opposed by Indonesia, which fearing competition for its own diesel factories requested that Singapore limit its production to engines of over 500 horsepower. Singapore argued that most of ASEAN demand was for smaller engines and the size restriction would make the Singaporean factory unprofitable. While this debate continued, Indonesia, the Philippines and Thailand all expanded their diesel engine production, to the point that Singapore abandoned its AIP. Indonesia and Thailand squabbled over the overlap between their projects to produce diesel engines of differing sizes, until Thailand dropped its AIP and, outside the program, built a diesel engine plant competing with the Indonesian plant (Pomfret, 2001, 300n).

Singapore had effectively dropped out of the program by the time that the first AIPs were coming on stream in 1984. Singapore opted out of participation in other countries' AIP's, agreeing only to make a one percent token contribution to AIPs so that they would still meet the conditions for Japanese soft loans (Lim, 2009, 216). The ASEAN phosphate fertilizer project in the Philippines ran into similar problems as the diesel engine projects as Indonesia expanded its own superphosphate production; falling phosphate prices after the initial decision in 1976 further undermined the viability of this AIP. Thailand's AIP went through a long gestation period before being abandoned/modified to a project that competed with Indonesia's AIP.

The reasons for AIP failure ranged from technical to political. Given the obligation of other ASEAN countries to purchase the output of AIPs, pricing was a major issue, and conflicts arose over the extent to which infrastructure costs could be included when calculating fair prices. Because AIPs were import-substituting projects that were not competitive at world prices, the concept of a "fair" price was unclear. The non-producing countries were expected to pay a mark-up over the world price to support their partner's industrialization, but there were no criteria to determine how much value should be placed on promoting an infant industry elsewhere in Southeast Asia, especially when it might inhibit one's own future industrialization (as in the dispute over diesel engine production). A symptom of failure was the lack of private sector interest in investing in AIPs.

An attempt to revive co-ordinated industrial policies by establishing complementary production within sectors began in 1981 with automobile components, but this was scuppered by Malaysia's decision to proceed with its own integrated car industry. The Industrial Complementation scheme was replaced in 1988 by the Brand-to-Brand Complementation scheme providing incentives (primarily a 50% tariff reduction on intra-ASEAN trade) to multinational corporations to allocate their production facilities across different ASEAN countries. With eight approved projects, this scheme claimed more successes than the AIPs or the Industrial Complementation Scheme, but the Brand-to-Brand Complementation scheme still had limited impact, and especially so as Indonesia did not participate. This scheme was, in turn, superseded by the ASEAN Industrial Cooperation Scheme in 1996 which permitted two or more companies to sign an agreement which, if approved, qualifies them for preferential duties on intra-ASEAN trade; the 145 agreements approved by 2007 were mostly in the auto sector plus a handful from electronics (Lim, 2009, 218).

The fundamental problem with all of these schemes to co-ordinate industrial policies was that members wanted to support their own import-competing industries, but were unwilling to support their partners' uncompetitive industries. Partner countries were reluctant to buy the output of an AIP if more suitable or cheaper alternatives were available from a non-ASEAN country. Regional cooperation to promote import-substituting industrialization by overcoming problems of small national market size failed for similar reasons in RTAs in the Americas (e.g. the Central American Common Market) and Africa (e.g. the East African Community).[14]

---

[14]Trade diversion is the key concept in explaining the economic cost of such RTAs. Preferred treatment for internal suppliers diverts trade from more efficient external suppliers at a cost not

Preferential tariffs introduced after 1977 were of little economic importance. Countries tended to offer preferential tariff reductions only on items where there was no threat of increased competition for domestic producers. These were typically items with low MFN tariffs and hence small preference margins, or goods not produced in ASEAN. Empirical studies (e.g. Imada, 1993, 4–8) found that tariff preferences had minimal impact on trade flows. As the ASEAN countries shifted towards more outward-oriented economic development strategies in the 1980s, their exports went to markets outside the region. Intra-ASEAN trade as a percentage of members' total trade was smaller in 1989 than it had been in 1970 (Ariff and Tan, 1992, 254).

ASEAN was generally inactive during the 1980s. No summit was held for a decade after 1977 (Table 2.1). At the 1987 summit, it was decided to meet every five years, and to accelerate implementation of preferential trading arrangements and the various industrial comple-mentation schemes. The decision at the 1992 summit to meet every

Table 2.1   ASEAN Summits.

Number	Date	Place	Number	Date	Place
1st	Bali	1976	7th	Brunei	2001
2nd	Kuala Lumpur	1977	8th	Phnom Penh	2002
3rd	Manila	1987	9th	Bali, Indonesia	2003
4th	Singapore	1992	10th	Vientiane	2004
5th	Bangkok	1995	11th	Kuala Lumpur	2005
1st informal	Jakarta	1996	12th	Cebu, Philippines	2007
2nd informal	Kuala Lumpur	1997	13th	Singapore	2007
6th	Hanoi	1998	14th	Thailand	2009
3rd informal	Manila	1999	15th	Vietnam	2010
4th informal	Singapore	2000			

Source: http://www.aseansec.org/4933.htm (accessed 13 October 2009).
Note: The 12th summit, scheduled for December 2006, was postponed for a month due to Typhoon Seniang. The 14th summit was originally scheduled for December 2008, but due to political events in Thailand postponed until April, when it was disrupted by demonstrators; it was finally held in October in Cha-am and Hua Hin.

---

only to the external suppliers, but also to buyers within the RTA. In the CACM and EAC, and probably with respect to AIPs, the trade diversion costs outweighed the benefits to the sheltered producers. Pomfret (2001) provides more details. The only example of successful pursuit of this type of trade-diverting regionalism was the Common Agricultural Policy of the European Union which gave internal producers preferred access to the whole EU market; the policy was politically driven, and implemented at a very large cost to the EU budget and to European consumers.

three years signalled more serious interest in ASEAN. After informal summits had been called in every non-summit year after 1995, the summits became officially annual in 2001.[15] In 1994, the ASEAN Regional Forum (ARF) was created, bringing together the dialogue partners (ASEAN members, Australia, Japan, New Zealand, South Korea, the EU and the USA), China, Russia, Laos, Vietnam and, in 1995, India to discuss security issues. Complementing the various bilateral alliances and dialogues, the ARF provides a setting in which members can discuss regional security issues and develop cooperative measures to enhance peace and security in the region.[16] At the December 1995 summit, ASEAN members signed the Treaty on the Southeast Asian Nuclear Weapon-Free Zone.

ASEAN finally moved towards becoming an RTA with the 1992 announcement that an ASEAN Free Trade Area (AFTA) would be established by 2008. Even this was a hesitant step. Within 15 years, internal tariffs would be reduced to 5 percent or less rather than full tariff-free intra-ASEAN trade, preferential tariff reductions were back-loaded to take effect as late in the transition period as possible, and lengthy lists of commodities were excluded.[17] Indeed, the initial exclusion lists were so long that AFTA was relaunched in 1993 with fewer exclusions and a target date for completion of 2003. Relative to the limited benefits from the preferential tariffs, however, the paperwork was often sufficiently disincentive that traders did not claim the preferential tariff rate even if they were eligible. At the same time, ASEAN countries (the Philippines and Thailand, in particular) unilaterally cut tariffs on a large range of goods, reducing the margin of preference

---

[15] The location is alphabetical by country (Table 2.1), but in 2006 Myanmar was skipped in deference to US and EU concerns about human rights.

[16] The ARF today comprises of 27 countries: ten ASEAN member states, ten ASEAN dialogue partners (Australia, Canada, China, the EU, India, Japan, New Zealand, South Korea, Russia and the United States), one ASEAN observer (Papua New Guinea), and Bangladesh, Mongolia, North Korea, Pakistan, Sri Lanka and Timor-Leste. Taiwan has been excluded, and issues regarding the Taiwan Strait are neither discussed at the ARF meetings nor stated in the ARF Chairman's Statements.

[17] Unprocessed agricultural goods and services were explicitly excluded from the original proposal, although some ASEAN members voluntarily included some agricultural goods. The agreement on the ASEAN Investment Area (AIA) was signed in 1998, but implementation was not required until 2010 for ASEAN investors and 2020 for non-ASEAN investors.

(Ando and Kimura, 2005). The net result was that AFTA's preferential tariffs had a very small impact on trade in the 1990s (Manchin and Pelkmans-Balaoing, 2008).

AFTA was the only RTA in East Asia in the second half of the twentieth century. Sub-regional economic zones (SRZs) emerged in the Pearl River Delta (the PRD involved Hong Kong, Macau and Guangdong Province of China) and around Singapore (Sijori, or Singapore, Johor and Riau), but these were market-driven, with some public policy measures to facilitate cross-border trade and investment. Other sub-regional zones or "growth triangles" tried to replicate the success of the PRD or Sijori, with more state involvement and less economic impact (e.g. BIMP-EAGA and IMT-GT were created in 1993–1994).[18] In Northeast Asia, the Tumen River Project, a state-driven sub-regional zone involving the Koreas, China, Japan and Mongolia, had little economic effect. The SRZs will be discussed in greater detail in Chapter 4.

Although AFTA had little impact as a conventional RTA with preferential tariffs, cooperation among ASEAN members did have economic effects during the 1990s. Singapore already had liberal and efficient trade arrangements, but Indonesia, Malaysia, Thailand and, to a lesser extent, the Philippines all began to streamline their border facilities as they adopted more outward-oriented development strategies. Much of this trade facilitation could be done unilaterally, but there were benefits from coordination and standardization between neighbours and on a regional basis. Coordination among customs officials and initiatives such as the ASEAN Single Window were aimed at reducing the time and cost of trading across ASEAN borders. Individual steps can be listed, but their impact is hard to measure. At the aggregate level, however, trade costs of the five countries declined substantially, converging on the best practice of Singapore (see Figure 4.1 below).[19]

---

[18] BIMP-EAGA (Brunei, Indonesia, Malaysia, Philippines East ASEAN Growth Area) became bogged down with issues such as territorial demarcation. IMT-GT (Indonesia–Malaysia–Thailand Growth Triangle) had private sector origins in the desire of Malaysian businesspeople to trade more with northern Sumatra, but was stifled by government control (and by border tensions between Malaysia and southern Thailand).

[19] Pomfret and Sourdin (2009) provide evidence that trade costs of the ASEAN countries fell substantially during the 1990s and significantly faster than other countries' trade costs, suggesting that national policies as well as technical change were responsible. See the Appendix for details of their methodology.

ASEAN's five founder members were joined by Brunei Darussalam when it became fully independent in 1984, but the big challenge of enlargement came in the final years of the twentieth century. Vietnam joined ASEAN in 1995, Laos and Myanmar in 1997, and Cambodia in 1999. The accession of Cambodia and Myanmar was controversial because of their governments' records on human rights, and Cambodia's accession was delayed on political grounds. Geographically, the 1995–1999 enlargement may represent the natural limits of ASEAN, which is now bordered to the north by China, to the west by India and to the south by Australia, none of whom are likely to become full members (Map 1). The only unclear frontier is to the east where Papua New Guinea and Timor-Leste are contiguous to ASEAN.[20]

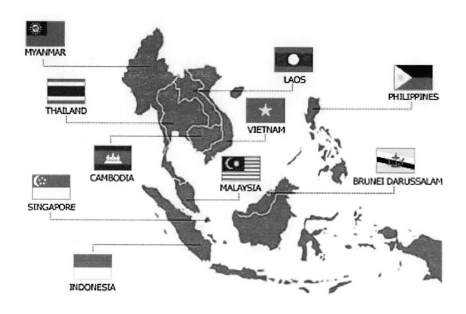

Map 1:   ASEAN

---

[20]Papua New Guinea was granted Observer status in 1976. Timor-Leste became a member of the ASEAN Regional Forum in 2005 and is actively pursuing full ASEAN membership.

Regional Trading Arrangements outside Southeast Asia

The most far-reaching regional trading arrangement in the Asia–Pacific region is that between Australia and New Zealand. Building on an earlier and more limited Australia–New Zealand Free Trade Agreement, the 1983 Closer Economic Relations (CER) agreement went beyond preferential tariff reductions. All quantitative restrictions on bilateral trade were removed by 1990, and the CER also covers a wide range of other non-tariff barriers to trade, the application of anti-dumping and countervailing duties, subsidies and government procurement, while additional protocols in 1988 and 1992 extended the CER to services and to the harmonization of business law and competition policy (McLean, 1995; Scollay, 1996). The timing of the CER coincided with the major reform programs in the two countries which moved them from being among the most highly protected high-income countries to having among the most liberal trade policies; there was little scope for preferential tariff policies as MFN tariffs plummeted. However, the extent of the coverage marks the CER as the leading example of deep integration outside Europe. The broader lessons from this process may, however, be limited by the closely shared history of the two Australasian countries.

Australia and New Zealand have also figured prominently in integration agreements in the South Pacific. The South Pacific Forum was founded in 1971 by Australia, the Cook Islands, Fiji, Nauru, New Zealand, Tonga and Western Samoa, and later joined by Niue, Papua New Guinea, Kiribati, Palau, Solomon Islands, Tuvalu, Federated States of Micronesia, the Republic of the Marshall Islands and Vanuatu. The Forum's main activities consisted of the coordination of fishing and transport policies, disaster relief, and trade and aid negotiations with non-member countries — the last effectively referring to Australia and New Zealand. The South Pacific Regional Trade and Economic Co-operation Agreement (SPARTECA, signed at the Forum 1980 summit) guarantees duty-free and unrestricted access on a non-reciprocal basis for a wide range of Forum island economies' products into Australian and New Zealand markets. In 2000, the Forum was renamed the Pacific Islands Forum (PIF) with a more formal organization, including a secretariat based in Suva, Fiji.[21]

The South Asia Association for Regional Cooperation (SAARC) was launched in 1985 by Bangladesh, Bhutan, India, the Maldives, Nepal and Pakistan and a framework preferential trading agreement was signed in 1993. However, the agreement was not ratified until 1995 and only limited preferential treatment was granted. Indeed, until 1995, trade between the two largest SAARC members had been at worse than MFN treatment, and only in 1995 as one of its commitments as a charter WTO member did Pakistan agree to grant MFN treatment to imports from India. Related to these bilateral problems, India was more active in promoting other regional initiatives such as the South Asian Growth Quadrangle launched in 1997 by Bangladesh, Bhutan, India and Nepal or BIMSTEC (Bangladesh, India, Myanmar, Sri Lanka and Thailand Economic Cooperation), which was also launched in 1997 and is SAARC minus Pakistan plus Myanmar and Thailand.[22]

In Southwest Asia, Iran, Pakistan and Turkey founded the Economic Cooperation Organization (ECO) in 1985 to promote economic, technical and cultural cooperation.[23] After the death of the Ayatollah

---

[21]New Caledonia and French Polynesia, previously Forum Observers, were granted Associate Membership in 2006. Forum Observers include Tokelau (2005), Wallis and Futuna (2006), the Commonwealth (2006), the United Nations (2006) and the Asian Development Bank (2006), with Timor Leste as Special Observer (2002). Fiji's membership was suspended in May 2009 for failing to make commitments about holding elections.

[22]The Indian Ocean Rim Initiative could also be seen as an attempt by India to pursue an option unconstrained by the presence of Pakistan. The Indian Ocean Rim Initiative dates from a 1995 meeting of Australia, India, Kenya, Mauritius, Oman, Singapore and South Africa. The group was extended in 1996 to include Indonesia, Madagascar, Malaysia, Mozambique, Sri Lanka, Tanzania and Yemen, and formally launched in 1997. The Indian Ocean Rim-Association for Regional Cooperation (IOR-ARC) now has 18 member states (the above 14 plus Bangladesh, Iran, Thailand and the United Arab Emirates — Seychelles joined in 1999 but withdrew in 2003). The Association's work programs are conducted by member countries with shared interests under the umbrella of three working groups: the Working Group on Trade and Investment, the Indian Ocean Rim Business Forum, and the Indian Ocean Rim Academic Group.

[23]ECO is the successor organization to Regional Cooperation for Development (RCD), which was functional from 1964 to 1979 and whose charter, the 1977 Treaty of Izmir, remains the basic document of ECO. RCD was the economic and social arm of the Central Treaty Organization (CENTO), whose origins lay in the 1955 Baghdad Pact, a counterpart of NATO and the

Khomeini in June 1989, the Iranian leadership, as part of a general policy of liberalizing international economic relations and reintegrating Iran into the wider community, led initiatives to boost ECO's activities. Implementation of the 1991 Protocol on Preferential Tariffs was limited.[24] However, enlargement of ECO from three to ten members, in November 1992, gave the organization new impetus.[25] The accession of Afghanistan, Azerbaijan, Kazakhstan, the Kyrgyz Republic, Tajikistan, Turkmenistan and Uzbekistan gave ECO a cultural cohesion, incorporating all of the non-Arab Islamic countries of Western and Central Asia. The ECO summits in the 1990s typically included grand declarations, but the concrete achievements of ECO were modest. ECO probably had greatest potential in the area of trade facilitation, but statements of intent outran practical achievement.[26] In sum, the

---

Southeast Asia Treaty Organization (SEATO), with the primary goal of limiting the expansion of Communism. When Iraq withdrew in 1959, the Baghdad Pact was renamed CENTO. Iran and Pakistan withdrew in 1979, CENTO was disbanded, and the RCD became dormant. In 1985, the RCD was revived as ECO, a trilateral organization of Iran, Pakistan and Turkey to promote multi-dimensional regional cooperation with a view to creating conditions for sustained socioeconomic growth in the member states. After revision of the Treaty of Izmir in 1990, ECO was fully launched in 1991.

[24] Application of the May 1991 Protocol on Preferential Tariffs, by which the signatories agreed to offer a 10 percent preferential tariff reduction on selected items, was disappointing; the lists of items were extremely limited, and even after national implementation began in May 1993 there were doubts that the preferential treatment was actually being applied. The ECO Committee on Preferential Tariffs met several times between 1993 and 1995, but was unsuccessful in persuading the signatories to extend their lists or to offer more substantial preference margins. The new members showed no interest in acceding to the preferential tariff arrangements. After little progress had been made on this front by 1996, the ECO Secretariat took the initiative in trying to reorient attention to include discussion of the implications of the Uruguay Round and the World Trade Organization for the ECO region. This initiative was formalized in the Almaty Declaration at the 1998 ECO summit when all members were urged to take steps towards WTO membership. In effect, the organization had abandoned regionalism in favour of multilateralism so far as trade policy is concerned.

[25] For the historical background on ECO, see Pomfret (1999) and Afrasiabi (2000). Although the 1992 enlargement created a bigger ECO, for the Central Asian countries this period was one of regional disintegration following the collapse of the Soviet Union (Linn, 2004). The ECO members committed themselves to establishing nine regional institutions and, in 1996, the Council of Ministers approved a restructuring, which included the establishment of a permanent ECO Secretariat in Tehran, but these institutions remain weak.

[26] At the 1995 ECO Summit, the heads of state signed the ECO Transit Trade Agreement and an Agreement on the Simplification of Visa Procedures for the Businessmen of ECO Countries, but

achievements of ECO have been modest. Some of the ECO summits, notably that of 1996 where the main debates featured disputes between Uzbekistan and Iran and delegates left a day earlier than planned, have been divisive. Such disputes highlighted the disparity between statements of cultural unity (an association of non-Arab Islamic countries west of India) and the differences between the Islamic Republics of Iran or Pakistan and more secular Islamic states of Central Asia. A fundamental obstacle to economic integration within ECO is the similarity of the member countries' economies, which all specialize in a small group of primary products (oil, gas, minerals, and cotton). In the twenty-first century, ECO leaders and ministers continue to meet at irregular intervals and make declarations of progress, but there is little evidence of actual achievements or of significant commitment to the institution by Central Asian countries.

The arrangements described in this section were tangential to the process of East Asian regionalism. They reflect an environment in which the regions of Asia were narrower and more distinct than they would become in the twenty-first century. The South Asian and Southwest Asian countries had little connection to East Asia, and the new independent Central Asian countries were more concerned with nation-building and playing off larger neighbours than in becoming part of an Asian region. Australia and New Zealand had an ambivalent position, not really part of Asia, but not wanting to be excluded at a time when their traditional economic links to the UK had been shattered by Britain's EU accession and their attitude towards the USA was mixed.[27] Moreover, none of the RTAs apart from the CER had any significant economic impact.

---

the transit agreement was only signed by eight countries, and the two non-signatories, Uzbekistan and Afghanistan, straddle important crossroads in the region. At the Fifth ECO Summit in Almaty in May 1998, Uzbekistan again refused to sign a much watered down transit agreement. A decade later, establishment of the ECO Trade Promotion Organization, headquartered in Tehran, met with a lukewarm response in Central Asia.

[27]While becoming more economically integrated with Asia, Australia's political position, varied with the government; the Labor governments of 1983–1996 and post-2007 sought to position Australia in Asia, while the 1996–2007 Liberal government put more weight on historical ties with the UK and USA.

Conclusions

Before 2000, regionalism in the Asia–Pacific region was distinguished by its absence. Apart from the Australasian CER agreement, the only functioning regional trading arrangement, ASEAN, had minimal economic impact. The primary goal of peaceful coexistence both within and beyond Southeast Asia was reflected in the 1971 Zone of Peace, Freedom and Neutrality Declaration and the 1976 Treaty of Amity and Cooperation in Southeast Asia, and recognition of security interdependence in the Asia–Pacific region led to the establishment in 1994 of the ASEAN Regional Forum (ARF). These security-related aspects will not be dwelt upon in this book, but given the organization's history the fact that there has been no military conflict between ASEAN members is a major achievement.[28]

The high-performing East Asian economies — Japan, Hong Kong, South Korea, Taiwan and Singapore — owed their success to exporting labour-intensive manufactured goods to the high-income countries of North America, Western Europe and Australasia. Access to these markets was on the basis of MFN tariffs, and the successful exporters did not strive for preferential treatment.[29] They also had no interest in negotiating preferential access to one another's markets. Indeed, when Malaysia floated the idea of an RTA covering the ASEAN countries,

---

[28] If this achievement is an ASEAN success, it is because ASEAN has provided a forum in which problems can be pre-empted, rather than being due to ASEAN institutions. The Treaty of Amity and Cooperation has not been operationalized beyond a general renunciation of the use of force to settle disputes, and ASEAN has no formal dispute settlement or conflict resolution mechanisms. Bilateral disputes are taken to other fora, e.g. the dispute between Indonesia and Malaysia over Sipidan and Ligitan islands was taken to the International Court of Justice in the Netherlands in 2002, or are treated as a bilateral affair, e.g. as tensions escalated along the Thai–Cambodia border in 2009–2010 neither side invoked ASEAN.

[29] Some of the new industrializing economies received preferential treatment under importing countries' Generalized System of Preferences (GSP) schemes which were introduced in the 1970s. GSP tariff preferences were, however, limited and subject to unilateral change by the importing country; in the 1980s, the new industrializing economies were being graduated out of GSP schemes (Kirkman, 1989). A more important issue for the exporters was minimizing non-tariff barriers to their exports, which heightened their sensitivity to not upsetting rich-country trading partners by joining an RTA such as the EAEC.

Japan and Korea, the other countries showed no interest in alienating the USA by granting preferential access to non-US imports.

The open (i.e. non-preferential) regionalism of Asia–Pacific Economic Cooperation (APEC), which was established in 1989, was not regionalism in the normal sense of RTAs. Politically, APEC was driven by US opposition to, and Australian fear of, being sidelined by an Asian RTA, such as that being proposed by Malaysia. These developments will be discussed in the next chapter.

Chapter 3

The Rise and Decline
of Open Regionalism

Asia in the second half of the twentieth century was characterized by an absence of regional trading arrangements. There were, however, cooperative activities, such as the Executives' Meeting of East Asia–Pacific Central Banks (see Chapter 5), and a growing sense of regional identity. Outside ASEAN, the cooperative activities were often led by Japan and Australia, the two high-income countries in the western Pacific. This alignment, at times, conflicted with other ideas of the composition of the region. The conflict climaxed in the early 1990s with the choice between Malaysian Prime Minister Mahathir's vision of an East Asian grouping and the wider Asia–Pacific Economic Cooperation (APEC).

The conflict was resolved in favour of the broader APEC, as most East Asian countries saw little benefit from a narrower RTA and much to lose from alienating the USA. The open (i.e. non-preferential) regionalism of Asia–Pacific Economic Cooperation (APEC), which was established in 1989, was not regionalism in the normal sense of RTAs, and the membership encompasses a range of countries with no common features beyond a Pacific coastline (Map 2).[1] Nevertheless, despite its informality and diverse membership, APEC did play a role in the evolution of East Asian regionalism by encouraging unilateral trade liberalization during the first half of the 1990s.

---

[1] APEC now includes Australia, Brunei, Canada, Chile, China, Hong Kong, Indonesia, Japan, Korea, Malaysia, Mexico, New Zealand, Papua New Guinea, Peru, the Philippines, Russia, Singapore, Taiwan, Thailand, the USA and Vietnam.

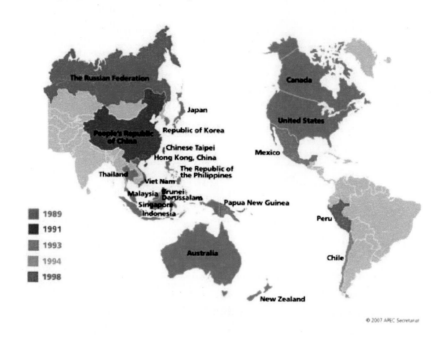

Map 2:   APEC

APEC was, however, a poor forum for convincing governments to proceed any faster or further with trade liberalization than they felt comfortable with. This weakness was highlighted when the USA over-reached in attempting to open markets with the 1996 Early Voluntary Sectoral Liberalisation (EVSL) initiative. Combined with the irrelevance of APEC as an institution to address the Asian Crisis which erupted in July 1997, the EVSL debacle sounded the death knell of APEC as an important economic institution. APEC summits continue to provide a meeting place for many of the world's most important leaders (to the chagrin of Europeans) and APEC provides useful network opportunities for officials involved in, for example, trade facilitation. However, by the turn of the century, APEC was on the sidelines as East Asian regionalism began to flourish.

Origins of Asia–Pacific Economic Cooperation

Early steps towards cooperation in the Asia–Pacific region during the 1960s were informal and non-governmental. The Pacific Basin

Economic Council (PBEC) was founded in 1967 as an independent business association for the Asia–Pacific region. The Pacific Trade and Development Conference (PAFTAD) is an informal private academic organization whose annual conferences have, since 1968, been organized around important economic policy questions facing the region; PAFTAD has a secretariat at the Australian National University. In 1980, at the initiative of the prime ministers of Japan and Australia, a "Pacific Community Seminar" was held in Canberra, Australia. The Seminar was attended by eleven delegations (from Australia, Canada, Indonesia, Japan, South Korea, Malaysia, New Zealand, the Philippines, Singapore, Thailand and the United States) and three Pacific Island states (Papua New Guinea, Fiji and Tonga); representatives of the Asian Development Bank, PBEC and PAFTAD were also present. Typically, each delegation comprised of one senior government official, one business leader, and one academic or professional member. This became the blueprint for the Pacific Economic Cooperation Council (PECC), and the Seminar was relabelled PECC-1 (i.e. the first meeting of PECC).

The Pacific Economic Cooperation Council is an independent tripartite body in which senior representatives from government, business and academia participate.[2] The aim was for PECC to serve as a forum for cooperation and policy coordination to promote economic development in the Asia–Pacific region. It remains informal and independent and provides a forum for furthering ideas generated by the two pre-existing independent groupings representing business and academia (PBEC and PAFTAD).[3] Singapore hosts the PECC secretariat.

In the late 1980s, as global trade negotiations (the Uruguay Round) faltered and regionalism appeared to be strengthening in Western Europe, as the European Union was creating its single market (the

---

[2]The articles collected in Pacific Economic Cooperation Council (2005) provide background on the formation of PECC and early years of cooperation in the Asia–Pacific region.

[3]PECC's membership consists of national committees, which in 2009 numbered 22: Australia, Brunei Darussalam, Canada, Chile, China, Colombia, Ecuador, Hong Kong, Indonesia, Japan, Malaysia, Mexico, New Zealand, Peru, the Philippines, Singapore, South Korea, Taiwan, Thailand, the USA, Vietnam and the Pacific Islands Forum. PECC also has two associate members, France (representing its Pacific territories) and Mongolia, and two institutional members, PAFTAD and PBEC.

EC92 program), and the USA, Canada and Mexico were negotiating the North American Free Trade Area (NAFTA), many in Asia felt they were being disadvantaged by the creation of large preferential trading blocs in the rest of the world. In this environment, two alternative visions were floated: the wider Asia–Pacific concept of open regionalism proposed by Australia in 1989, and the narrower more traditional RTA proposed by Malaysia's prime minister, Mohamed Mahathir, in 1990. In the event, Japan's rejection of Mahathir's proposal, which would include the ASEAN countries and northeast Asian countries, made it a non-starter.[4]

In January 1989, Australian prime minister Bob Hawke proposed intergovernmental cooperation in the Asia–Pacific region and Asia–Pacific Economic Cooperation (APEC) was launched later in the year, drawing on the experience of PECC and ASEAN. The twelve founder members of APEC were the PECC countries: Australia, Brunei, Canada, Indonesia, Malaysia, Japan, South Korea, New Zealand, the Philippines, Singapore, Thailand and the United States (i.e. ASEAN plus Japan, South Korea, Australia, New Zealand, the USA and Canada). Politically, APEC was driven by US opposition to and Australian fear of being sidelined by an Asian RTA, such as the East Asia Economic Group proposed by Malaysia. The 1990 Kuching Consensus laid out the basis for ASEAN members' participation in APEC on the basis of enhancing ASEAN's economic contribution. The 1991 Seoul APEC Declaration laid out four objectives of APEC:

- promoting sustained growth and development;
- enhancing the gains from increased global interdependence by encouraging the flow of goods, services, capital and technology;
- strengthening an open multilateral trading system;
- reducing barriers to trade in APEC member countries without detriment to other economies.

---

[4]Mahathir's original proposal was for an East Asia Group, operating as a trade bloc with preferential treatment of members. After Japan's cool reception, it was repackaged as a less threatening East Asia Economic Caucus (EAEC), and in 1994 the EAEC countries formed a caucus within APEC.

The last feature, in contrast to the Western European model of treaty-based discrimination against the rest of the world, defined the concept of "open regionalism" (Drysdale, Elek and Soesastro, 1998). The APEC process was explicitly informal, opening the way to participation from Hong Kong or Taiwan without raising issues of recognition, and these economies joined with China in 1991.[5]

Although the USA had supported the formation of APEC, this was primarily as a negative response to the threat of an East Asian RTA and the positive contribution of the 1989–1992 Bush administration was limited. The USA continued to push aggressive unilateralism, although the East Asian targets of its super 301 market-opening trade measures were pursued less aggressively than India or Brazil. President Bush Sr. himself was best remembered for collapsing at a banquet table in Japan during a futile mission to open Japanese markets to US car exports. Secretary of State Baker's most memorable Asian trip was to Mongolia in search of trophies from shooting rare animals. President Clinton signalled an end to the neglect of Asia by announcing that his first year in office would be the Year of Asia in US policy, and the USA hosted the first summit of APEC leaders (Table 3.1).[6]

The 1993 APEC summit sent important messages, although they were received differently in different capitals. For Asian leaders, it was a signal that the USA was not in single-minded pursuit of a Western Hemisphere bloc. This probably had less impact on the APEC region than in facilitating the completion of the Uruguay Round of multilateral trade negotiations, which happened in 1994 and led to the creation of the World Trade Organization (WTO) in 1995. For European leaders, the message was less positive, as they observed a meeting of many of the world's most powerful leaders, but without a

---

[5]Formally they joined under the names of Hong Kong, China, and Chinese Taipei. Mexico and Papua New Guinea joined APEC in 1993, Chile in 1994, and Peru, Russia and Vietnam in 1998. A moratorium on new members was imposed in the late 1990s and extended for a decade after the 1997–1998 Asian Crisis. As of 2010, Colombia and Ecuador are expected to become members in the near future and other economies have expressed interest in joining (e.g. India, Laos, Guam, Mongolia and Bangladesh).

[6]Before 1993, the highest level APEC meetings were at ministerial level: Canberra 1989, Singapore 1990, Seoul 1991 and Bangkok 1992. Starting in 1993, ministerial meetings were accompanied, and overshadowed, by economic leaders meetings (summits).

Table 3.1   APEC Summits.

Year	Location	Year	Location
1993	Blake Island (near Seattle), USA	2003	Bangkok, Thailand
1994	Bogor, Indonesia	2004	Santiago, Chile
1995	Osaka, Japan	2005	Busan, Korea
1996	Subic Bay, Philippines	2006	Hanoi, Vietnam
1997	Vancouver, Canada	2007	Sydney, Australia
1998	Kuala Lumpur, Malaysia	2008	Lima, Peru
1999	Auckland, New Zealand	2009	Singapore
2000	Brunei	2010	Yokohama, Japan
2001	Shanghai, China	2011	To be determined, USA
2002	Los Cabos, Mexico	2012	Vladivostok, Russia

Notes: The first four annual meetings (Canberra 1989, Singapore 1990, Seoul 1991, Bangkok 1992) were attended by ministerial-level officials. Since 1993, the annual APEC Economic Leaders' Meetings have been attended by the heads of government from all member economies except Taiwan, which is represented by a ministerial-level official.

European presence — in contrast to the G7 summits where a majority of participants were European. For Europeans, the APEC summit highlighted the shift in the global economic centre of gravity from the North Atlantic to the Pacific.

The Bogor Declaration and APEC's Heyday, 1994–1997

Open regionalism was popular in the context of many Asian countries seeking to liberalize their own trade policies and hoping for reciprocal multilateral liberalization on the part of other countries beyond what was being achieved in multilateral trade negotiations. This was especially true for some of the larger Asian economies such as China, Indonesia, the Philippines and Thailand, which were reorienting their economies from earlier inward-looking development strategies. The centrepiece of this process was the declaration at the 1994 Bogor Summit that APEC members would create a free and open trade and investment zone, with the specific goal that members would remove their tariffs by 2010, with extensions for developing countries to 2020. The Bogor Declaration was the high-point of open regionalism.

APEC contributed to trade liberalization in East Asia. Leaders such as Suharto in Indonesia, Ramos in the Philippines and Jiang Zemin and Zhu Rongji in China used the Bogor Declaration to influence domestic policy debates and accelerate unilateral trade liberalization. By encouraging transparency in trade policy, APEC may have also had a less direct positive impact on trade.[7] Such concerted liberalization was attractive in the specific conditions of the early and mid-1990s, when many leaders saw the East Asian model of outward-oriented development to be dependent on both national policies and an open multilateral trading system that might be under threat from discriminatory regional trading arrangements.[8]

As economic conditions began to deteriorate in some APEC members in 1996–1997, trade liberalization became less attractive (Garnaut, 2000).[9] This was already visible at the 1995 Osaka summit when proposals for action on anti-dumping polices were rejected, but leaders agreed to proceed with drawing up individual action plans based on the Bogor Declaration goals. The action plan adopted at the 1996 summit in the Philippines emphasised six main areas of work: market access in goods, market access in services, open investment regimes, reduced business costs, efficient infrastructure, and economic and technical cooperation. Individual action plans presented at the 1997 Vancouver summit were, however, short on specifics and, although most did proceed beyond WTO commitments, they fell short of the Bogor Goals on trade liberalization.

In the face of perceived foot-dragging in individual action plans, the USA tried to push trade liberalization further in 1996 with the Early

---

[7]Analysing trade between APEC countries, Helble, Shepherd and Wilson (2009) found that transparency significantly increases trade flows.

[8]The commitment was not universal. Poorer APEC members wanted to maintain protection of infant industries, and this view was shared by more nationalist policymakers in Taiwan or South Korea. Other countries' leaders, e.g. Malaysia, argued for greater flexibility, such as interpreting trade liberalization in the AFTA sense of reducing tariffs below five percent rather than eliminating them and of permitting lengthy exclusion lists. Views on what open regionalism meant for foreign investment were even more diffused.

[9]Concerted unilateralism within APEC may have become less attractive as WTO charter members engaged in implementing their obligations under the 1994 Final Act of the Uruguay Round of multilateral trade negotiations. Also, the enthusiastic trade-liberalizing APEC members may have come to the end of their lists of tariffs that they were willing to reduce unilaterally.

Voluntary Sectoral Liberalisation (EVSL) initiative. As tabled at the 1997 Vancouver summit, the EVSL called for APEC liberalization in 15 sectors, of which nine were high priority and six were second-tier. In the first tier were chemicals, rubber and plastics, energy, environmental goods and services, forestry products, fisheries, gems and jewellery, medical equipment and instruments, telecommunications, and toys. The second tier consisted of the automotive sector, civil aircraft, fertilisers, food, rubber, and oilseeds.

The Early Voluntary Sectoral Liberalisation Initiative, the Asian Crisis and APEC

The EVSL initiative quickly ran into opposition led by Japan, which was unhappy that the USA considered EVSL provisions as binding for developed countries. Japan insisted on opting out from liberalization of the fisheries and forestry sectors, which had been designated as high-priority sectors. Japan was supported by China, South Korea and Taiwan, for all of whom agricultural trade liberalization was too politically sensitive to make sweeping liberalization commitments with respect to the food sector. By 1998, the EVSL had collapsed acrimoniously. At the 1998 APEC summit, Indonesia, Malaysia and Thailand joined the other sceptics in refusing to support the initiative. In brief, APEC members were unwilling to accept pressure to liberalize beyond what they would have done unilaterally, and the scope for concerted unilateral liberalization had narrowed by the late 1990s.

APEC was further discredited by its failure to address the 1997 Asian Crisis. At the 1999 summit, in Auckland several members were paying more attention to exploring bilateral trade agreements, including the host country which initiated negotiation of a Singapore–New Zealand FTA at the summit. By the turn of the century, open regionalism had lost the significance that it attained in the mid-1990s. Although APEC summits continue to provide a venue for leaders from the USA, China, Japan, Russia and other members to meet in a fairly informal setting, the economic impact of APEC had diminished.[10]

---

[10]Proposals to establish a Free Trade Area of the Asia–Pacific region were rejected at the 2004 and 2006 summits in the face of opposition from East Asian APEC members. Attempts to address

The most important APEC trade initiative in the first decade of the twenty-first century has concerned trade facilitation. At the 2001 Shanghai summit, APEC members committed to reducing their trade transactions costs by 5% between 2002 and 2006. The Trade Facilitation Action Plan (TFAP-1) was deemed successful and in TFAP-2 a commitment was made to reduce trade costs by a further 5% over the period 2007–2010. This is a useful exercise, encouraging governments to catalogue their trade costs and think of measures to reduce them in national Trade Facilitation Action Plans, and it complements multilateral negotiations on trade facilitation in the WTO's Doha Development Round.

The TFAPs are, however, no more than a framework for encouraging voluntary national action to reduce trade costs and for transparency in publicizing trade facilitation measures that have been introduced by APEC members. Without any agreed measure of trade costs, a quantitative target such as a 5% reduction is operationally meaningless.[11] Moreover, it was explicitly agreed that a "one-size-fits-all' approach to trade facilitation is inappropriate, so each country can select a different array of trade costs to be reduced, making it difficult to even determine whether one country's reduction in aggregate trade costs is larger or smaller than another country's reduction in trade costs. The announcement of TFAP-2 in July 2007 mentioned streamlining electronic customs documentation, establishing single windows as an entry point where import, export and transit requirements can all

---

the rise of FTAs by establishing best practice guidelines were also ineffective, in the face of the members' insistence that any best practice recommendations would be non-binding. After September 2001, the USA tried to link economics and security, and at the 2002 summit the Secure Trade in APEC initiative was launched, but following the 2003 invasion of Iraq, which was condemned by many APEC leaders, a majority position emerged that APEC was not the appropriate forum for security matters; at subsequent summits, reassurances about efforts to combat terrorism have not been accompanied by concrete measures.

[11] In February 2009, Hong Kong agreed to donate $200,000 to the APEC Secretariat to develop a way to measure the outcome of its Trade Facilitation Action Plan. However, without an agreed definition of trade facilitation this goal is a chimera. Quantitative work such as that carried out at the World Bank (e.g. Wilson, Mann and Otsuki, 2003) deduces changes of trade costs from trade flows rather than measuring trade costs directly. Analysis of the cif-fob gap as a measure of trade costs is in its infancy (Hummels, 2007; Pomfret and Sourdin, 2009); to be operationally useful in a context such as the APEC TFAPs, we need a better understanding of the breakdown between the part of the gap which may be responsive to policy and the exogenously determined part (e.g. related to distance or landlockedness). See the Appendix for discussion of this measurement issue.

be fulfilled, making business travel within APEC easier,[12] harmonizing food safety and standards and protecting data privacy; but there is no contractual obligation for APEC members to address any or all of these areas. This flexibility may be more acceptable to APEC members than a commitment such as the Bogor Declaration, which sounded acceptable in 1994, but had to be rejected as it became clear that APEC members would fail to meet the target of zero tariffs by 2010.[13] In practical terms, the TFAPs signal a return to APEC's *de facto* 1993–1996 role as a talking shop where desirable unilateral policies may be coordinated.

Conclusions

In the early years after APEC was established in 1989, the organization played a valuable role in bringing Asian economies together and encouraging unilateral trade liberalization. APEC kept the USA engaged in the region and forestalled the formation of a potentially discriminatory regional arrangement, such as the East Asia Economic Caucus (EAEC) proposed by Malaysian Prime Minister Mahathir. The high point was the Bogor Declaration, which envisaged tariff-free trade among APEC members. However, in 1997/8 APEC's substantive influence faded with the debacle of the EVSL and the organization's failure to respond

---

[12]The APEC Business Travel Card Scheme gives holders priority immigration and customs clearance on arrival and departure from international airports, and provides multiple-entry three-year visas to participating economies. In 2007, however, only 17 APEC members participated in the Scheme (Australia, Brunei Darussalam, Chile, China, Hong Kong, Indonesia, Japan, Korea, Malaysia, New Zealand, Papua New Guinea, Peru, Philippines, Singapore, Taiwan, Thailand, and Viet Nam). By March 2008, the active number of cards was more than 34,000, with Australia responsible for nearly 40% of all cards issued. Mexico began issuing cards in 2007–2008. A goal of TFAP-2 was to encourage US participation, but by 2010 the card only allowed access to the fast-track air-crew lanes at US airports and cardholders still needed to obtain visas as required by United States law, although the card is recognized for expedited visa interview scheduling at US embassies. For more information on the Scheme, see http://www.apec.org/apec/business_resources/apec_business_travel0.html.

[13]APEC supporters have finessed this failure by claiming that the Bogor goals "targeted liberalisation of trade and investment by industrialised economies (like Australia and Japan) by 2010 and developing countries (like China and ASEAN) by 2020" rather than being commitments to eliminate tariffs, and the Bogor goals can be "put to bed" by the Japanese government reducing agricultural trade barriers and by all APEC members "shifting the focus decisively towards deeper integration through a regional commitment to structural reform and institutional harmonisation" (Drysdale, 2009).

to the Asian Crisis. Since 1998, APEC has been marginalized as an institution for addressing key economic issues facing the region (Bergsten, 2009).

After the turn of the century, APEC remained useful as a high-profile meeting place for the leaders of the USA, China, Japan, Russia, Australia and other countries. As with any such club, it created dissatisfaction among those excluded. European leaders responded by establishing the biennial Asia Europe Meeting (ASEM) in 1996 as an inter-regional forum consisting of members of the European Union and ASEAN, plus China, Japan and South Korea.[14] A more select set of world leaders met at the G7 summits for the seven largest market-based economies, which was enlarged to include Russia but excluded large emerging economies such as China, India and Brazil. The establishment in 2008–2009 of the G20 as the principal economic meeting place of the world's leaders was a response, but this group may be too large to provide a suitable meeting place for the major powers.

From an East Asian perspective, the evolution of APEC can be explained in terms of shifting balances of regional economic power. In 1989, Japan's economic pre-eminence was at its peak. Japan's main security relationship was with the USA, which was also the number one market for Japanese exports. Cooperation within the western Pacific was primarily with Australia; the two countries' central bankers saw themselves as the leaders in the region's monetary sphere. Thus, Japan was strongly opposed to an exclusively East Asian arrangement such as the EAEC and embraced Australia's proposal for a wider organization that included the USA. For the East Asian region as a whole, trade in 1989 was overwhelmingly with partners outside the region, primarily the high-income countries of North America, Western Europe and Australasia.

By 2000, the situation had changed dramatically, with the rising economic weight of China and closing of the economic gap between

---

[14] ASEM meetings alternate between Asia and Europe: ASEM1 Bangkok 1996, ASEM2 London 1998, ASEM3 Seoul 2000, ASEM4 Copenhagen 2002, ASEM5 Hanoi 2004, ASEM6 Helsinki 2006. India, Mongolia and Pakistan were invited to ASEM7 in Beijing in 2008, bringing the number of participants to 43 countries plus the European Commission and ASEAN Secretariat. Australia and Russia were invited to ASEM8 in Belgium in 2010.

Japan and China. Asian trade patterns were transformed by the rapid growth of Chinese exports during the 1990s and by the emergence of intra-Asian trade flows, and the two trends converged in the late 1990s as China played a more central role in regional value chains. China's principal trade policy focus during the 1990s was WTO accession, a process which lasted 15 years from its application in 1986 to conclusion in 2001, during which time China established its credentials as a country committed to the rules-based multilateral trading system. This commitment, shared by Japan, underpinned gradual improvement in bilateral relations and increased economic interaction between China and Japan.[15] By the end of the decade, when China's WTO negotiations were effectively concluded, the time was ripe for a revival of an East Asian grouping.

---

[15]The political relationship had been normalized in 1972, but economic relations had not been smooth in the 1970s, e.g. after Mao Zedong's death in 1976, many turnkey projects purchased from Japanese firms by the government of Hua Guofeng were cancelled after Hua's ouster by Deng Xiaoping in 1978. The only formal agreements between China and Japan are a 1978 Long Term Trade Agreement and a 1988 Bilateral Investment Treaty, both of which were irrelevant by the end of the century. Nevertheless, economic relations flourished in the 1990s as Japanese firms looked for offshore suppliers and investment opportunities as well as seeing a growing market.

Chapter 4

Market-driven Regionalization: The Emergence of Subregional Zones

Until the 1990s, the trade of Asian countries was largely with countries outside the region. The global division of labour typically involved low-wage Asian countries providing labour-intensive value-added in a fairly simple global value chain. A large retailer or an intermediary from North America or Western Europe would provide the product specifications and perhaps organize the delivery of some intermediate inputs; the East Asian producer would assemble the product (e.g. sew the shirts, stitch the baseballs or fix the copper wire in the semiconductors); and the foreign firm would arrange the transport and marketing to the consumer in the high-income country.

Japan broke out of this pattern in the 1950s and 1960s when firms such as Toyota or Honda or Sony established their own identity and internalized the value chain. This was a successful strategy through the 1970s and first half of the 1980s when Japan's share of world trade increased rapidly despite protectionist moves in North America and Western Europe (e.g. limiting the number of Japanese cars that could be imported). After 1985, with the falling value of the US dollar and rapid appreciation of the yen, Japanese exporters faced declining competitiveness. Japan then initiated a trend towards integrated production chains within East Asia when it invested heavily in Southeast Asia.

Economic growth in the high-performing East Asian economies has been export-oriented and heavily concentrated in a handful of large port cities (Pomfret, 1994; 1995a). For the larger economies such as South Korea and Taiwan in the 1960s and 1970s or China, Indonesia and Thailand in the 1980s and 1990s, the process involved rural-urban labour migration as agricultural workers shifted to higher productivity employment in manufacturing. Income gaps between the cities and countryside drove the internal migration as average incomes increased but large numbers of low-wage workers were still available. For the cities of Hong Kong and Singapore with no rural hinterland, their comparative advantage in labour-intensive manufactures quickly encountered a shortage of low-wage labour. The solution was to relocate the labour-intensive activities to contiguous regions of neighbouring countries while continuing to take advantage of their accumulated skills in producing and marketing labour-intensive goods. The phenomenon of sub-regional economic zones is analysed in the first section of this chapter.

As a result of Japanese offshore investment, the growth of sub-regional economic zones and China's greater economic diversity and complexity, intraregional trade and investment in East Asia began to increase rapidly during the 1990s. By 1996, intraregional trade accounted for 50% of the East Asian countries' total trade, compared to about a third at the start of the 1980s. The share of intraregional trade in total exports dipped after the Asian Crisis, but climbed back to 52% in 2004, when the import share was 57% (Munakata, 2006, 47).[1] This pattern partly reflected the increasing importance of Asian markets as incomes and demand rose, but more importantly it reflected the emergence of regional value chains which is described in the second section of this chapter.[2]

The emergence of regional value chains was an example of market-driven regionalization, but it had policy implications. Fragmenting production by locating different activities according to countries' comparative advantage is only feasible if transport and other trade

---

[1] These are higher than equivalent measures for NAFTA and similar to those for the EU in the mid-1980s. Trade intensity indices, which declined in the three decades up to 1985 and were then flat for a decade (Petri, 1993), also show increasing trade within the East Asia region during the second half of the 1990s and the first half of the 2000s (Sohn, 2002; Ng and Yeats, 2003; Petri, 2006).

[2] The increased regionalization of the East Asian economy is described in Frankel and Kahler (1993), Hatch and Yamamura (1996), Aggarwal and Morrison (1998, 65–86), Lincoln (2004, 42–113), Munakata (2006, 37–61), Rajan (2006) and Dean and Lovely (2008).

costs are low. In particular, cumbersome procedures when goods cross national borders are the kiss of death for international value chains, and any country which has excessive at-the-border costs will play little role in such value chains. In the 1990s, the emergence of regional value chains placed pressure on governments to facilitate trade if their country was to participate in these chains, and this was especially apparent within the original ASEAN members. Evidence is presented in the third section of this chapter.

Sub-Regional Economic Zones (SRZs)

Rapid growth in East Asia was heavily concentrated round a handful of coastal areas, mostly based on the great port cities. Hong Kong and Singapore were city states, and Taiwan and South Korea as an island and a peninsular economy were surrounded by water. Chinese development was heavily concentrated in coastal areas around Guangzhou, Shanghai, Tianjin, Xiamen, Dalian and a handful of other ports. In Thailand, Greater Bangkok, with an eighth of the country's population, produced over half of the country's output. For China and Thailand, unskilled labour could be brought into the manufacturing sector by rural-urban migration, but this option was not available to Hong Kong. Instead, Hong Kong's entrepreneurs moved their production facilities offshore.

The first phase of China's economic reforms after 1978 centred on increased agricultural productivity. The labour released from more productive agriculture and the savings accumulated by farmers went into local businesses, collectively known as township and village enterprises (TVEs), which largely produced the kind of manufactures that local families would buy with their higher incomes (utensils, construction materials for home improvements, and so forth).[3] By 1983–1984, many TVEs were running up against demand constraints as their local market became saturated. This coincided with rising wages and land prices in Hong Kong and adverse exchange rate developments which were making Hong Kong uncompetitive in markets for labour-intensive

---

[3] The TVEs were an institutional response to the restrictions on labour movement and on financial institutions imposed in the still heavily regulated Chinese economy of the 1980s.

manufactures. The solution was to combine Hong Kong's managerial and marketing expertise with the TVEs' low-wage but literate labour by shifting sewing machines and other equipment from Hong Kong across the border. Most of this occurred in Guangdong, the province adjacent to Hong Kong with a shared language and many family ties. The web of economic linkages that quickly emerged between Hong Kong, neighbouring counties of Guangdong and Macau created the Pearl River Delta (PRD) economic region (Map 3). Creation of the PRD economic region was market-driven by Hong Kong entrepreneurs and TVE managers, although the Hong Kong authorities and local Chinese officials took positive steps to facilitate the process.[4]

A similar phenomenon began to emerge around Singapore in the late 1980s and 1990s as Singapore lost its comparative advantage in labour-intensive goods. Singaporean businesses moved their labour-intensive activities to neighbouring parts of Malaysia (Johor) and Indonesia (Riau Province), while Singapore remained the financial and commercial hub of the region, which was soon dubbed Sijori after the initial letters of the three component parts (Map 4). Johor is linked to Singapore by a causeway and had a pre-existing industrial base, with wages significantly lower than in Singapore. Riau province has abundant and relatively cheap land, and labour-intensive activities were transferred to industrial parks newly developed by large Indonesian conglomerates and government-linked Singaporean firms (e.g. the Batamindo Industrial Park in 1991 and Bintan Industrial Estate in 1993 were jointly developed by Singapore's Sembcorp Industries and JTC International and Indonesia's Salim Group).[5]

A characteristic of the PRD and Sijori is that these regions were the result of a bottom-up process rather than a top-down creation of an

---

[4]Jurisdictional competition in China was important. Any county in the Pearl River Delta area of Guangdong whose administration did not support the establishment of joint ventures with Hong Kong quickly found its living standards slipping behind those of its neighbours. The central government played a role by creating special economic zones, notably in Shenzhen and Zhuhai, adjacent to Hong Kong and to the Portuguese colony of Macau respectively, but many towns outside the special zones were just as successful. For more details, see Vogel (1989) and Pomfret (1991, chapter 5).

[5]The two parks cover 430 hectares and employ 92,000 workers, generating over $6 billion per year in exports (Lim, 2009, 226). Batam and Bintan Islands have excellent boat connections to Singapore.

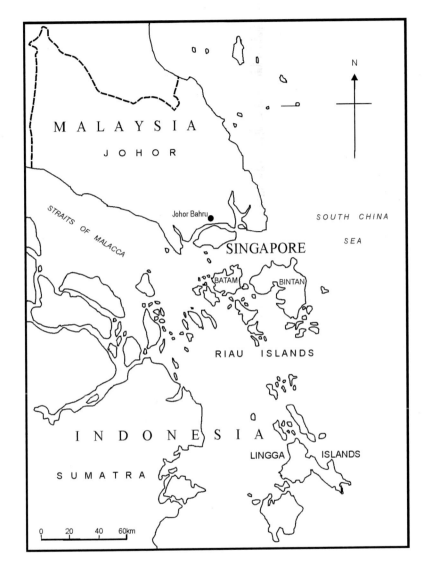

Map 3:   Sijori.

RTA by national governments. In Sijori's case, a Singapore–Indonesia intergovernmental agreement preceded the establishment of the industrial parks, but the activities have been driven by profit-seeking corporations. Moreover, the PRD and Sijori were not groupings of nation states, but included small parts of China or of Malaysia and Indonesia.

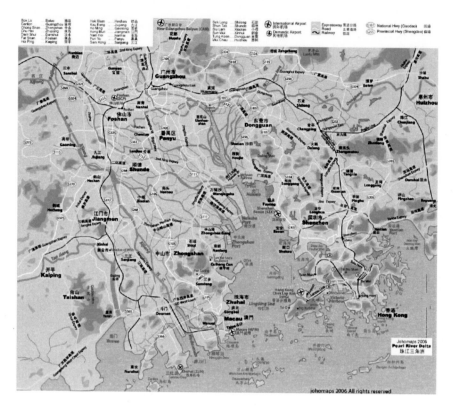

Map 4:   Pearl River Delta.

These characteristics spawned the name 'subregional economic zones', or SRZs (Pomfret, 1996a).

Policymakers in ASEAN sought to emulate the economic success of Sijori by creating other SRZs among neighbouring regions of countries, often with the goal of stimulating economically backward areas. The Indonesia–Malaysia–Thailand Growth Triangle (IMT-GT), launched in July 1993, included North Sumatra in Indonesia, three northern states of Malaysia (Penang, Kedah and Perlis) and southern Thailand. The Brunei, Indonesia, Malaysia, Philippines East ASEAN Growth Area (BIMP-EAGA), launched in March 1994, included Brunei, the Indonesian provinces of Kalimantan and Sulawesi, the Malaysian states of Sabah and Sarawak, and southern Philippines. IMT-GT had some private sector origins with the desire of Malaysian businesspeople to trade more with northern Sumatra, but both it and BIMP-EAGA were top-down creations intended to stimulate growth in parts of South-east Asia that were lagging far behind Sijori. Neither has been very successful; BIMP-EAGA became bogged down in issues such as terri-torial demarcation, while IMT-GT was stifled by government control (and by border tensions between Malaysia and southern Thailand). More fundamentally, neither of these SRZs has the complementarities that differentiate the three components of Sijori, nor do they have a hub comparable to Singapore.

An even more top-down approach was adopted in Northeast Asia with the creation of the Tumen River SRZ. In the decades up until the 1980s, apart from bilateral trade between Japan and South Korea, inter-national economic relations in Northeast Asia were severely repressed; the Korean peninsula was divided, relations between the Soviet Union and China had been tense since the early 1960s (which also affected Mongolia which was in the Soviet sphere of influence), and Japan, South Korea and Taiwan had limited economic relations with the Peo-ple's Republic of China. The situation was transformed in the early 1990s by the dissolution of the Soviet Union and the end of central planning in Russia and Mongolia, and by the establishment of diplo-matic ties between China and South Korea, which was followed by a rapid increase in recorded trade between China and South Korea.[6] At an international conference in Changchun in 1990, China called for coordinated measures to promote economic activity in the area where China, the USSR and North Korean borders meet; and in follow-up conferences in 1991 in Ulaanbaatar and Pyongyang, the United Nations Development Programme (UNDP) approved a $3.5 million two-year project to assist a Programme Management Commit-tee consisting of the three countries plus Japan, Mongolia and South Korea (Map 5). The six countries had complementary economies; Japan and South Korea were high-income capital-abundant countries, while

---

[6]Already by 1989, Chinese trade with South Korea, as well as with Taiwan, flourished, based on the attraction of foreign investment in China by entrepreneurs in Korea or Taiwan whose equip-ment was no longer profitable in their homeland but was still profitable at Chinese wage rates. However, for political reasons, the origins of the trade and investment flows were often hidden by, for example, passing through Hong Kong or using relatives as sleeping partners (Pomfret, 1991, 110–11).

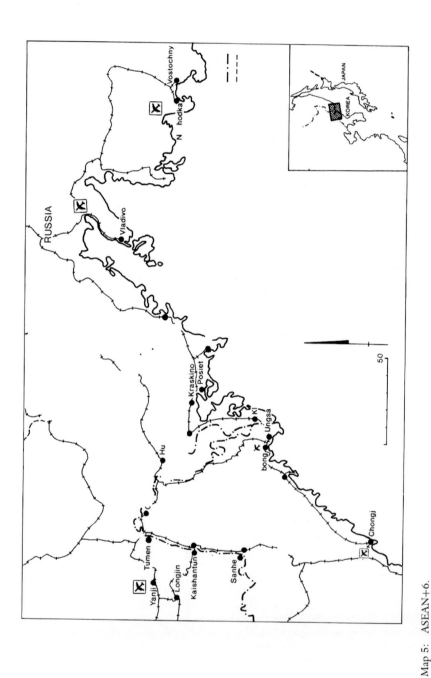

Map 5:   ASEAN+6.
Note: The map covers the narrow area of the Tumen River Area Development Programme covering Yanbian Autonomous Prefecture (China), the southern part of Primorski Krai (Russia), and the northest corner of the DPRK. The inset indicates the wider area covered by the programme when it had six partners (China, Japan, Mongolia, Russia and the two Koreas).

Mongolia and the Russian Far East were abundant in natural resources, and northeast China and North Korea had abundant literate low-wage labour. Initial agreements in 1992–1993 called for the three contiguous countries to lease land to an internationally managed Tumen River Economic Zone. However, when it came to implementation, the national governments had doubts about leasing land to a supranational corporation and several partners appeared unwilling to provide the promised funding. In 1994, the project appeared to be stalled, a situation not helped by the death of North Korean President Kim Il-sung. The UNDP had nothing to show for its $3.5 million expenditure, apart perhaps for some confidence-building in one of the tensest corners of Asia.[7]

The Greater Mekong Subregion (GMS), established in 1992 by Cambodia, Laos, Myanmar, Thailand, Vietnam and Yunnan Province of China, represented a different approach to subregional cooperation. The GMS was not a preferential trading arrangement, nor was it based on bringing together complementary economies as in the SRZs just described. Instead, it was aimed at promoting cooperation among countries that should have been tied together by geography, but whose infrastructure had been destroyed by the lengthy Indochina wars which lasted until the late 1970s. A primary activity, coordinated by the Asian Development Bank, has been to develop transport corridors across the GMS in order to reduce the costs of international trade.[8]

---

[7] Pomfret (1995b; 1996b; 130–142; and 1997/8) provides details of the evolution of the Tumen River project in the 1990s. The Tumen River Area Development Programme continued to exist and be supported by the UNDP and other donors. In 2005, it was rebadged as the Greater Tumen Initiative (GTI) with five member countries: China, North and South Korea, Mongolia, and the Russian Federation. The geographical coverage of the Greater Tumen region now covers China's three northeast provinces and Inner Mongolia, North Korea's Rason Economic and Trade Zone, eastern provinces of Mongolia, eastern port cities of South Korea, and part of Russia's Primorsky province. See http://www.tumenprogramme.org/.

[8] Coordination is desirable because transport infrastructure is less valuable if it stops at national borders or is not accompanied by trade facilitating measures. After the first road bridge across the Mekong River linking Vientiane to northeast Thailand was opened in 1993, its economic value was much reduced by regulations aimed at protecting the Lao trucking industry; goods had to be unloaded in the middle of the bridge and transferred from a Thai truck to a Lao truck. When this requirement was finally lifted in 2008, cross-border transport costs were reduced by 30%; reported in Agency for International Trade Information and Cooperation (Geneva), *Aitic Information Brief No. 13*, September 2008, 4–5.

Regional Value Chains[9]

Regional value chains are a natural outgrowth from the subcontracting that US electronics firms pioneered in the 1960s and the off-shoring of automobile assembly by Japanese produces when the yen appreciated in the second half of the 1980s. The subcontracting process in Asia started with foreign transnational corporations or purchasing houses outsourcing production stages in the 1960s (e.g. US semiconductor firms in Hong Kong and Singapore or footwear firms in Korea) and some non-Asian firms developed Asian networks (e.g. Nestlé coordinates its processed food production in southeast Asia across Indonesia, Malaysia, the Philippines and Thailand). However, the establishment of regional value chains accelerated notably in the 1990s.

When Japanese firms began to produce and export transistors in the late 1950s at a lower cost than the leading US producers, two US firms pursued different reactive strategies. Philco invested in automated production technologies to offset high US labour costs, and suffered disastrous losses due to the rapid obsolescence of their expensive equipment. Fairchild set up a manufacturing plant in Hong Kong in 1961 to assemble US-made components for re-export to the USA. The second strategy was so successful that it was soon copied by other US corporations, who located design and fabrication in the USA, sent the components to Mexico or Asia for assembly, and returned the finished product to the USA for testing and marketing; semiconductor technology was ideally suited to this model because it involved discrete steps with differing requirements, and at all stages, the product had a high

---

[9]The value chain concept has been used in the business studies literature, most prominently by Michael Porter (1985; 1990). The chain metaphor highlights the sequential and interconnected structures of economic activities, with each link in the chain adding value to the process, although Porter's conceptualization is bounded by the firm or inter-firm network. Related concepts are used in the international political economy literature, dating especially from the 'new international division of labour' literature of the early 1980s (e.g. Fröbel *et al.*, 1980), and in the global commodity chain literature (e.g. Borrus *et al.*, 2000) reviewed by Henderson *et al.* (2002), which distinguishes between a chain and a network: "A chain maps the vertical sequence of events leading to the delivery, consumption and maintenance of goods and services — recognising that various value chains often share common economic actors and are dynamic in that they are reused and reconfigured on an ongoing basis — while a network highlights the nature and extent of the inter-firm relationships that bind sets of firms into larger economic groupings" (Sturgeon, 2001, 10).

value/weight ratio so that transport was a minor cost.[10] Competition forced producers to search for the least-cost reliable assembly locations and to move more steps offshore as skills were developed. Some design and testing activities were moved to Hong Kong and Singapore, which also became regional marketing centres for the finished products.

The process could be conducted within a firm through direct foreign investment in production facilities overseas or it could be done by subcontracting to local producers. The choice depends upon the trade-offs between retaining control over things like proprietary technology and quality control and the extent to which a local firm or joint-venture partner may be better able to deal with local labour regulations or relations with governments.[11] Whether via subsidiaries or by subcontracting, the separation of production steps quickly spread to other branches of the electronics industry and to other industries. Initially, this largely involved sewing, whether using copper wire in electronic equipment or making garments or travel goods or baseballs. In some manufacturing sectors, first-tier suppliers, whose names are virtually unknown to the final consumers, coordinated the production process while the brand-name company focussed on design and marketing. For Levi jeans, for example, Li & Fung of Hong Kong coordinate a value chain in which Korean yarn is woven and dyed in Taiwan, cut in Bangladesh, sewn in Cambodia, where Japanese zippers are inserted, and dispatched into Levi's marketing network. Singapore-based Flexitronics plays a similar role for Ericsson and Visteon for Ford Motors or Denso for Toyota, organizing the supply chain by a mix of subcontracting, subsidiaries and direct purchases from worldwide sources.

A second important stimulus for the creation of regional value chains was the large-scale off-shoring of Japanese manufacturing activities following the rapid appreciation of the yen after 1985. A prime

---

[10]The development of subcontracting was also facilitated by tariff reform, which exempted the US-made components from import duties when the assembled product was imported into the USA.

[11]Producers in the follower countries also had choices. Mathews and Cho (2000) analyse the evolution of the semiconductor industry in Korea, Taiwan, Singapore and Malaysia, emphasising how local firms acquired experience and knowledge through a mix of strategies which included joint ventures, licensing of technologies, and original equipment manufacturing.

example was the rapid growth of the automobile industry in Thailand led by Japanese car producers (Fujita and Hamaguchi, 2008, 28–30; Dent, 2008, 52–8).[12] With the expansion of car production, many Japanese components manufacturers established production facilities near the assembly plant; by the early 2000s, over 100 Japanese automotive components manufacturers were producing in Thailand (Dent, 2008, 53).[13] In 1996, Japanese companies produced over half a million cars in Thailand, but the severe crisis in 1997 reduced domestic demand in Thailand and the output of the Japanese affiliates dropped below 200,000 in 1998. Although China overtook Thailand as the largest offshore producer of Japanese companies' cars in Asia (Gokan, 2008, 261–3), production in Thailand rapidly recovered, with over 400,000 units produced in 2005. In China, car joint ventures in the 1980s were dominated by US and European partners in locations determined by the Chinese government, but in the 1990s, as output grew rapidly and several hundred Japanese car and automotive component firms established affiliates in China, the industry became concentrated in coastal areas around Guangzhou, Shanghai and the Bohai Gulf to facilitate shipping of components in and out. Output of Japanese carmakers in China, Thailand and, to a lesser extent, Taiwan continued to grow rapidly after the turn of the century.

A similar phenomenon occurred on a more muted scale as South Korean firms faced currency appreciation and declining competitiveness in unskilled-labour-intensive activities in the late 1980s and early 1990s. Restrictions on capital flows were lifted as Korea joined the OECD in 1996, but this was followed by over-optimistic and poorly judged foreign borrowing and overseas investment which contributed to a severe

---

[12] Japanese producers had begun to assemble cars in Thailand from completely knocked down kits in 1962 (Nissan) and 1964 (Toyota). Honda began producing motorcycles in Thailand in 1967 and cars in 1984, while Hino, Isuzu, Mazda and Mitsubishi all established production facilities in the 1970s. These simple operations were, however, greatly expanded from the late 1980s onwards.

[13] Japanese firms own 90% of the Thai industry which is concentrated within 200 kilometres from central Bangkok. Local conditions interact with the subcontracting/value chain aspect in that Thai production is concentrated in compacts and pick-up trucks. Thai domestic demand was growing rapidly by the late 1980s as many families' incomes rose sufficiently that they could afford their first car and demand was skewed towards pick-up trucks (in part due to local preferences in rural areas, but also because the sales tax was 3% on pick-ups and 30–50% on passenger cars).

financial crisis in the second half of 1997. Despite the restrictions in the first half of the decade and the crisis in the second half of the decade, foreign direct investment (FDI) was significant during the 1990s, with both outward and inward FDI averaging around $3 billion per year.[14] China was the number-one destination for Korean FDI, with Indonesia and Vietnam as the next largest Asian destinations.

The fragmentation of production processes has been facilitated by declining transport and communication costs over the last half century. Some of these changes were endogenous, as firms trying to develop ever more efficient global value chains explored ways to reduce their costs. Reduced inventories through just-in-time deliveries are one striking example; the more the value chain is split up, the more vulnerable it is to hold-ups, but keeping many days' worth of inventories at every step is expensive, so with the increased complexity of value chains a wider range of delivery modes emerged with real-time tracking systems that were increasingly sophisticated and reliable.[15] Other logistical advances such as improvements in intermodal transport have put pressure on governments to deregulate trucking, rail freight, shipping and air transport so that users have flexibility to determine the best means of combining and operating their transportation needs.

Regional networks in East Asia became denser in the 1990s. Early evidence of this was found by Menon (1996), who examined intra-industry trade within ASEAN and found it mainly to be driven by transnational corporations seeking lower wage costs for labour-intensive parts of the production process. Steps towards creating an ASEAN Free Trade Area may have helped the process by allowing easier movement of components among ASEAN countries, but Athukorala and Menon (1996) found little evidence of this in the early 1990s.

In the 1990s and early 2000s, intra-industry trade (IIT) increased rapidly. Kimura, Takahashi and Hayakawa (2007), Haddad (2007) and Gruenwald and Hori (2008) provide evidence that Asian IIT is vertical intra-industry trade associated with fragmentation of production

---

[14]Data from UNCTAD *World Investment Report 2006*, quoted in Kim (2008, 213).

[15]The rapid expansion of FedEx, DHL, UPS, etc., indicated the latent demand for such services, and their growth put pressure in institutions such as postal services' monopolies and regulated air freight services. See Pomfret (2008, 60–5).

rather than the horizontal intra-industry trade due to product differentiation observed in Europe. Ando and Kimura (2005) calculate very high shares of machinery (HS84-92) in East Asian countries' trade in 1996 and 2000, and conclude that this structure is especially suited to production fragmentation.[16] Xing (2007) calculates intra-industry trade, measured at the 3-digit SITC level, to have accounted for 6% of China's bilateral trade with Japan in 1980, 18% in 1992 and 34% in 2004, and finds that Japanese foreign direct investment performed a significant role in enhancing IIT.[17]

The studies of the 1990s tended to focus on the role of Japanese transnational companies. Some of the initiative for fragmentation also came from the original Gang of Four newly industrialized economies who were all facing rising costs of unskilled labour as their economies developed. However, as China's rapid economic growth resumed after 1992, China played an increasingly central role in the Asian division of labour.[18] A much quoted example was the Barbie dolls exported from China, whose production involved inputs from Japan (Barbie's nylon hair), Taiwan (the vinyl plastic pellets to make Barbie's body) and elsewhere, all coordinated from Hong Kong with final assembly in China.[19]

The regional value chains consist of increasing trade in intermediate goods, a pattern documented in the "Emerging Asian Regionalism" report (ADB, 2008, chapter 3), which claims that the share of parts and components in East Asian trade and especially in the trade of Malaysia, the Philippines, Singapore and Thailand is among the highest in the world.[20] The ADB illustrates the process with the example of a hard disk

---

[16]Fragmentation is analysed in Arndt and Kierzkowski (2001).

[17]Zhang *et al.* (2005) have comparable estimates.

[18]Gaulier, Lemoine and Ünal-Kesenci (2006) and Athukorala (2009) emphasize China's growing role in this process.

[19]The example highlighted the difficulty of identifying where a good is made; in the mid-1990s, the 'Made in China' Barbie dolls retailed for $9.99 in California, of which about 35 cents was earned in China (Feenstra and Taylor, 2008, 5 — citing a syndicated US newspaper article from 1996). Trade data are, however, collected and reported by gross value, not value-added as in other components of GDP.

[20]In ASEAN, the share of parts and components rose from 35% of trade in manufactures in 1996 to 43% in 2006 and in China from 12.5% in 1996 to 24% in 2006; over the same period,

drive manufactured by a company in Thailand: eleven components are sourced domestically, and 19 within ASEAN (seven from Malaysia, five from Singapore, four from the Philippines and three from Indonesia), six are sourced from China, one each from Hong Kong and Taiwan, and twelve from Japan, while four parts come from outside Asia (three from the USA and one from Mexico).[21] The hard disk drive is a relatively simple product, which is itself essentially an intermediate good with most of the firm's output being used in electronic products assembled by other Asian firms.[22]

The increasing complexity of regional value chains increased Asian competitiveness in world markets, but the region remained heavily dependent on the high-income countries for final sales. Input-output analysis of the destination of Asian exports of final goods reinforces the conclusion that the region still relies on markets beyond the region; Pula and Peltonen (2009) estimate that only 7% of emerging Asia's GDP was ultimately sold as exports to another emerging Asia country, while 22% went to the USA, the EU and Japan.[23] Exposure to external markets was highlighted in 2008 when East Asia experienced little financial contagion from the crisis in the USA, UK and elsewhere, but suffered from reduced import demand in the crisis economies.

---

the world average increased only slightly, from 19.6% to 20.2%, and in India the share remained constant at around 10% (ADB, 2008, 64).

[21] The numbers are from the ADB (2008, 63) map, which is based on the research of Daisake Hiratsuka (in Hiratsuka, 2007). Some components are sourced from several countries, e.g. 'base' (from China, Malaysia and Thailand), 'disk' (from Japan, Malaysia and the USA) and 'head' (from China, Mexico and the USA). Whether this reflects different sub-components, differing quality inputs or spreading of risk across several suppliers is unclear from the source.

[22] Linden *et al.* (2007) document the importance of global production networks in the assembly of an iPod sold by the US company Apple. They estimate that the hard-drive, produced by the Japanese company Toshiba using affiliates based in China accounts for 51% of the cost of all iPod parts. Japanese companies in Japan produce the display module and display driver, accounting for 16% of input costs. Samsung supplies 2% of the value of inputs from factories in Korea. The final assembly, accounting for 3% of the input cost, is carried out by a Taiwanese company in a plant in China. The source of 20% of inputs cannot be determined. This leaves 9% of input costs that are supplied by US firms, who provide the video/multimedia processor and the portal player CPU; the former input is produced in either Singapore or Taiwan, while the CPU may come from production plants in either the USA or Taiwan.

[23] ADB (2008, 72) reports estimates based on the GTAP computable general equilibrium model that the ratio of final demand outside the region to final demand within the region was 2:1 in 2006.

Trade Facilitation

The emergence and rapid growth of regional value chains created pressures for trade liberalization and facilitation because fragmentation of
the production process is only profitable if the cost of moving components across borders is low in terms of both money and time. In the
pre-1990 setting, there was no pressure for preferential tariff reductions
within an RTA, because East Asian countries were not selling within the
region, and indeed the import-competing industries opposed reduction
in their protection whether the liberalization was preferential or multilateral. With the shift to more outward-oriented development strategies in the 1980s and 1990s, such opposition was less effective and
many MFN tariffs were reduced unilaterally, often presented within
the framework of APEC open regionalism.

Pressures for trade facilitation were addressed predominantly by
national measures, such as improved customs administration or the
creation of special economic zones with reduced red tape and exemp-
tion from trade taxes. National measures could favour sector-specific
value chains, e.g. Thailand helped the car industry by improving
conditions for foreign investors and infrastructure along the eastern
seaboard southeast of Bangkok where many Japanese auto firms were
concentrated and, most of all, by eliminating local-content rules on
automotive products in 2000.[24] Sometimes there was bilateral cooperation, as between Singapore and Johor (Malaysia) and between
Singapore and Riau (Indonesia), to facilitate trade within the Sijori sub-
regional zone. ASEAN provided a forum for setting regional standards
for integrated border management, and explicitly encouraged steps
such as the Single Window for goods entering a country, as opposed
to separate stops for customs, quarantine and other checks.

Although trade facilitation consisted of many discrete measures of unknown individual impact, aggregate measures suggest that

---

[24]During the 1990s, local content had increased as car assemblers purchased more components
from local suppliers (usually subsidiaries of Japanese firms or joint ventures with Japanese producers), but local content rules did impinge on assemblers' flexibility, and were becoming more
restrictive as Chinese participation in regional value chains began to increase at the end of the
decade.

trade costs fell substantially in Indonesia, Malaysia, Philippines and Thailand during the 1990s, converging towards Singapore's trade costs of around 5 percent of the value of internationally traded goods (Figure 4.1). There is evidence that, during the 1990s, trade costs within ASEAN fell faster than in other parts of the world (Pomfret and Sourdin, 2009; Shepherd and Wilson, 2008).

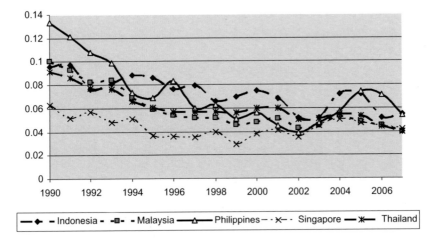

Fig. 4.1   Average ad valorem Trade Costs, ASEAN5 Countries, 1990–2007.
Source: Pomfret and Sourdin (2009), based on Australian import data.
Note: Trade costs are measured by the gap between free-on-board (fob) values of a good at the port of exit from the exporting ASEAN country and import values which include cost, insurance and freight (cif). The cif-fob gap is an economically meaningful measure of the price wedge due to trade costs, but the cif and fob values, which must be collected on the same quantity of trade and appropriate data, are only collected and reported by a few countries; Hummels (2007) describes such datasets for Australia, New Zealand, the USA and some Latin American countries. See the Appendix for further discussion of measurement issues.

The focus on trade costs rather than tariffs is appropriate because MFN tariffs had been reduced unilaterally and by the 1990s what mattered more was the absence of delays and unexpected costs when crossing borders. Nevertheless, in sectors in which regional value chains were especially strong, particular steps were taken to liberalize trade. In the important area of information technology products, for example, many Asian countries have eliminated tariffs by signing the voluntary WTO Information Technology Agreement (ITA), which entered into force in 1997.[25] The most important tariff reductions in the trade agreement between Japan and Thailand, negotiated between 2001 and 2005, concerned reductions in tariffs on automotive component imports into Thailand.

Conclusions

The 1990s was a crucial decade for the Asian economy as regionalization gathered force. The process was overwhelmingly market-driven as firms responded to competitive pressures to reduce costs by relocating stages of production in lower-cost locations. Some of the regionalization was assisted by public policies, but these were narrowly local and amounted to little more than cooperation on cross-border infrastructure (e.g. Singaporean agreements with Indonesia to promote links between the city state and Batam and Bintan islands in Riau Province).

The most important enabling condition was the strength of multilateral trading arrangements as the conclusion of the Uruguay Round led to the creation of the WTO in 1995, with members' commitments subject to a dispute resolution mechanism. The mandatory WTO Technical Barriers to Trade (TBT) Agreement, which provides a code of good practice for the preparation, adoption and application of standards, and the 1997 Information Technology Agreement (ITA) are especially important for Asian regional value chains. Also significant during the 1990s was the long but steady process of Chinese WTO accession, which was accompanied by domestic reforms in China to make its economy more transparent and WTO-compatible, as well as establishing a credible commitment to global trade norms and diminution of the discretionary power of customs and other officials.

---

[25] Australia, China, Hong Kong, India, Indonesia, Japan, Korea, Malaysia, New Zealand, the Philippines, Singapore, Taiwan, Thailand and Vietnam are all signatories of the ITA, which was concluded at the Singapore Ministerial Conference in December 1996. ITA participants must abide by three basic principles: 1) all products listed in the Declaration must be covered; 2) all must be reduced to a zero tariff level; and 3) all other duties and charges must be bound at zero. There are no exceptions to product coverage, although an extended implementation period is possible for sensitive items. The ITA is solely a tariff-cutting mechanism; while the Declaration provides for the review of non-tariff barriers, there are no binding commitments concerning NTBs. For more details, see http://www.wto.org/english/tratop_E/inftec_e/itaintro_e.htm.

Successful promotion of regionalism was not a feature of the 1990s. ASEAN appeared to be an ineffective economic organization as creation of the ASEAN Free Trade Area (AFTA) proceeded spasmodically with high-profile exceptions to internal tariff liberalization, although ASEAN did provide a useful forum for coordinating trade facilitation. APEC, with its open regionalism, better captured the spirit of the times by rejecting discriminatory exclusive regional arrangements, but lost influence when it appeared to be forcing governments to do what they did not wish to (the EVSL initiative) and when it played no role in responding to the 1997–1998 Asian Crisis. The Crisis provided the catalyst for Asian governments to reassess Asian regionalism.

Chapter 5

The Asian Crisis, Monetary Integration, and ASEAN+3

Advocates of closer economic integration in Asia in the 1990s were concerned that Asia was being left behind in a global movement to regionalism represented by an expanded EU and a putative Free Trade Area of the Americas.[1] Nevertheless, during the first half the 1990s despite increased regionalization, there was little movement towards regional integration on the part of policymakers. ASEAN's free trade area was characterized by freer trade in areas where members chose to reduce their MFN tariffs, but other goods were placed on lengthy exclusion lists. APEC was a meeting place where members announced voluntary non-discriminatory trade liberalization, but it covered both sides of the Pacific and began to lose relevance when it tried to push Asian members to liberalize trade faster than they desired in the EVSL initiative.

The catalyst for more purposeful East Asian regionalism was the economic crisis that hit many countries in the region in the second half of 1997, and led to deep recessions in some countries in 1998 and 1999. The Asian Crisis was a major shock for countries that had grown accustomed to high growth rates. Although rapid growth resumed

---

[1] "Clearly, the Asian FTA effort is a belated example of a trend that has been widespread throughout the world for some time. Regionalism has become a critical part of the new international trade order. The world has seen a surge in regional arrangements since the early 1990s. The GATT-WTO has been notified of over 250 regional trading agreements up to December 2002" (Naya, 2004, 4).

within a few years even in the hardest-hit countries, in 1997–1998, it seemed like a bottomless pit in countries such as Thailand, Indonesia, Malaysia and South Korea. Searching for a scapegoat, many Asians felt that the global institutions provided too little assistance too late, and contrasted with the generous support that had been given in the recent past to Latin American countries or Russia by the International Monetary Fund (IMF). Japan latched on to this to propose the creation of an Asian Monetary Fund.[2] Following the momentum gathering in Western Europe towards the creation of the euro, there was even talk of an Asian currency.[3]

China was relatively little affected by the Asian Crisis and, in 1997, was a staunch supporter of the multilateral institutions, willing to follow the US lead in matters of global economic architecture. This support started to flag as China perceived itself receiving little credit for its position and for self-effacing measures such as not joining the competitive devaluations of 1997–1998. The US bombing of the Chinese embassy in Belgrade in May 1999 was a catalyst for re-evaluation of China's position and a decision to shift China's support in favour of regional institutions. The conjuncture of both Japan and China looking favourably on regional options created a unique window of opportunity for East Asian regionalism at the end of the twentieth century.

Substantive progress in monetary coordination, notably the Chiang Mai Initiative in 2000 among the ASEAN+3 group of the ten ASEAN countries plus China, Japan and South Korea, was accompanied by calls from some quarters for even closer monetary integration.

---

[2] Japan floated the idea of an Asian Monetary Fund at the ASEM Finance Ministers' meeting in Bangkok in September 1997. Subsequently the head of the Hong Kong Monetary Authority, Joseph Yam raised the possibility of an eventual Asian currency unit and the Philippine President Joseph Estrada put the issue on the Agenda of the 1999 ASEAN summit, and several academics, including Robert Mundell, advocated the creation of an Asian euro. For references, see Henning (2002), Eichengreen (2004) and Hamanaka (2009). More limited currency union has also been considered, especially within Southeast Asia (Madhur, 2002).

[3] The euro was launched on 1 January 1999 for non-cash transactions, and the European Central Bank took over the conduct of monetary policy for the eleven member countries. Euro banknotes were issued in 2002. Emphasis on the euro as evidence of a pattern towards currency consolidation was, however, a selective reading of the European experience as Eastern Europe was undergoing an even more dramatic monetary disunion with the disintegration of the Czechoslovak, Yugoslav and Soviet currency areas. In total, Europe had more currencies in 2002 than it had a dozen years earlier (Pomfret, 2003).

The twenty-first century reality, however, was of slow progress in Asian monetary integration. Even the Chiang Mai Initiative proved largely irrelevant. When the US and European financial crises of 2007–2009 led to a downturn in the global economy, Asian financial policymakers relied on their own resources or credit lines from the USA, rather than on regional institutions. The idea of an Asian currency seemed no closer to realization despite the success of the euro, which was gradually being adopted by more EU members.

Monetary and Financial Integration before 1997

Before 1997, central bankers and finance ministers from the region met to discuss monetary coordination, largely in response to Japanese initiatives.[4] To some extent, this was a consequence of events in the second half of the 1980s (e.g. the dramatic fall and rise of the yen before and after 1985 and the Japanese financial crisis of the late 1980s), as well as of longer term trends such as the emergence of Tokyo as an international financial centre and the status of the yen as an international currency. The various meetings were low-key and technical, rather than undertaking any grand initiatives. Two harbingers of issues to come were the bureaucratic competition between different arms of the Japanese government (in this case, the central bank and the Ministry of Finance) and ambivalence over which countries to include in regional fora.

The Executives' Meeting of East Asia–Pacific Central Banks (EMEAP) was established in 1991, with the first meeting hosted by the Bank of Japan and twice yearly meetings thereafter.[5] The group was composed of central bankers from Australia, Japan, South Korea, Indonesia, Malaysia, New Zealand, the Philippines, Singapore and Thailand. The People's Bank of China joined in 1992, and the Hong Kong Monetary Authority in 1993. The Japanese name *Higashi Ajia-Oseania*, which means "East Asia-Oceania," highlighted the exclusion

---

[4]This section draws heavily on Hamanaka (2009).
[5]There was an unspoken rule that the Bank of Japan would host every second meeting and provide a temporary secretariat.

of the USA (Hamanaka, 2009). EMEAP started as a deputy-level meeting and initally sought mainly to nurture relationships among member central banks and to exchange economic/financial information, including macroeconomic surveillance. Regular contact, rather than ad hoc meetings, was considered essential for mutual understanding and economic surveillance.

In a September 1995 speech, Bernie Fraser, governor of the Reserve Bank of Australia, proposed upgrading regional financial cooperation, including the establishment of an Asian version of the Bank of International Settlements (BIS), i.e. an institution with its own capital, subscribed by member central banks, and its own balance sheet. This proposal led to the institutionalization of EMEAP, with the first governors' meeting held in July 1996 in Tokyo. The governors agreed to establish three working/study groups on financial markets, central banking (later changed to payment and settlement systems), and bank supervision, i.e. a structure parallel to that of the BIS. However, unlike the BIS, EMEAP did not have its own capital and balance sheet.

A separate initiative from the Japanese Ministry of Finance led to the first meeting in Hong Kong in May 1992 of the Four Markets Group, which aimed to strengthen the relationship among regional financial authorities and to exchange market information, with regard to foreign exchange markets in particular. The members of the group were financial authorities of Japan, Hong Kong, Singapore and Australia.[6] Shortly afterwards, the Japanese Ministry of Finance participated in the first APEC Finance Ministers' Meeting, held in Honolulu in March 1994; this initiative did not lead far, and the Honolulu meeting was not the start of regular meetings. The Japanese Ministry of Finance's relations with Asian counterparts were upgraded to minister-level in October 1994 with the first Japan–ASEAN Finance Ministers' Meeting, but this forum also did not assume great importance.

---

[6]The Bank of Japan was excluded. The Hong Kong Monetary Authority and Monetary Authority of Singapore were deemed to be central banks within a government and the Reserve Bank of Australia was represented because it holds responsibility for international finance. However, these justifications seem to be excuses for the Ministry of Finance to exclude the Japanese central bank from this forum.

In March 1997, the Four Markets Group was expanded to the Six Markets Group, as the USA and China joined, and the level of the participants was raised to vice ministers or vice governors.[7] While APEC had grown dysfunctional, the Six Markets Group might have grown into an Asian G6, but the group lost momentum soon after the upgrade, holding no meetings after February 1999. Japan's Ministry of Finance revived the Four Markets Group in September 1999, without the participation of the USA and the China, but as an Asian forum the Four Markets Group's membership was too limited. In 2000, the ASEAN+3 financial process took priority over the Four Markets Group, although the achievements of the Four Markets Group, such as discussions of a regional bond market and regional credit agency, became the agenda of the ASEAN+3 financial process.

From AMF to CMI[8]

The Asian Crisis which followed the Thai devaluation in July 1997 was a major shock to the region. The East Asian model had become widely recognized as a more or less unqualified success, and countries adopting the model had come to expect self-sustained growth as the norm.[9] Although there were warning signs in a slowdown of Thai exports in the first half of 1997 and real estate bubbles in Bangkok and other cities, the suddenness and scale of the downturn were not anticipated. The outbreak of the Asian Crisis in July 1997 was signalled by Thailand's central bank no longer being able to support the national currency; the Thai baht lost 50 percent of its value in the foreign exchange markets and many financial institutions went bankrupt. The contagion effects included competitive currency depreciations and reassessment by foreign investors of portfolio investment in other East Asian countries; foreign investors found Indonesia, South Korea and

---

[7]This regional financial meeting was greeted with suspicion by Korea and Taiwan, who considered themselves more financially important than China at the time.
[8]This section is based on Pomfret (2005).
[9]The widely read *East Asian Miracle* report by the World Bank (1993) sat on the fence in explaining the causes of the miracle, but left little doubt that a miracle was occurring.

Table 5.1   Economic Growth before and during the Asian Crisis: Indonesia, Malaysia, South Korea and Thailand, 1988–2000 (annual growth in real GDP).

Country	1988–95 Annual average	1996	1997	1998	1999	2000
Indonesia	7.9	7.8	4.7	−13.1	0.8	4.9
Malaysia	9.4	10.0	7.3	−7.4	6.1	8.9
South Korea	8.1	7.0	4.7	−6.9	9.5	8.5
Thailand	10.0	5.9	−1.4	−10.5	4.4	4.8

Source: Asian Development Bank — online at www.adb.org.

Malaysia especially wanting and these countries were the epicentres of the crisis.[10]

The decline in output in the four hardest-hit economies was dramatic (Table 5.1). As well as being unexpected, policymakers had no idea how long the negative growth would last. Indonesia, Korea and Thailand sought temporary relief from the International Monetary Fund, while Malaysia introduced capital controls. The subsequent recession was especially hard for the poorer members of society, and in Thailand and Indonesia it led to protests and major political change.[11] In this context, IMF conditionality which included raising interest rates to discourage capital outflows was deeply unpopular. A Keynesian response of stimulating domestic demand was pursued in 1998, especially by Malaysia and South Korea, which alleviated the fall in economic activity, but the strong recovery in 1999 (2000 in Indonesia which was wracked by political turmoil) was driven by renewed export growth. With hindsight, a lesson of the 1997–1998 Asian Crisis

---

[10]Liberalization of international capital flows, which had taken place in Thailand, Indonesia and South Korea in the 1980s and early 1990s, was a crucial precondition for financial contagion. China, India and other countries with capital controls suffered less from contagion, whether or not their financial institutions had shaky balance sheets. The other economies less affected by contagion were those with liberalized capital flows and more robust financial sectors, e.g. Hong Kong, Singapore, Taiwan, Australia, New Zealand and Japan (whose financial sector was still adjusting to the decade-long slump since the bursting of the late 1980s bubble).

[11]From 1992 until the early 2000s, Thailand had the most vigorous democracy in East Asia with several peaceful changes of government and a free press (on all issues apart from the monarchy), but after the landslide victory of Thaksin Shinawatra's populist party in the 2001 election the country became polarized and suffered a coup d'état in 2006; although democracy was restored in 2007, the victory of Thaksin's party in the December 2007 election was followed by continued instability centred on conflict which had regional and class foundations. By contrast, the political upheaval in Indonesia during the 1997–1998 economic crisis led to the overthrow of the autocratic New Order regime of President Suharto and within a decade Indonesia had a functioning and lively democracy.

was that the East Asian growth model was built on firm foundations, although breakneck outward-oriented growth with substantial capital inflows could encounter sudden short-run setbacks if the capital was poorly invested.[12]

Japan seized on the response of the International Monetary Fund, which was widely perceived to have been inadequate, to propose the formation of an Asian Monetary Fund (AMF).[13] Japanese arguments in support of the AMF were fourfold (Ogawa, 2001). First, the IMF financial support for the crisis-hit countries was too little and too late. Second, East Asian countries are underrepresented in the IMF. Third, an AMF could help prevent regional contagion in future crises. This argument is related to criticisms of the tardiness of the IMF's responses in 1997:

> A 'currency meltdown' occurred on July 24 when all of the countries faced severe speculative attacks. Thus, the Thai baht crisis had the contagion effects on the other ASEAN countries before the IMF decided its financial support to Thailand (Ogawa, 2001, 235).

The weight to be placed on this argument depends on the extent to which one accepts the contagion hypothesis, as well as on whether one believes that faster or bigger or better directed assistance could have forestalled contagion. Fourth, an AMF could better conduct regional surveillance and muster peer pressure to forestall crises than could an institution based in Washington, DC.

The four arguments struck some chords with policymakers outside Japan, but they are not conclusive arguments for a new institution. The apparent inequity in Asian countries' IMF representation was solely a Japanese issue; other countries and the region as a whole had a representation appropriate to its economic size. The scale of

---

[12]Lessons about the appropriate exchange rate regime are less clear. A catalyst for the Crisis was inappropriate attempts to maintain exchange rates pegged to the US dollar (Corden, 2007, 8–9), but after the turn of the century most of the high-performing Asian economies had returned to a de facto dollar peg and no currencies were truly freely floating with market-determined exchange rates.

[13]Perceptions were important. A lasting image from the crisis was of IMF Managing Director Michel Camdessus standing arms-folded over Indonesia's President as he signed the January 1998 IMF agreement. For many Asians, the image evoked memories of European nineteenth century imperialism.

IMF assistance in 1997–1998 varied, with Korea receiving much more assistance than any other country because its financial crisis was seen as the only one posing a threat to the global financial system. Malaysia chose to impose controls on short-term capital flows in 1998, rather than to accept IMF support with conditionality. Thailand and Indonesia may have preferred more short-term assistance in dealing with their liquidity problems, but this was gradually forgotten by the early 2000s as the Crisis receded much faster than had been anticipated in 1998.[14] Regional surveillance could be handled within existing institutions; in 1998, the Southeast Asian countries proposed an ASEAN Surveillance Process and requested ADB technical support, and the ADB has subsequently taken on a regional surveillance role through its Asia Recovery Information Center.[15]

The fundamental reason for the AMF's lack of progress was opposition from other IMF members, notably the USA, to duplication of roles. Support within the region was also lukewarm, although the episode generated new initiatives and speculation about Asian monetary arrangements.[16] A weaker version of the AMF proposal emerged at a meeting of Asia–Pacific finance ministers and central bankers in Manila in November 1997; the 14 economies represented in Manila were the first six ASEAN members, China, Hong Kong, Japan, South Korea, Australia, New Zealand, Canada and the USA. The Manila Framework called for a regional surveillance mechanism, enhanced economic and

---

[14]Corden (2007, 110) makes the point that it would have been harder to manage a Korean-sized injection from the IMF in Thailand or Indonesia, because the major foreign lenders were harder to identify and the rollover of short-term loans by creditor banks which contributed to the brevity of Korea's recession would have been difficult to coordinate.

[15]The IMF's surveillance mechanism is bilateral, so the regional nature of the ASEAN proposal was innovative. The ASEAN Surveillance Process became operational in March 1999 with a coordinating unit at the ASEAN Secretariat in Jakarta and national units in the ten member countries (Manupipatpong, 2002, 112–115). At a meeting in Sydney in March 1999, the Australian government proposed that a regional surveillance information facility be based at the ADB in Manila, and provided financial assistance through AusAID. Staff of the ADB's Regional Economic Monitoring Unit now prepare the *Asia Recovery Report* twice a year and maintain a website at http://www.adb.org/REMU/aric.asp.

[16]In October 1998, the Japanese government launched the New Miyazawa Initiative, offering a $30 billion extended liquidity provision to East Asian economies in a future economic crisis; this was superseded by the 2000 CMI. The following paragraphs draw on Henning (2002), Manupipatpong (2002) and Murase (2002) for information about the various developments and on Bird and Rajan (2002) for policy options raised in the process.

technical cooperation in strengthening domestic financial systems and their regulation, and measures to strengthen the IMF's response to financial crises. Although the topics are reminiscent of the AMF proposals, the tone was in terms of supplementing the central role of the IMF rather than displacing the IMF.

A more important forum for regional financing arrangements emerged out of meetings among the ASEAN+3 countries, i.e. ASEAN plus China, Japan and South Korea. This was the alignment proposed by Malaysia for an East Asian Economic Group in 1991, which had existed since then as the East Asia Economic Caucus within APEC, and it was also the group of Asian countries that participated in the first Asia Europe Meeting (ASEM) in Bangkok in 1996. China, Japan and South Korea were invited to have separate meetings with ASEAN at the December 1997 informal summit in Kuala Lumpur. However, it was only in the context of a meeting of deputy finance ministers and deputy central bank governors in March 1999 that the term ASEAN+3 came into general use. At the November 1999 ASEAN summit in Manila, the 13 heads of government issued a Joint Statement on East Asia Cooperation, and the list of areas for joint action included financial and monetary cooperation (Dent, 2008, 153).

A catalyst for the formation of ASEAN+3 and for its attention to financial and monetary cooperation was, of course, the 1997–1998 Asian Crisis, but the driving force behind the changing impact of the group between 1998 and 2000 was China's changing relations with the USA (and IMF) and with Japan. China supported the IMF's approach to the 1997 crisis and its "mainstay" role was acknowledged at the December 1998 APEC summit in Kuala Lumpur. China, however, felt that it received little practical reward and relations with the United States soured in the first half of 1999 over the US intervention in Kosovo and the bombing of the Chinese embassy in Belgrade. At the same time, China's attitude towards Japan became warmer, e.g. Bowles (2002) contrasts the coolness of Jiang Zemin's visit to Japan in December 1998 with the conciliatory nature of Zhu Rongji's visit in October 2000. Improved bilateral relations between East Asia's two major powers were critical for East Asian regionalism.[17]

---

[17]Although there is strong evidence of China's willingness to play a leadership role in Asian regionalism since the 1997 crisis, some commentators (e.g. Medeiros and Fravel, 2003) interpret

The most significant of the ASEAN+3 meetings was that of the 13 countries' finance ministers in Chiang Mai in May 2000, where a regional financing arrangement was established with US$1 billion in commitments. The Chiang Mai Initiative (CMI), which became effective in November 2000, allows countries to swap their local currencies for major international currencies for up to six months and for up to twice their committed amount.[18] The CMI is framed in terms of supplementing the IMF's role insofar as countries seeking liquidity support must also look for IMF assistance although bilateral swaps under the CMI are not conditional on IMF negotiations being completed. By March 2002, six bilateral swaps, worth $14 billion, had been concluded under the CMI (Manupipatpong, 2002, 118), and by the end of 2003, this had increased to 16 bilateral swaps amounting to $35.5 billion (Wang, 2004, 944). The CMI has the potential to evolve into the role foreseen for the AMF as a lender of last resort in crises, and, with combined foreign exchange reserves of around $800 billion, the ASEAN Plus Three countries have financial resources which dwarf the assistance given in 1997–1998. Nevertheless, from the participating countries' public pronouncements, it remains unclear how far some of them are willing to see the CMI evolve towards an AMF, or how they view the relationship of the CMI to the Manila Framework.[19]

Monetary policy coordination made even less progress.[20] A case is often made for exchange rate fixity to forestall competitive devaluations by countries competing with one another across a range of traded goods and also to encourage direct foreign investment. In the years before 1997, such fixity was more or less maintained among the ASEAN

China's more active diplomatic engagement since the mid-1990s in a global rather than a regional context.

[18]The CMI superseded the ASEAN swap arrangement, which had been in place since 1977 but at its maximum the ASEAN facility only amounted to $200 million. It also superseded bilateral swap arrangements such as that between Japan and South Korea.

[19]Although garnering fewer headlines, the Manila Framework remains in place and raises questions of coordinating activities under the CMI and financial activities involving Australia, Canada, New Zealand, the USA and the ASEAN+3.

[20]The CMI agreement provided for information exchange and regular meetings between deputy ministers of finance and a dialogue framework for future discussions of the international financial system. While these may be useful confidence- and cooperation-building mechanisms, they have had little practical impact.

countries, China, Hong Kong, South Korea and Taiwan by their *de facto* pegs to the US dollar, but this led to, disastrous in some cases, swings against the yen. Proposals for a common currency see that as the best solution to the competitive devaluation threat.[21] The simplest solution would be region-wide pegs to the US dollar, or even dollarization; McKinnon and Schnabl (2003), for example, conclude that East Asia is a "natural dollar zone." In addition, a larger currency area could reduce the required level of foreign exchange reserves, because offsetting shocks would reduce the need for a lender of last resort. A single currency is also advocated as allowing the East Asian countries to speak with a single voice in international financial fora.[22] Despite these benefits and the long-attested finding that East Asia satisfies some of the criteria for being an optimum currency area at least as well as Western Europe (Goto and Hamada, 1994), many obstacles to Asian monetary union remain.

Advocates of a common Asian currency have not addressed the institutional question of how the common exchange rate is determined (and hence how monetary policy is conducted for the entire currency area), who would determine when the lender of last resort acts, and who would speak with the single voice. Eichengreen (2004) lists four real preconditions for monetary union, in contrast to pseudo conditions such as numerical deficit ceilings or convergence criteria:

1. the capacity to delegate monetary policy to an international institution, which should be accountable, representative, efficient and effective;
2. a culture of monetary policy transparency;
3. open capital accounts;
4. a common transmission mechanism.

East Asia is far from achieving these preconditions. The 1997 crisis exposed the variation and weakness of financial systems, which would

---

[21] Despite the experience of 1997–1998, the attraction of a dollar peg seems to remain strong in these countries. McKinnon (2004, 326) pointed out that by early 2004 "the day-to-day volatility of each country's dollar exchange rate is not significantly different from its pre-crisis level."

[22] This point, which addresses the Japanese concern about its low voting weight in the IMF, has also been raised by Korean economists (Oh and Harvie, 2001, 261).

make realization of the last two preconditions difficult without substantial financial reform. Political cultures also need to change in many of the Asian countries, including some of the large ones, if the second condition is to be obtained. Most distant of all is the prospect of agreeing on an international monetary policy institution; how would the huge variations in economic and demographic size be dealt with and, assuming that China and Japan would have the largest weight, what are the prospects for genuine trust and cooperation in the near future.[23]

Despite these obstacles to monetary union in Asia, the fact remains that the regional integration agenda in East Asia was kick-started by the post-1997 currency union debate. Monetary agreements, the CMI in particular, were concrete achievements. The urgency of pursuing regional initiatives towards monetary integration was underlined after the turn of the century by a feeling that reform of the international financial architecture and the IMF, which was in the air after the 1997 Asian Crisis, had now gone off the G8 radar screen (Wang, 2004, 940).[24] Nevertheless, the main response to the possibility of future balance of payment uncertainties was national; all East Asian countries built up their foreign currency reserves, implying distrust of any external support, regional or global, in the event of a balance of payments crisis.

After the Chiang Mai Initiative

In the 2000 Chiang Mai Initiative (CMI), the ten ASEAN countries, China, Japan and Korea agreed on currency swap arrangements in the

---

[23]Some observers point to the parallel of the role of former enemies France and Germany in playing a locomotive role in European integration, but the continuing antipathy between China and Japan on many levels (highlighted by the riots at the 2004 Asian soccer championship finals when Japan defeated China in Beijing) suggests how different the Asian situation in the early twenty-first century was to that of Europe half a century earlier.

[24]The view that the IMF was biased and could not be relied upon in an Asian crisis was reinforced for some observers by the 2007–2009 Atlantic Crisis, when the IMF acted much more boldly than in 1997, offering quick and substantial assistance to Iceland and hard-hit countries of eastern Europe. This was made possible by the increase in IMF resources authorized by the G20 (i.e. by a body in which Asia is well-represented), but it still contrasted sharply with the slow and parsimonious IMF assistance during the 1997–1998 Asian Crisis. The difference may reflect a learning process in which the Asian countries were unfortunate guinea pigs, but it did not completely erase the belief that Asia had been hard-done by at the hands of a US- and European-dominated IMF in its hour of need.

case of a balance of payments crisis. The CMI was the first East Asian regional agreement in banking and finance; although there had been informal arrangements, such as the Executives' Meeting of East Asia–Pacific Central Banks (EMEAP), none had the formal status or explicit regionalism focus of the CMI. The CMI's ASEAN+3 membership recalled the EAEC proposal, and was in stark contrast to the pan-Pacific composition of APEC. The Asia–Europe Meeting (ASEM) which began to hold biennial summits in 1996 may also have contributed to a sense of Asian-only regionalism encapsulated in ASEAN+3, although the EU was more concerned about its own exclusion from groups like APEC than in promoting Asian solidarity.

In the financial sphere, the Asian Bond Market Initiative (ABMI) was launched at the EMEAP central banks forum and endorsed by ASEAN+3 finance ministers in 2003. The ABMI is intended to mobilise the region's currency reserves for the region's own needs, but the value of bonds issued remains small. The first Asian Bond Fund pooled one billion US dollars from the eleven EMEAP members for investment in US-dollar denominated bonds issued by sovereign or quasi-sovereign borrowers from eight of the EMEAP economies. In June 2005, the second Asian Bond Fund invested $2 billion in local currency denominated sovereign and quasi-sovereign bonds from the same eight economies. The ABMI's main role has been to highlight both cross-border and domestic market impediments (e.g. capital controls and variations in withholding and other taxes) to bond market development in the region.[25]

In early 2009, the ASEAN+3 finance ministers decided to multilateralize the CMI swap arrangements, so that a country with balance-of-payments problems can access the entire pool, which the ministers agreed should amount to a total of US$120 billion. The biggest issue concerned the size of contributions and the associated voting rights, foreshadowing a key issue in any Asian monetary fund or common currency area (i.e. who would determine monetary policy?). With the multilateralization of the CMI in early 2009, Japan contributes $38.4 billion, or 32% of the $120 billion total, while China

---

[25]For more details, see *Box4.3: Building Asian Bond Markets* in ADB (2008, 134–135).

contributes $34.2 billion and Hong Kong $4.2 billion.[26] Thus, equal weights for Japan and China were achieved by a fudge: the share of China plus Hong Kong is equal to that of Japan, although Hong Kong is in many respects a separate economic entity and was not party to the CMI. Even beyond the tensions between the established and rising economic power for supremacy, it is uncertain what the weight should be of the mid-rank economic powers, led by Korea but also including the larger ASEAN economies; in 2009, Korea's contribution to the multilateralized CMI was set at $24 billion and other contributions at less than $5 billion per country. Although agreement was reached on the contribution weights, issues such as economic surveillance before the release of CMI funds and monitoring to ensure due diligence after disbursement remain unresolved. To be more effective, the process needs an institutional form rather than being run by part-timers, but there is fierce competition over where a secretariat should be located.

A more fundamental reason for the slow progress on monetary integration was the deterioration of China–Japan bilateral relations and competition for primacy in international monetary arrangements, of which the haggling over contributions to the multilateralization of the CMI in early 2009 was a symptom. China's position on international monetary arrangements is national and global rather than regional. In response to the 2008–2009 financial crisis, China promoted the use of the renminbi as a settlement currency while resisting external pressure to appreciate the currency's value and advocated broadening the currency base of the IMF's special drawing rights (SDRs) and increasing the SDR's role as a reserve currency. The proposal for increased use of the SDR as a reserve currency was viewed by the Japanese Ministry of Finance as a ploy to increase the presence of the renminbi in Asian trade and payments, and the Ministry responded by offering bilateral swap arrangements in yen to other Asian countries. At the first official summit between China, Japan and Korea in December 2008, China increased its bilateral swap arrangements with Korea from $4 billion

---

[26]These shares contrast to earlier arrangements such as the funding of the Asian Development Bank, in which China's share is less than half of Japan's.

to $30 billion, including a contribution from Hong Kong, while Japan increased its bilateral swap commitments to Korea from $13 to $30 billion. Superficially, this was a prelude to the CMI multilateralization contest on who pays how much, but the bilateral arrangements with Korea were about currency competition between the yen and renminbi rather than being part of a regional initiative.

Conclusions

In practice, both the CMI and the ABMI have made only minor contributions to Asian monetary integration. The CMI played a minimal role in the 2008–2009 crisis because the Asian countries' own reserves were more than adequate, i.e. governments had learned national rather than regional lessons from the 1997–1998 Asian crisis.[27] Even with the Chiang Mai Initiative Multilateralization, the amounts available are small. As a reference point, Korea's bilateral swap agreement with the US Federal Reserve is for up to $30 billion (i.e. a quarter of the entire CMI funds), while Japan's liquidity swap agreement with the US Federal Reserve is unlimited. More substantive steps towards monetary integration, such as the proposal for an Asian Monetary Unit (AMU), have made no progress, and an Asian Monetary Fund (AMF) or Asian currency remain distant.

The evidence on financial integration in East Asia is mixed. Asset markets can be considered to be integrated when assets are priced by the same stochastic discount rate (Flood and Rose, 2005). Kim and Lee (2008) emphasise the convergence of interbank interest rates and of government bond yields in East Asia in the decade after 1998. Nevertheless, the spreads remain significant — larger than, for example, in the EU before the introduction of the euro. Covered interest parity (i.e. the requirement that the domestic interest rate equal the world interest

---

[27]The US Federal Reserve's provision of a guaranteed credit line to four emerging economies (Brazil, Mexico, Singapore and South Korea) was more important in 2008–2009 than the CMI. The Fed was concerned that, as many foreign investors liquidated their assets, the monetary authorities of these countries might have trouble accommodating a fire-sale of domestic currency; the credit line made clear that there would be no problem satisfying increased demand for US dollars from Singapore or South Korea.

rate plus the forward discount on domestic currency) as an indicator of financial market integration tends to be rejected.[28] It is widely believed that Asian financial markets are more integrated with global financial centres than with other regional financial markets; gravity model analysis of asset-holdings suggests a small but significant within-region bias in East Asia (Lee, 2008), but that result may be driven by short-term trade finance. There is even less evidence of integration of the market for financial services, as national banking systems in East Asia remain distinct.

Some writers have seen monetary integration as a way of promoting regional economic integration by differentially facilitating intra-regional trade flows.[29] Priority to monetary integration was proposed as a specifically Asian approach, and the conventional sequence of economic integration progressing from free flows of goods, to factor market integration and then to economic union was dismissed as Euro-centric.[30] In practice, however, when Asian regionalism stepped up a gear after 2000, it was led by trade agreements.

---

[28]For more details on financial integration and macroeconomic policy coordination, see Cavoli (2007) and Cavoli and Rajan (2009). The survey of East Asian financial integration by the Asian Development Bank (ADB, 2008, 108–148) has a more positive interpretation of the evidence behind the statements in this and the following sentence.

[29]Wang (2004, 952–954) starts his discussion of the sequencing issue by observing that: "The euro area pursued trade integration first, but from a theoretical point of view there is no clear reason for this. Furthermore, there are many good reasons for forming a monetary union before an FTA." Pomfret (2005) discusses the sequencing debate.

[30]The stages of regional integration were set out by Balassa (1961), although he saw preferential trading arrangements, a free trade area (= a preferential arrangement with zero tariffs on internal trade), a customs union (= FTA plus a common external trade policy), a common market (= customs union plus free movement of capital and labour), and economic union (= common market plus common economic policies) as a taxonomy of the depth of integration rather than a sequencing map. The trade-first model captures, very approximately, the sequencing of western European integration since 1957.

Chapter 6

Asian Regionalism Resurgent: FTAs after 2000

The emergence of Asian regionalism can be dated from the aftermath of the 1997 Asian Crisis and to dissatisfaction with the role of the International Monetary Fund which led to the monetary focus described in the previous chapter. In the final year of the twentieth century, there were also developments which provided a catalyst to regional trade agreements. The collapse of the 1999 WTO meetings in Seattle and the diminishing significance of APEC (including the half-hearted attempt by the United States to kick-start further trade liberalization at the 1999 APEC summit through its P5 initiative with Australia, Chile, New Zealand and Singapore) led to new approaches to trade liberalization in the Asia–Pacific region.[1] The principal manifestations were the deepening of ASEAN and rapid growth in the number of bilateral trade agreements.

The ASEAN countries had already begun to reduce the number of protected activities that were excluded from the ASEAN Free Trade Area, and this process accelerated after the turn of the century. Bilateral trade negotiations were begun in 1999/2000 by Japan with Singapore, South Korea, Canada and Mexico, by South Korea

---

[1] President Clinton's 1997 Trade Policy Agenda had included negotiation of bilateral trade agreements with individual Asian countries and the P5 proposal (for RTAs with Australia, Chile, New Zealand and Singapore) was on the table, but divisions within the administration had limited follow-up (Munakata, 2006, 188, n5).

with Chile and New Zealand as well as with Japan, and by Singapore with New Zealand (concluded in 2000), Australia, Canada and other countries. In the final months of 2000, the leaders of China and Japan individually approached ASEAN with proposals for a free trade agreement, and in the following year China, Japan and Korea discussed a coordinated ASEAN+3 FTA.[2] However, China became impatient with the slow progress and negotiated a bilateral FTA with ASEAN in 2002. Meanwhile, ASEAN moved beyond the ASEAN Free Trade Area by announcing in 2003 the establishment of an ASEAN Economic Community.

Apart from the major ASEAN+1 agreement with China, dozens of bilateral trade agreements were concluded by East Asian countries. With any preferential trading arrangement, the welfare effects are ambiguous, depending primarily on whether new trade is created or whether trade is diverted from the existing exporter to a preferred supplier. Additionally, with a complex web of agreements there may be problems of conflicting rules of origin and so forth; the phenomenon of tangled preferential arrangements was labelled the "spaghetti bowl" effect by Jagdish Bhagwati, initially in the European context. It is often referred to as the "noodle bowl" effect in the Asian context.[3]

Concerns about the negative noodle bowl effects did not, however, dampen the proliferation of bilateral and plurilateral trade agreements in the first decade of the twenty-first century. These agreements are extremely diverse and some have minimal impact, but a common thread is a focus on trade facilitation rather than tariff reduction, sometimes focussing on very specific sources of trade costs. A consequence is that many of the terms are not discriminatory. The agreements address issues of particular concern to the countries concerned, but

---

[2] Lee, Koo and Park (2008) describe the dramatic change in the three countries' positions on trade agreements. Using a gravity model, they conclude that the three have not been adversely affected by the existence of major regional RTAs, which implies that the post-2000 increase in RTAs in East Asia is internally driven rather than a defensive response to developments elsewhere. For China, the priority in the 1990s was WTO accession negotiations, which were effectively completed in 2000 with formal accession in 2001; only then did China turn to bilateral trade agreements.

[3] Bhagwati (2008) provides a statement of his views on preferential trading arrangements. On the Asian noodle bowl, see Baldwin (2006), Feridhanusetyawan (2005), Plummer (2007), Tumbarello (2007), ADB (2008) and Kawai and Wignaraja (2009).

outcomes such as simplifying border procedures or removing a behind-the-border obstacle to trade apply to all trading partners. Even when tariffs are addressed, the goal is not necessarily preferential treatment. The reduction in tariffs on imports of automotive components in the Thai–Japan agreement was to facilitate trade between Japanese carmakers' factories in Thailand and their regular component suppliers in Japan; competition between those suppliers and non-Japanese component producers was not at issue. After examining the main agreements, this chapter will conclude by assessing the nature of East Asian regional trade agreements.

ASEAN: From Free Trade Area to Economic Community

The pace of establishing AFTA noticeably accelerated in the late 1990s. AFTA was formally completed in 2002, when internal tariffs had been reduced to 5% or less, but the real issue was the number of excluded sensitive items. This number was substantially reduced in the late 1990s and early 2000s as unprocessed agricultural products were phased into AFTA and 'sensitive' manufactured and processed agricultural products were transferred to inclusion lists. The climax was Malaysia's removal in 2005 of assembled and knocked-down automobiles from its exclusion list, signalling that even its most high profile import-competing industry would be opened up to free trade within ASEAN.[4] By 2006, all temporary exclusions had been brought on to the inclusion lists of the original ASEAN members and the unprocessed agricultural products still considered 'sensitive' (less than 150 tariff lines) were to be included by 2010, leaving only a General Exceptions List of 377 tariff

---

[4]The impact of removing goods from the AFTA exclusion list was sometimes offset by non-tariff measures such as targeted excise duties. Malaysia raised excise duties on cars at the same time as it brought cars off its AFTA exclusion list, ensuring that little or no increase in domestic demand would occur and give exports from other ASEAN countries an opportunity to establish market-share. Thailand's excise duty on sports utility vehicles, justified as an environmental policy measure, primarily affected imports of Ford vehicles assembled in the Philippines and was seen by the Philippines authorities as a ploy to encourage Ford to shift its production base to Thailand (Dent, 2008, 100–101). Nevertheless, the shift from protectionist trade barriers to taxes which did not discriminate between domestic and imported goods was a major step.

lines, representing less than one percent of all tariff lines and mainly connected to the protection of national security, public morals and articles of historical significance (Hedi Bchir and Fouquin, 2006).[5]

The growing practical usefulness of AFTA was reflected in increased utilization rates after the turn of the century. In 2000, about one tenth of Thai exports to ASEAN partners (excluding Singapore) entered under AFTA preferential rates. By 2008, this proportion was over a third. The increase between 2000 and 2008 was most striking for Thai exports to Indonesia (up from 10% to 60%), Vietnam (up from close to zero to almost half) and the Philippines (up from around 15% to 45%).[6]

Reflecting the accelerated pace of regional integration, an initiative to establish an ASEAN Economic Community by 2020 was launched at the 2003 ASEAN summit in Bali.[7] The ASEAN Economic Community project was an attempt to unify and extend the ASEAN Free Trade Area, the ASEAN Investment Area[8] and the ASEAN Framework Agreement on Services, and is clearly aimed at facilitating trade within a single ASEAN market. Twelve priority sectors were identified for fast-track integration: electronics, information and communications technology, healthcare, wood-based products, autos, rubber-based products, textiles and clothing, agro-based products, fisheries, air travel, tourism and logistics.

At the January 2007 summit in Cebu, the target date for the creation of a single ASEAN market was brought forward to 2015. At the November 2007 ASEAN summit in Singapore, the ASEAN Charter and ASEAN Blueprint were launched. The Blueprint provides a road map for establishing the ASEAN Economic Community by 2015,

---

[5]The four newest ASEAN members had later deadlines for bringing tariffs on the included items below 5% — 2006 for Vietnam, 2008 for Laos and Myanmar, and 2010 for Cambodia.

[6]Ando, Estevadeordal and Volpe Martincus (2009, 23), reporting numbers from the Japan External Trade Organization (JETRO) *Daily World News*, 9 March 2009, http://www.jetro.go.jp/biznews/ (in Japanese).

[7]The Community was the realization of the ASEAN Vision 2020, declared as a goal at the second informal summit in December 1997. The collections edited by Denis Hew (2007) and by Michael Plummer and Chia Siow Yue (2009) provide further information on the ASEAN Economic Community.

[8]The ASEAN Investment Area (AIA) aims to ensure national treatment for ASEAN investors by 2010 and for all investors by 2020 (Plummer, 2009, 170–182).

while the Charter provides the legal documentation for creating a more formal rules-based structure for ASEAN. The Blueprint has four parts:

A. Creating a single market in which goods, services, investment, capital and skilled labour flow freely, with more rapid liberalization of the twelve priority integration sectors (wood-based products, automotive, rubber-based products, textiles and clothing, electronics, agro-products, fisheries, e-ASEAN, healthcare, air travel, tourism and logistics).

B. Creating a competitive region with a clear competition policy to establish a level playing field, consumer protection, protection of intellectual property rights, and coordinated infrastructure development (in transport, energy and mining, information and communications technology, taxation and e-commerce).

C. Fostering equitable economic development through support for small and medium-sized enterprises (SMEs), and by enhancing the Initiative for ASEAN Integration (IAI) which was launched in 2000 to narrow development gaps between the six older members and the four most recent ASEAN members.[9]

D. Working towards ASEAN-centrality in external economic relations and fostering enhanced participation in global supply networks through the adoption of best international practices and international standards.

In establishing the AEC, agreements need to be concluded and ratified, institutions must be established, infrastructure put in place, and so forth, and ASEAN members agreed to a Scorecard approach to

---

[9]The IAI launch was followed by the 2001 Hanoi Declaration on Narrowing the Development Gap for Closer ASEAN Integration and by the introduction of an IAI Work Plan at the November 2002 summit. The Work Plan called for the funding of projects in the four poorest countries (Cambodia, Laos, Myanmar and Vietnam) by the richer ASEAN members; by 2006, of the $28.2 million committed, $21.6 million was from Singapore, $4.1 million from Malaysia and $1.5 million from Brunei. The amounts were much smaller than bilateral assistance from the ASEAN6 to the CLMV countries, $159.5 million by 2006, of which $100.4 million was from Thailand, $52.5 million from Singapore, and $5.9 million from Malaysia. Even these numbers are small compared to the $4 billion committed by Japan under the Japan–ASEAN Economic Partnership Agreement to narrow economic gaps among ASEAN countries (Dent, 2008, 103–104).

checking their individual progress in meeting targets and deadlines set out in the Blueprint.

In moving towards the deeper integration of the AEC, ASEAN members have accepted the need for change in the political decision-making process. The "ASEAN way" of reaching decisions by consensus is too susceptible to hold-up. Decisions necessary to create a single market in the face of opposition from vested interests in a small number of member countries can now be pushed through by a qualified majority; the necessary majority is ASEAN10–x, where the number of countries equal to x depends on the issue. To establish whether decisions are actually implemented, monitoring is important; individual member countries must be accountable for completing actions at the appropriate time, and some kind of Scorecard or account-keeping is essential. Whether these innovations, in fact, lead to more decisive actions will depend upon the political will of the countries involved when a serious conflict arises.[10]

An alternative approach to the hold-up problem inherent in the pre-AEC consensus approach is for members who want to push ahead with integration to move faster and let the others catch up later. This approach has been promoted by Singapore, e.g. at the 2003 ASEAN summit, Singapore's Minister for Trade and Industry argued that "it is better to catch up with those who are faster than to be dragged back by those who are slower" (Dent, 2008, 107). Under Prime Minister Thaksin Shinawatra, Thailand responded to this approach by establishing in 2003 the Singapore–Thailand Enhanced Economic Relationship to strengthen cooperation, liberalization and integration across a number of sectors which overlapped with the AEC priority integration

---

[10] Indicative of the potential problem was the difficulty encountered in implementing the Scorecard approach as a way of monitoring progress towards establishing the ASEAN Economic Community. Each member should be assessed by their progress in meeting targets and deadlines set out in the Blueprint, but when a scorecard for 2008 (with on average 67 components graded pass or fail for each country) was drawn up by the ASEAN Secretariat in 2009, its publication was suppressed by the member governments. There may be reservations about comparing numerical results when the list is not identical for each country (e.g. the four newest members may have received higher percentage scores because their targets were less demanding) and achievement or non-achievement of some qualitative targets may be difficult to determine objectively on a pass/fail basis, but the main reason for secrecy was that ASEAN members did not like to be shown to be below average on a numerical grade.

sectors. The Enhanced Economic Relationship encountered strong opposition from Malaysia, Indonesia and Brunei, who saw it as further fragmentation beyond the ASEAN6/CLMV division of ASEAN, and the bilateral relationship achieved little before crumbling when Thaksin lost power in September 2006.[11] Nevertheless, between 2003 and 2006 the Singapore–Thailand Enhanced Economic Relationship may have contributed to Singapore's goal of speeding up regional economic integration in Southeast Asia.

The ASEAN–China FTA and the Weakening of ASEAN+3

At the same time, as ASEAN was deepening its own regional integration, it looked for new institutional arrangements with its northeast Asian trading partners. Towards the end of 2000, the leaders of the three major trading nations of the North Pacific announced steps to initiate bilateral trading agreements within the region, in a sharp break from their previous practice. On October 22, the prime ministers of Japan and Singapore agreed that on 1st January 2001 they would launch negotiations of a 'new age' preferential trade agreement to be known as the Japan–Singapore Economic Partnership Agreement (JSEPA).[12] On November 16, the US president and Singapore's prime minister announced that they would start negotiations on a bilateral free trade agreement. On November 25, at the fourth ASEAN+China summit, China's premier Zhu Rongji called on the ASEAN members "to explore the establishment of a free trade relationship" with

---

[11] The bilateral relationship and Thaksin's downfall were linked by the controversial sale of Shin Communications, Thailand's largest telecommunications company 49.5% owned by Thaksin, to the Singapore government's investment company, Temasek, run by the Singaporean prime minister's wife, which became public knowledge in January 2006. Backlash against the sale of such a national asset in a non-transparent deal between close political allies contributed to Thaksin's falling popularity in Bangkok, paving the way for the September coup d'état.

[12] Japan intended initiating negotiations for bilateral trade agreements with South Korea (a move prompted by Korean President Kim Daejong's bold attempt at reconciliation between the two countries and reflected in the agreement to co-host the 2002 football World Cup) and Singapore. The attempt to improve bilateral relations with South Korea made slow progress (Munakata, 2006, 109–110), but a Singapore free trade agreement was quickly concluded because there were no significant obstacles (e.g. agriculture was irrelevant to Singapore).

China (Munakata, 2006, 8–9). In 2000–2001, following the CMI in the monetary arena, ASEAN was considering a proposal for trade integration among ASEAN+3, but foot-dragging by Japan and Korea (Munakata 2006, 117–118) led to ASEAN and China moving swiftly in 2001 towards negotiating an ASEAN+1 trade agreement.[13]

In November 2002, ASEAN and China signed the framework agreement on Comprehensive Economic Cooperation, which foreshadowed the establishment of an ASEAN–China Free Trade Area within ten years. In June 2003, China and Thailand signed an "early harvest" agreement to eliminate tariffs on 108 edible vegetables and 80 edible fruits and nuts from 1 October 2003, and early harvest measures involving other ASEAN members were introduced on 1 January 2004. In November 2004, the formal Agreement on Trade in Goods, between ASEAN and China was signed; it envisaged the establishment of a free-trade area by 2010 for six ASEAN members and by 2015 for the four newest ASEAN members. In addition, the framework agreement foresaw more comprehensive liberalization with agriculture, human resource development, information and communication technology, investment, and the development of the Mekong River Basin identified as priority areas (Sen, 2004, 76) and collaboration on illegal immigration, drug smuggling, counterterrorism and other security concerns also on the agenda (Kwei, 2006, 121).

Implementation of the ASEAN–China FTA has not been smooth sailing. Several ASEAN members fear that key sectors of their economies may be swamped by Chinese goods.[14] In 2009 Indonesia,

---

[13]China had an advantage over Japan and Korea insofar as its FTA with ASEAN could obtain a WTO waiver of most-favoured nation treatment under the Enabling Clause which governs preferential arrangements among developing countries, whereas any Japanese or Korean FTAs have to gain waivers under the stricter conditions of Article XXIV.

[14]Some of the anti-Chinese sentiment is distinct from the FTA, but does not provide a congenial background for closer economic ties. Plans by the Aluminium Corporation of China in 2008 to mine bauxite in Vietnam ignited a public debate characterized by nationalist attacks on China. In December 2009, demonstrations in Laos against the granting of a 50-year lease on the outskirts of Vientiane to a Chinese development company forced the government to reduce the concession from 1,600 to 200 hectares. In the same month, Cambodia refused to bow to Chinese pressure to extradite 20 Uighur asylum-seekers, despite a visit from Chinese Vice-President, Xi Jinping, who signed cooperation projects involving $1.2 billion. Territorial disputes remain unsettled in the South China Sea, where islands claimed by China are also claimed by Brunei, Malaysia, the Philippines and Vietnam.

for example, delayed implementation of the FTA in steel and textiles, and in October 2009, after accusing China of dumping nails, Indonesia imposed a punitive tariff of 145%.

China's ASEAN+1 agreement and the bilateral FTAs signed by some ASEAN members (notably Singapore and Thailand) with countries within and outside the region undermined the role of the ASEAN+3 grouping in regional trade liberalization. This was exacerbated by the slow and partial progress of negotiations between both Korea and Japan and ASEAN.

The Comprehensive Economic Cooperation Agreement between South Korea and ASEAN has struggled to be comprehensive in each of its four components. The agreement on goods trade signed in 2006 was boycotted by Thailand, which was concerned about the omission of agriculture and negotiated a separate agreement in 2009. The agreement on services trade negotiated in 2007 was only signed by six ASEAN countries (Brunei, Malaysia, Myanmar, the Philippines, Singapore and Vietnam). The investment agreement signed in 2009 contained statements of intent to encourage investment flows rather than specific commitments. As of 2010, agreement on a dispute settlement mechanism had yet to be reached.

The ASEAN–Japan Comprehensive Economic Partnership Agreement, which entered into force in December 2008, removed tariffs on Japanese exports from one ASEAN country to another, aiming especially to benefit electronics and automobile manufacturers. Japan agreed to repeal tariffs on 93 percent of imports from ASEAN by value within ten years, while the ASEAN6 will eliminate tariffs on 90 percent of imports from Japan within ten years; the four newest ASEAN members have a more gradual tariff elimination table. These terms are repetitive of liberalization that had already occurred or leave out sensitive areas where trade barriers are significant, i.e. the 7 or 10 percent of imports not covered by the agreement.

The ASEAN+3 framework became used not for trade issues, but for various other functional areas such as finance, information technology, standards, the environment, health (after the SARS outbreak in 2003), and energy security (after the oil price hikes in 2004). At the eighth ASEAN+3 summit in 2004, it was agreed to convene a regular East Asian Summit. After arguments about whom to invite, with China favouring a guest list limited to ASEAN+3, Japan argued successfully for Australia, India and New Zealand to be included, so that the East Asian Summit configuration became ASEAN+6. There was no clarification of the relative roles of the East Asian Summits and the ASEAN+3 summits in the evolving regional architecture, but the evolution of trade agreements after 2001 reduced the centrality that the ASEAN+3 grouping had briefly attained with the Chiang Mai Initiative.

Bilateral Trade Agreements

In the opening years of the twenty-first century, a new wave of RTAs centred on bilateral agreements and focussing on non-tariff barriers to trade originated in East Asia (and was taken up energetically by the Bush Administration in the USA).[15] The spread of trade agreements in Asia has been documented by Menon (2007), Kawai and Wignaraja (2007), Lee *et al.* (2008) and ADB (2008). From effectively one RTA before 2000, there were dozens a decade later. Menon (2007) reports that, by October 2006, the number of bilateral agreements signed between individual ASEAN members and other Asian countries and between Asian countries and other countries had reached 176, of which 50 had been implemented. Table 6.1 reports the number recorded by 2010 for selected countries on the Free Trade Agreement Database maintained by the Asia Regional Integration Center at the ADB.

Although often listed as regional trading arrangements (e.g. on the WTO website), many of the bilaterals were not regional. When Thailand embarked on a policy of negotiating bilateral trade agreements, it began with Bahrain and Australia before moving on to the United States and Japan; this pattern is weakening Thailand's *regional* trading arrangements by eroding the degree of preferential treatment negotiated within ASEAN.[16] South Korea's experimentation with bilaterals started with Chile and New Zealand — willing collocutors, but hardly regional neighbours and never likely to generate large bilateral

---

[15]On the genesis of the new bilateral agreements see Rajan, Sen and Siregar (2001).

[16]In the early 2000s, Malaysian ministers frequently criticized ASEAN members (i.e. Singapore and Thailand) for concluding non-regional RTAs, which were a distraction from regional integration and against the spirit of ASEAN (Dent, 2008, 212).

Table 6.1　Free trade agreements proposed, under negotiation, signed or implemented, selected countries, as of early 2010.

Country	Proposed	Under negotiation	Signed	Under implementation	Total
Afghanistan	1	0	2	1	4
Australia	6	6	0	7	19
Bangladesh	0	3	1	2	6
Brunei Darussalam	4	1	0	6	11
Cambodia	2	1	0	4	7
China	8	6	1	9	24
Fiji	1	1	0	3	5
Hong Kong	0	1	0	1	2
India	12	10	1	8	31
Indonesia	6	2	1	5	14
Japan	4	5	0	11	20
Kazakhstan	2	1	3	5	11
Korea, Republic of	8	9	1	5	23
Kyrgyz Republic	1	0	2	7	10
Lao PDR	2	1	0	6	9
Malaysia	3	6	2	6	17
Myanmar	2	2	0	4	8
Nepal	1	1	0	2	4
New Zealand	4	3	1	6	14
Pakistan	10	8	2	6	26
Papua New Guinea	1	1	0	4	6
Philippines	4	1	0	5	10
Singapore	5	9	2	16	32
Sri Lanka	2	1	1	4	8
Taiwan	1	2	0	4	7
Tajikistan	2	0	7	2	11
Thailand	6	3	1	9	24
Turkmenistan	0	0	1	2	3
Uzbekistan	1	0	7	3	11
Vietnam	2	2	2	4	11

Source: ADB Asia Regional Integration Center Free Trade Agreement Database for Asia, at http://www.aric.adb.org/10.php (accessed 5 February 2010).
Notes: Proposed = parties are considering a free trade agreement, establishing joint study groups or joint task force, and conducting feasibility studies to determine the desirability of entering into an FTA; Under Negotiation = parties begin negotiations with or without a framework agreement; Signed = parties sign the agreement after negotiations have been completed (some FTAs still require legislative or executive ratification); Under Implementation = when the provisions of an FTA becomes effective, e.g. when tariff cuts begin.

trade flows. The recurrence of Chile among Asian countries' bilateral agreements reflects a willing partner rather than a regional agreement. Similarly, the FTAs with the USA are about US policy and the importance of the US market, rather than regionalism.

Listing the agreements as FTAs (as on the ADB website cited in Table 6.1) is also a misnomer, because none of these "free trade" agreements calls for the elimination of restrictions on trade between the signatories. Although negotiations towards bilateral trade agreements are mushrooming in the Asia–Pacific region, the agreements' coverage and actual implementation are often limited. Sensitive items are excluded, which matters more for some agreements than others. Japan could happily leave agriculture outside their bilateral with Singapore, but omitting agriculture is more contentious when they negotiate with a country like Thailand. South Korea insisted that rice be omitted from any agreement with ASEAN on trade in goods, which led Thailand to opt out of the ASEAN–Korea negotiations in 2006. Similarly, the United States refusal to include sugar in its "free trade" agreement with Australia greatly reduced the trade-creating potential of the agreement.

In general, it is difficult to monitor the progress or content of these bilateral negotiations. Many of the agreements lack serious content (Pomfret, 2007). Some cross-regional agreements involve trade flows that are, and always will be, tiny, such as Korea–EFTA or Thailand–Bahrain,[17] and some agreements are paper agreements which have never actually entered into force. Even those agreements between substantial trading partners that have come into force have often been driven by a small number of specific, and sometimes apparently minor, issues. The Japan–Thailand agreement, for example, excluded areas with significant trade barriers such as rice; its principal results were to reduce the tariff on components imported by the mainly Japanese-owned carmakers in Thailand and to ease restrictions on temporary migration of Thai chefs into Japan. China has demanded as a precondition for entering into a FTA with Australia that it be granted market economy status by Australia.[18] Many countries have long had bilateral arrangements on double taxation, coordinated strategies to fight money laundering and other financial matters without making the claims to

---

[17]The European Free Trade Association (EFTA) consists of Iceland, Liechtenstein, Norway and Switzerland.

[18]Market economy status ensures fairer treatment in anti-dumping cases because actual Chinese prices are used as the benchmark rather than constructed prices that can be manipulated by the importing country. That, however, should be almost automatic since China's WTO accession and on its own scarcely justifies calling an agreement an FTA.

be furthering liberalization that the recent bilateral negotiations have attracted.

The use of a range of context-specific RTAs to address trade facilitation issues can be illustrated by the terms in Japan's RTAs concerning technical barriers to trade. The eleven RTAs notified by Japan to the WTO which had come into force by October 2009 (Table 6.2) included the 2008 ASEAN–Japan FTA and seven RTAs with individual ASEAN members (all except Cambodia, Laos and Myanmar). Although the ASEAN FTA came after five of the seven RTAs with individual ASEAN countries, it does not supersede the individual bilaterals, some of which contain varying "ASEAN Plus" items. The RTAs with Singapore, the Philippines and Thailand contain mutual recognition of conformity assessment procedures on a sectoral basis (all three target electrical equipment, and the Japan–Singapore RTA also targets telecommunication equipment), while the Brunei and Indonesia RTAs have no such provisions. Other agreements simply affirm commitment to obligations under the WTO Technical Barriers to Trade (TBT) Agreement concerning transparency, etc.[19] In sum, Japan's RTAs with southeast Asian countries contain a menu of commitment to trade facilitation in the TBT area, reflecting the relative importance of the issue in bilateral trade and of implementation costs, which may be increased by distance between two countries' regulatory regimes and by language difficulties, and business interest.[20]

As with the second global wave of RTAs in the 1980s, which was characterized by proponents as a "new regionalism," the third wave has novel features. The agreements are not primarily about traditional tariff

---

[19] Such commitments are trivial in that the TBT Agreement was part of the Single Undertaking in the Uruguay Round which means that its observance is mandatory for all WTO members. Laos is the only ASEAN country that is not a WTO member.

[20] Mutual recognition agreements are more prevalent among high-income countries where trusted conformity assessment bodies are likely to be more numerous. Japan signed stand-alone mutual recognition agreements with the EU (January 2002) and the USA (November 2007), which were not considered to be RTAs. The RTA with Switzerland, which is part of the European Economic Space, contains TBT provisions, but the other two non-Asian RTAs in Table 6.2, with Mexico and Chile, do not. Among Japan's RTAs with ASEAN countries, mutual recognition goes furthest in the RTA with Singapore, where implementation costs could be expected to be lowest, although in fact the governments overestimated demand; by 2009, there was a single recognized conformity assessment body in Singapore and none in Japan (Naiki, 2009, 3).

Table 6.2   RTAs Notified by Japan to the WTO, as of October 2009.

Partner	Entry into Force	TBT Provisions
Singapore	November 2002	Yes
Mexico	April 2005	No
Malaysia	July 2006	Yes
Chile	September 2007	No
Thailand	November 2007	Yes
Indonesia	July 2008	No
Brunei	July 2008	No
ASEAN	December 2008	Yes
Philippines	December 2008	Yes
Switzerland	September 2009	Yes
Vietnam	October 2009	Yes

Source: Naiki (2009, Table 1).

barriers, but more often about reducing border and behind-the-border trade costs. The bilateral agreement negotiated between Singapore and Japan, for example, focused on areas such as financial services, capital flows and the coordination of regulatory systems, which are analytically more difficult areas, often with inherently less transparency than the traditional trade barriers of tariffs or quotas. Nevertheless, the thrust of the analysis of the first two waves remains valid. Even in the new areas, multilateral non-discriminatory trade liberalization is usually the best approach not only from a cosmopolitan global perspective, but also often for the net economic welfare of the participants in regional arrangements. The lack of transparency and the selective coverage may make it more likely, given the political economy of trade policy, that trade-creating opportunities will be passed over because they hurt domestic producers while trade diversion will be permitted because domestic producers do not suffer. On the other hand, trade facilitation measures, by their nature, tend to be non-discriminatory, even if a particular trade cost may have been especially burdensome for the country negotiating the trade agreement.

Conclusions

In the twenty-first century, East Asian regional agreements have primarily concerned trade. However, tariffs are no longer the main issue. The substantial tariff cuts negotiated in the Uruguay Round of multilateral trade negotiations which ended in 1994, and the unilateral tariff cuts which many Asian countries implemented in the 1990s, have left low MFN tariffs with little scope for preferential treatment.[21] Moreover, and especially important in the context of regional value chains, import of intermediates is frequently exempt from duties as long as the product is eventually exported. Thirdly, the multilateral Information Technology Products Agreement (ITA) signed at the 1996 WTO Ministerial in Singapore covers much of the shipping of electronics components that dominates, for example, Korea–China trade (Nicolas, 2009).

Already, in the second half of the 1990s, the emphasis within ASEAN had shifted to trade facilitation measures. The deepening of ASEAN integration towards formation of an ASEAN Economic Community continues this pattern in the twenty-first century. Similarly, the accelerated pace and broad scope of China–ASEAN negotiations in the early years of the twenty-first century reflected the growth of regional value chains involving China and Southeast Asian nations and the corresponding need to reduce trade costs. Among ASEAN members, the leader in implementing trade agreements since 2000 has been Singapore with 16 agreements in effect by 2010 (Table 6.1); countries signing trade agreements with Singapore cannot have been concerned about preferential access to what was already essentially a tariff-free economy. It is also noteworthy that, apart from the ASEAN FTA, China's earliest trade agreements were with Australia, Chile, Hong Kong, Macau and New Zealand — all low-tariff economies where preferential tariff treatment would be of minor significance.

The bilateral and plurilateral trade agreements are hard to classify, but preferential tariff rates are not the centrepiece and the terms are more commonly aimed at addressing specific concerns about trade costs. The ASEAN–Australia–New Zealand FTA signed in February 2009, for example, has a very short chapter on tariffs and

---

[21]The Japan–Singapore Economic Partnership Agreement, the longest running of the Japanese bilaterals (Table 6.2), had by 2006 a negligible impact on goods trade, whether tested by a gravity model (Urata and Okabe, 2010) or by a variety of more descriptive criteria (Ando, 2010). These results are consistent with the earlier study by Hertel, Walmsley and Itakura (2001), who found no gains from tariff reductions and that all benefits came from cost-reducing trade facilitation measures.

country-specific schedules for tariff reductions, while the other twelve chapters concern measures to improve the environment in which trade occurs, with improved customs procedures, smoother quarantine processes, more transparent rules and regulations, the alignment of standards and so forth. The bilateral agreements are often scoffed at for their failure to reduce tariffs and for claiming to be WTO-Plus, but the latter label is accurate insofar as the agreements address trade facilitation measures which have not been part of past rounds of WTO multilateral trade negotiations, and are only weakly represented on the Doha agenda.[22] On the other hand, despite often claiming to go beyond trade in goods, the coverage of services trade and of foreign direct investment in post-2000 agreements has been limited, either because of restrictive conditions or narrow sectoral coverage.[23]

Although preferential tariffs appear to be a minor issue, two issues are hotly debated: the low utilization of preferential tariffs and the desirability of consolidation. Take-up of ASEAN tariff preferences has been very low (Manchin and Pelkmans-Balaoing, 2008), primarily due to small margins of preference relative to the added bureaucracy of claiming preferential rates of import duty. As mentioned above, however, take-up rates of AFTA preferences increased in the 2000s (Ando *et al.*, 2009), presumably because many formerly excluded items were brought within AFTA.[24] Overall, low take-up has characterized most bilateral trade agreements.[25] It has become commonplace to blame

---

[22]Whalley (2008, 525–529) makes a similar point. Although the section of his paper is entitled "Beyond Goods and Services: The example of ASEAN and ASEAN country agreements," the focus is on competition policy (or "Anti-Competitive Business Conduct, Designated Monopolies and Government Enterprises" as the clauses are labelled in one Singaporean agreement) and related areas of mutual recognition, TBT/SPS and anti-dumping, all of which are about trade in goods and, to a lesser extent, services. He also notes that "the relative ease of customising agreements to cover non-trade barrier issues" explains the complexity and diversity of post-2000 agreements.

[23]The treatment of services in Asian trade agreements is reviewed by Ochiai, Dee and Findlay (2010) and the restrictions on foreign direct investment are analysed by Urata and Sasuya (2010).

[24]Kawai and Wignaraja (2009) conclude from interview data that the slow take-up before the mid-2000s was temporary because it took years for traders to respond to AFTA.

[25]It is, however, likely that specific targeted measures in bilateral agreements were utilized. For example, the lobbying by Japanese carmakers for reduced tariffs on component imports into Thailand indicated that this was important to them; they surely took advantage of this item in the Japan–Thailand FTA to further integrate their assembly plants in Thailand into regional value chains.

the complexity of the "noodle bowl" of overlapping trade agreements with their varied tariff rates and rules of origin, but when most trade between parties to an agreement is conducted under low or zero MFN tariffs, it is unsurprising that few traders bother to find out about, let alone avail themselves of, preferential tariff rates.[26] Is it any surprise that few Japanese firms report taking advantage of the Japan–Singapore Economic Partnership Agreement when Singapore's tariffs are close to zero?[27]

Many observers argue the need for consolidating trade agreements in Asia, because the "noodle bowl" of overlapping and inconsistent trade agreements is a sign of fragility (Baldwin, 2006) or of missed opportunities for efficient regionalism (ADB, 2008). Elsewhere, conflicting rules of origin have been found to be a negative consequence of spaghetti bowls. In East Asia, rules of origin are of less importance than in NAFTA or in US or EU agreements with third countries, because the Asian agreements are primarily targeted at facilitating trade that is already essentially tariff-free. Baldwin (2006) acknowledges the importance of low tariffs in Asian regionalism, but argues that because tariffs have not been bound at the WTO, this is a sign of fragility; in future times of trouble, countries may be tempted to raise tariffs and will be unconstrained by contractual obligations.

Among advocates of consolidation, there are, however, conflicting approaches. The ADB's Emerging Asian Regionalism project (ADB, 2008) recommended consolidation centred on ASEAN+3 or perhaps

---

[26]There is no single right answer to the question of what is the minimum effective preference margin because what matters more than the ad valorem margin is the net monetary benefit of claiming preferential treatment, which will differ by the size of shipment and the cost of claiming preferential treatment as well as by the preference margin. The consensus in the literature ranges from 4% (Francois et al., 2005) to 5% (e.g. Amiti and Romalis, 2006), which suggests that once MFN tariffs, have fallen below 5% any preferential rate is ineffective.

[27]Based on a November 2006 survey of Japanese firms, Takahashi and Urata (2010) report that 3.6% of firms engaged in international trade (17 out of 469 respondents) took advantage of the Japan–Singapore agreement and 5.5% (26 out of 469) utilized the Japan–Malaysia agreement. These low utilization rates are similar to those in earlier surveys of Japanese firms. If there are general (not commodity-specific) trade facilitating consequences of the Agreement, individual firms are unlikely to report themselves taking advantage of the Agreement. In the empirical assessment of the Japan–Singapore Economic Partnership Agreement by Hertel, Walmsley and Itakura (2001), virtually all the economic gains come from customs automation, security and harmonization measures for e-commerce, and liberalization of trade in business and construction services.

a wider grouping, guided by the Asian Development Bank. The UN regional commission, ESCAP, advocates extension of the Asia–Pacific Trade Agreement (APTA) under which seven Asian countries offer limited preferential tariff treatment to one another.[28] This institutional divide is unlikely to be bridged because the ADB and ESCAP are supported by Japan and China respectively, neither of which is likely to give way to the other's preferred institution, and the consolidation of preferential tariff arrangements is not sufficiently important for other countries to press for a resolution.[29] Indeed, any East Asia-wide RTA will, as with the monetary arrangements discussed in the previous chapter, be contingent on cordial relations between China and Japan; after improving in the late 1990s, bilateral relations deteriorated significantly in the half decade after 2001 when the new RTAs were proliferating.[30]

How important is the creation of an integrated Asian economic region? Some commentators see a limited but positive benefit in the consolidation of the complex web of arrangements described in the previous chapter. Patrizia Tumbarello (2007) of the IMF, for example, argues that a pan-Asian FTA among the 16 East Asian Summit countries (ASEAN+3 plus, Australia, India and New Zealand) might help to unravel the current 'noodle bowl' of overlapping trade agreements.

---

[28] APTA dates from the 1975 Bangkok Agreement which was signed by Bangladesh, India, Laos, South Korea and Sri Lanka. Laos has not issued customs notification of concessions granted and is thus not an effective participating member, although some other members have extended their APTA concessions to include Laos. The Agreement is open to any member of ESCAP and was boosted by China's accession in 2001. The name was changed to APTA in 2005. The Bangkok Agreement is acknowledged to have had a disappointingly small impact on intra-Asian trade before China's accession in 2001 and a 2006 commitment to revitalize APTA. Since then, the ESCAP Trade Division, which acts as APTA's Secretariat, has been actively soliciting new members and advocating deeper preferential tariff cuts.

[29] Japan is the largest shareholder in the ADB, contributes the largest slice of funding and provides the President. China is the only Asian country with a permanent seat on the UN Security Council, and hence a veto over UN decisions.

[30] History remains close to the surface. For China, a trigger was the 2001 visit by Japanese Prime Minister Junichiro Koizumi to the Yasukuni Shrine which honours Japanese soldiers and includes several war criminals executed after World War II. Prime Minister Koizumi repeated the visits, which also raised objections in South Korea, annually during his 2001–2006 term in office. Open hostilities erupted at football matches between China and Japan in 2005, after which Chinese leaders tried to leash the nationalism to which they had previously been content to provide tacit support. Relations improved in 2006–2007; Japanese Prime Minister Shinzo Abe visited China in October 2006 and Chinese Prime Minister Wen Jiabao visited Tokyo in April 2007 and gave the first speech by a Chinese Prime Minister to the Japanese Diet.

Joseph Francois and Ganeshan Wignaraja (2008), using a computable general equilibrium (CGE) model, predict large benefits from Asian integration, but these depend upon the assumed depth of integration, especially including China, Japan and Korea, in an arrangement removing barriers to trade in goods and services and reducing trade costs. They also find substantial gains from bringing India into the arrangement. This result is model-dependent,[31] but highlights the importance of the width of the region and of the depth of integration which are discussed in the next two chapters.

---

[31] CGE models provide *ex ante* estimates of the impact of changing parameters such as tariff rates, but the results depend upon the structure of the model, as well as the choice of scenarios. Some economists argue that CGE models underestimate the long-term impact of trade liberalization, including the effect of free trade agreements (e.g. DeRosa and Gilbert, 2005), but most *ex post* estimates using the gravity model find little impact of RTAs and the results are not robust; Ghosh and Yamarik (2004), using an extreme bounds test, conclude that "the pervasive trade creation effect found in the literature reflects not the information content of the data but rather the unacknowledged beliefs of the researchers." Baier *et al.* (2008) argue that the discrepancy is due to selection bias and that, although CGE estimates are generally too high, policymakers have selected into arrangements with partners where the effects will be large.

Chapter 7

How Wide is the Region?

Intertwined with the struggle for regional hegemony is the question of how the region should be defined. The core in recent decades has been ASEAN, but ASEAN itself reinvented its frontiers in the 1990s as the Cold War fault-line that ran through Southeast Asia lost meaning. ASEAN's expansion in the second half of the 1990s to include Laos, Myanmar, Vietnam and Cambodia reflected changing geopolitical realities a decade after the end of the Southeast Asian wars. In the late 1990s, ASEAN+3 emerged as a regional grouping which took the lead in monetary integration, culminating in the 2000 CMI, but monetary integration then lost steam. Meanwhile, after the turn of the century, Japan became increasingly concerned about China's weight in this grouping, and neighbouring countries such as India, Australian and New Zealand were concerned about being excluded. At the eighth ASEAN+3 summit in 2004, it was agreed to convene a regular East Asia Summit (EAS), which has been an ASEAN+6 grouping.

The membership issue remains fluid and subject to two sorts of pressures. On one hand, there is jockeying for influence among the major and the mid-level powers, which has focussed on the choice of forum or, for countries dissatisfied with how the forum-setting is proceeding, there may be a resort to arguments for variable geometry with overlapping institutions tackling different issues and allowing differential integration progress. The evolution of these struggles for institutional influence is analysed in the next section, which is followed by more specific treatment of the major countries and sub-regions outside the ASEAN+3 core.

On the other hand, membership in institutions for regionalism has an economic basis. Based on the analysis of previous chapters, we might expect the extent of the region to mimic the extent of the production networks which constitute Factory Asia. There is a two-way process insofar as membership in regional institutions may make it easier to participate in regional value chains, but it is not completely endogenous; some countries are absolutely disadvantaged by geography. What governments are prepared to bring to regional agreements also matters; many announced RTAs across the world have had no real impact, whereas ASEAN and ASEAN+China became serious regionalism steps when they facilitated the development of regional value chains by concrete targeted measures.

This chapter focuses on the first of these pressures — the jockeying for influence. The next chapter will concentrate on the nexus between regionalism, trade facilitation and the strengthening of production networks and regional value chains.

The East Asia Summit (ASEAN+6), Variable Geometry, and the G20

The geographical scope of East Asian regionalism expanded rapidly after the mid-1990s. Before 1996, the six ASEAN members were the only countries committed to any kind of regionalism and the actual economic content of their regional commitments was limited. This began to change in the second half of the 1990s as the existing members undertook trade facilitating initiatives and began to implement the ASEAN Free Trade Area more purposefully, and membership expanded from six to ten with the accession of Laos, Myanmar, Vietnam and Cambodia. This was close to the natural limit of an association of southeast Asian countries.[1]

---

[1] Timor-Leste has formally applied for ASEAN membership. Following independence in 2002, Timor-Leste was recognized as an Observer by ASEAN, and became a member of the ASEAN Regional Forum in July 2005 and acceded to the Treaty of Amity and Cooperation in Southeast Asia in 2007. Papua New Guinea has had Observer status since 1976, but only in 2009 started to express interest in pursuing full membership. While Australia and New Zealand often floated the idea of linking their bilateral Closer Economic Relations to ASEAN, they were never seriously viewed as part of a southeast Asian region.

The monetary integration talks which culminated in the 2000 Chiang Mai Initiative brought the ASEAN+3 grouping to centre stage. China proposed to hold an East Asia Summit in Beijing, but sensing a danger of diplomatic over-reach quickly back-tracked from the proposed location and supported Malaysia as the host. In 2004 and early 2005, the USA lobbied Japan not to cooperate with proposals for an East Asian Summit, because the summit was designed to enhance the influence of China, while others suspected that the goal was to exclude the USA (Munakata, 2006, 15). In general, however, the USA showed less concern about East Asian regionalism in the early 2000s than it had in the 1990s.[2] One consequence of the East Asia Summit was to highlight the competition for regional leadership; even though China backed down on playing host, the summit was a Chinese initiative and Japan felt a need to respond.

The First East Asia Summit, held in Kuala Lumpur on 14 December 2005, was preceded by arguments about whom to invite. China favoured a guest list limited to ASEAN+3. Japan, seeking counter-weights to Chinese influence, argued successfully for Australia, India and New Zealand to be included. Thus, the East Asia Summit (EAS) configuration is sometimes referred to as ASEAN+6. Russia attended the First EAS as an observer at the invitation of the host Malaysia, and its request to become a future member seems to be supported by China and India, but no agreement was reached. The Second EAS held in Cebu in the Philippines in January 2007 (postponed from December 2006 due to a typhoon), the Third EAS in Singapore in November 2007 and the Fourth EAS in Thailand had the same ASEAN+6 participants as the first EAS. Presumably any new member of ASEAN such as Timor-Leste would join the EAS, but more controversial cases such as Russia were on hold.

---

[2] This reflected other priorities, especially the war on terrorism after September 2001, but also the Bush administration appeared to have few principled opponents of discriminatory trade arrangements, whether signed by the USA or by other countries. Fostering ASEAN integration had become US policy (US Department of State *Fact Sheet* 'ASEAN Cooperation Plan' 4 December 2002), influenced by the increased involvement of US transnational corporations in Asian production networks. Within APEC, the USA shunned a 2003 Thai initiative to revive the Bogor Goals and a 2004 proposal for a Free Trade Area of the Asia–Pacific which was supported by Australia, New Zealand and Singapore.

At the Third EAS in Singapore in November 2007, the participants agreed to establish the Economic Research Institute for ASEAN and East Asia (ERIA). This Japanese-funded Jakarta-based institute is promoted as an Asian equivalent to the Organization for Economic Cooperation and Development (OECD). ERIA was tasked with reporting on the proposed Comprehensive Economic Partnership in East Asia and on the progress in establishing the ASEAN Economic Community, and, in particular, to evaluate the Scorecard approach to monitoring progress and to propose alternative measures of progress towards the AEC.

The Fourth EAS was delayed for almost a year due to political difficulties in the host nation, Thailand.[3] When it finally convened in October 2009, it was an anti-climax with a vaguely worded final statement. The Summit adopted two documents: a statement on disaster management, and the second related to the re-establishment of Nalanda University (a Buddhist institution on an ancient site in India).

Japan proposed a Comprehensive Economic Partnership in East Asia (CEPEA) among the sixteen East Asia Summit countries in 2006, clearly as a counter-proposal to an ASEAN+3 RTA which in Japanese eyes would be dominated by China. Inclusion of Australia, India and New Zealand diluted Chinese influence and a greater weight of democratic countries with market-based economies might make the grouping more acceptable to the USA. The CEPEA proposal made little progress in 2007–2009 as ASEAN focused on negotiating its own

---

[3]The Summit was originally to be held in Bangkok on 17th December 2008, but it was announced in late October 2008 that the Summit would be shifted to Chiang Mai due to concerns about political unrest in the capital city. It was decided on 2 December 2008 that due to the ongoing Thai political crisis, the Summit would be postponed until March 2009. The ASEAN Summit had been scheduled for 27th February 2009 to 1st March 2009, but those dates were not convenient for the ASEAN dialogue partners, and it was announced in January 2009 that the EAS and ASEAN+3 meetings would be held later, with the EAS re-scheduled for April in Pattaya. During the lead up to the Summit, there were several fatal border clashes between Thailand and Cambodia, and the Summit was to be used as an opportunity for sideline discussions between the two nations' leaders. On 11th April 2009, anti-Thai government protesters broke into the EAS meeting site, forcing the Thai Prime Minister, Abhisit Vejjajiva, to cancel the meeting; the leaders of China, Japan and Korea had to be airlifted out by Thai helicopters, whilst New Zealand Prime Minister John Key did not make it out of Bangkok airport and Australian Prime Minister Kevin Rudd turned back en route to Thailand. The Summit was initially rescheduled for 25th October 2009 in Phuket, but was moved again to Chaam and Hua Hin.

trade agreements with India (completed in 2008) and Australia and New Zealand (2009), after which ASEAN, suffering from negotiation-fatigue, seemed uninterested in pursuing the CEPEA. However, Risaburo Nezu, Chair of the CEPEA Expert Group, argues that the real obstacle is not so much ASEAN as the +6, which have concluded few bilateral FTAs among themselves, and he particularly highlights Japanese reluctance to open its market to sensitive imports.[4] Nezu (2009) contrasts China's role of importing components from its neighbours, completing assembly and exporting to the USA and Europe high-lighting that China has opened its market to its Asian neighbours and, in doing so, is facilitating their industrialization, with Japan's role of importing raw materials and maintaining trade surpluses, i.e. sucking in its neighbours' valuable foreign currency. China's open market plays a large part in expanding its regional economic influence, and agricultural exporters such as Australia and New Zealand show increasing interest in China (and South Korea) rather than in Japan. In sum, Japan's reluctance to open its markets undermines any Japanese-led regional integration proposals.

Proposals for a Free Trade Area of the Asia–Pacific among APEC members, which have been voiced in the Pacific Economic Cooperation Council (PECC), seem even less likely to be adopted. At the 2009 APEC summit, the United States Trade Representative announced that the USA would participate in negotiations to establish a Trans-Pacific Partnership (TPP) trade agreement, but the initial negotiations only involved eight countries: the P4 countries (Brunei, Chile, New Zealand and Singapore) plus Australia, Peru, the USA and Vietnam.[5] Most of the bilateral trade flows among these eight countries are already covered by bilateral trade agreements or involve tiny trade flows, with the

---

[4] Japan's bilateral FTA talks with South Korea, Australia, and India have made no progress, while negotiations with China and New Zealand have not even begun. Japan opposes liberalization of agricultural trade, while excluding agricultural products from negotiation was unacceptable to Australia and New Zealand.

[5] The origins of the TPP lie in the 1998 P5 proposal to spur trade liberalization among like-minded APEC members (Australia, Chile, New Zealand, Singapore and the USA), although after Australia, Chile and the USA failed to follow through, the only practical outcome of the P5 proposal was a Singapore–New Zealand bilateral trade agreement. In 2003, Chile expressed interest in trilateralizing the agreement and in 2005 Brunei Darussalam asked to participate, so that the agreement signed at the 2005 APEC Trade Ministers Meeting was P4. The P4 agreement

exception of the US–New Zealand and US–Vietnam links which are highly attractive to the smaller partner as long as important agricultural exports products (beef, lamb and dairy products for New Zealand, rice for Vietnam) are not excluded.[6] It is noteworthy that, apart from Singapore, none of the large and mid-sized Asian economies that have driven the regionalization process of the 1990s and 2000s showed interest in Trans-Pacific trade negotiations in 2009.

It is not essential that all functions of regional institutions be met by organizations with a common membership, and Australia, in particular, has pushed for "variable geometry" as a practical way forward for Asian and Trans-Pacific regionalism. However, if there is a core membership, there will inevitably be competition to be included in the core and for pre-eminence within the core. The various forums reflect Great Power competition, with Japan using the broader EAS membership to counterbalance China's success with a more functional approach towards relations with ASEAN. Trade agreements between ASEAN and the Closer Economic Relations countries (Australia and New Zealand) and between ASEAN and India also highlighted the broader region. However, the EAS raises questions about the trade-off between size and efficacy (is 16 countries too many to reach agreements?) and about the position of geographically cognate countries not in these arrangements, such as Bangladesh or Papua New Guinea.

The phenomenon of non-members wanting to be in the club ("the grass always looks greener beyond the fence") is illustrated by the expansion of EU membership and also by the recent flourishing of G (plus number) Groups. The G7 meetings, which began in 1975 in response to the economic shocks of the early and mid-1970s, brought

---

is comprehensive, including market access for trade in goods and services, TBTs, intellectual property, public procurement, competition policy, dispute settlement, and provision for future chapters on investment and financial services and a separate memorandum of understanding on labour and on the environment. The P4 agreement is open regionalism in that it is open to accession "on terms to be agreed among the parties, by any APEC economy or other state" (New Zealand Ministry of Foreign Affairs and Trade website at http://www.mfat.govt.nz/Trade-and-Economic-Relations/Trade-Agreements/Trans-Pacific/index.php).

[6]From the experience of the US–Australian FTA negotiations, it is likely that these goods will be excluded, given the political strength of the import-competing groups in the USA and the unimportance of New Zealand and Vietnam as markets for any US export industry that might supply countervailing lobbying.

together the leaders of the seven largest market economies in annual summits. In 1997, after replacing central planning by a market-based economy, Russia was invited to join what became the G8. By the twenty-first century, with the economic rise of China, India and Brazil, the G8 seemed anachronistic. The problem was addressed in 2009 by convening a G20 meeting which included not only the G8 countries but also the major Latin American economies, South Africa, Saudi Arabia, Turkey, India and Australia. From East Asia, the G20 included Japan, China, Korea and Indonesia. ASEAN was represented by Thailand which held the rotating presidency. However, in future, Thailand will not be represented and could legitimately question why Indonesia has a seat and it does not when their GDP is roughly equal.

The statement at the October 2009 G20 meeting in Pittsburgh that the G20 would henceforth replace the G8 as the main gathering of world leaders was generally welcomed in Asia, where the European preponderance in the G7/G8 has been viewed with suspicion. Australia and Korea, in particular, are vigorous supporters of the G20 grouping, because it represents a number which will just include them. With more exclusive membership, Australia and Korea would likely be excluded and, in a bigger group, each country's weight would be smaller.[7] Korea and Australia both favour the idea that the Asian G6 from the G20 countries should play a strategic agenda-setting role on Asian regional issues.[8]

Similar tensions surround the composition of the UN Security Council, where the five permanent members are jealous of their position while countries such as Japan, India, Germany or Brazil consider their claim to be at least equal to that of an existing member. In Asia, this plays out in competition between regional organizations. China has greater influence within the United Nations Economic and Social Commission for Asia and the Pacific (ESCAP). Japan has more influence, because it

---

[7] For similar reasons, Canada and Italy are the strongest supporters of maintaining a role for the G8, rather than a G20 in which their weight is diminished.

[8] Australian Prime Minister Rudd's proposals along these lines in Singapore (speech at the Shangri-La Dialogue summit on 29 May 2009) would not have been popular with his hosts who have seen Singapore, which is not a G20 member, as a hub for ASEAN and East Asian regionalization. Korea devoted much energy to hosting the G20 finance ministers meeting in 2010 and, as G20 chair for the year, was responsible for preparing for the 2010 G20 summit.

provides the largest share of funding, in the Asian Development Bank (ADB).

Australia and New Zealand

Australia and New Zealand embraced deep regionalism in 1983 with their Closer Economic Relations (CER) agreement. In the late 1980s and early 1990s, Australia played a leadership role in arrangements such as APEC or EMEAP, but under the 1996–2007 Liberal governments, Australia engaged less actively with Asia at the political level, even as economic ties continued to strengthen. Several overtures to link the CER and ASEAN were rebuffed in the 1990s and early 2000s. In 2006, Australia's government publicly stated that "if invited by ASEAN+3 members, Australia would be willing to make a financial and practical contribution to the Chiang Mai Initiative" (Corbett and Fitriani, 2008), but no invitation came and the CMIM remained an ASEAN+3 affair.

Apart from the CER, the most important bilateral trade agreement for Australia was the Australia–US Free Trade Agreement (AUSFTA) which came into force in 2005. Politically, the agreement signalled the zenith of close political relations between the Bush administration and the Howard government, reflected also in Australian support for the US-led 2003 invasion of Iraq. The AUSFTA was hotly debated in Australia, with a study commissioned by the government predicting large economic benefits and other studies finding minimal benefits.[9] The discrepancy arose because the AUSFTA has little to do with traditional trade barriers — barriers to Australian agricultural exports were either excluded (sugar) or phased in over very long time horizons (beef) and manufacturing trade between the two countries is not subject to significant tariffs — and the major impact of AUSFTA is

---

[9]During 2003–2004, four economic assessments of AUSFTA — by the International Monetary Fund, ACIL Tasman, the National Institute of Economic and Industry Research, and Philippa Dee of the Australian National University — found that the FTA would either have little economic impact or be bad for Australia's economy. The Australian government, keen to conclude an agreement for political reasons, ignored these studies and cited a report by the Centre for International Economics which predicted economic benefits from the FTA of around 0.7% of GDP. The quantitative literature is reviewed by Harris and Robertson (2009).

in difficult to quantify areas (i.e. extending copyright protection from 50 to 70 years, administrative changes to Australia's subsidization of prescription drugs, mutual recognition of qualifications in service sectors, and so forth).[10] Apart from questioning the value to Australia of what was seen as a one-sided agreement, critics of AUSFTA pointed to the potentially discriminatory nature of some of the service sector provisions, e.g. the relaxation of Australian screening of inward foreign direct investment in non-sensitive sectors or the US commitment to provide national treatment to Australian service sector exporters (Dee, 2007, 409n).

Meanwhile, New Zealand's embracing of bilateral trade agreements took it in different directions. The Singapore–New Zealand FTA, concluded in 2000, was the first of the new wave of bilaterals in Asia, and New Zealand's negotiations with South Korea were also among the earliest. The P4 trade agreement was signed in 2005 by Brunei, Chile, New Zealand and Singapore, and notably not by Australia or the USA which had been parties to the 1998 P5 proposal. Most dramatically, the 2008 China–New Zealand FTA was the first agreement signed between China and an OECD country. Particularly in the first half of the decade, these trade policy initiatives signalled New Zealand's Asian (or even global) focus at a time when Australia's attention was concentrated on the US relationship.[11] Progress towards deepening CER integration also moved at snail's pace for most of the

---

[10]Harris and Robertson (2009) argue that Australia traded items desired by the USA, e.g. on copyright protection and pharmaceuticals marketing, in return for guaranteed future access to the US market, which in their dynamic general equilibrium model turns out to be a major benefit. The argument that small countries sign RTAs with larger countries for market-access insurance (Perroni and Whalley, 2000) is difficult to assess quantitatively. In the 2007–2009 crisis in the USA, for example, it is unclear whether Australia avoided protectionist measures in the US market because of AUSFTA or because pressures for such measures would have been resisted by the US government even in the absence of AUSFTA; if protectionist measures would not have been imposed, then insurance turns out to be unnecessary.

[11]New Zealand is a friend but not an ally of the USA. After fighting with the USA in the Vietnam War, relations cooled in 1984 when New Zealand responded to concerns over nuclear testing in the Pacific by barring nuclear-armed and nuclear-powered warships from New Zealand ports, which was incompatible with US policy of neither confirming nor denying the presence or absence of nuclear weapons onboard its vessels. In 1986, the United States suspended its security obligations to New Zealand. Despite warmer relations in the 2000s, New Zealand's legislation prohibiting visits of nuclear-powered ships continues to preclude a bilateral security alliance with the US.

Howard governments' 1996–2007 tenure, only picking up in the final years.

Negotiations were initiated in 2005 for a trade agreement between ASEAN and the CER countries, and the ASEAN–Australia–New Zealand Free Trade Agreement (AANZFTA) was signed in August 2008. Australia and New Zealand will remove all tariffs on imports from ASEAN and ASEAN members will progressively remove tariffs on at least 90% of their tariff lines, with exemptions for Cambodia, Laos and Myanmar. AANZFTA provisions also cover trade in services, although less comprehensively than for goods, as well as investment, intellectual property, competition policy and economic cooperation; funding to support implementation will largely be provided by Australia and New Zealand.

After the 2007 Australian election, the Rudd government took a more proactive approach to Asia, proposing in 2008 the formation of an Asia–Pacific Community. The proposal was driven by concern that no institution existed that could deal comprehensively with regional economic, political and security issues. Thus, APEC does not include India and the ASEAN Regional Forum has 27 members but does not meet at Head of Government level, and when serious issues arise (such as North Korea's nuclear program) they are dealt with in an ad hoc fashion (in the Korean case, by the Six Party Talks). Nevertheless, the proposal met with little positive response, and Australia's status in the region was undermined by deteriorating relations with the major powers.[12] Only Australia's relations with South Korea were in good standing, largely due to a change of government in Korea, as well as mutual interest in promoting the success of the G20.

---

[12]China resented restrictions on its freedom to invest in Australian resource sectors, while Australia was upset by the arrest and non-transparent proceedings against an Australian executive working in China. Relations between Australia and India were damaged by high profile violence against Indian immigrants and students in Australia, and what the Indian government saw as half-hearted police action to identify and punish the perpetrators. Relations with Japan were damaged by Australian support for environmental groups opposing what the Japanese considered to be legitimate whaling activities. Each of these cases highlighted cultural gulfs between Australian and Asian attitudes towards individual rights, law and order, and discrimination, and perceptions of hypocrisy or duplicity.

India

For India, regional trading arrangements played little roles before serious reforms to open up the economy were implemented in the early 1990s. The South Asian Association for Regional Cooperation (SAARC), launched in 1985 by Bangladesh, Bhutan, India, the Maldives, Nepal, Pakistan and Sri Lanka, had little economic impact; trade between India and Pakistan was on worse than MFN basis until 1995, and even after the South Asian Free Trade Area entered into force in 2006, the regional trade liberalization was limited.[13] None of the initiatives launched in the late 1990s to bypass Pakistan (i.e. the South Asian Growth Quadrangle, BIMSTEC and the Indian Ocean Rim-Association for Regional Cooperation — see Chapter 2 for details) had much economic impact. More far-reaching bilateral agreements were implemented with Sri Lanka in 2000 and with Bhutan in 2005, but the markets of India's South Asian neighbours are generally small.

India adopted a Look East policy in the early 1990s in recognition of East Asia's growing economic might, and also perhaps in response to the fear of blocs forming in Europe and the Americas. India became an ASEAN dialogue partner in 1995 and joined the ASEAN Regional Forum in 1996. In 2004, ASEAN and India signed a framework agreement on economic cooperation, and they completed negotiations for an ASEAN+1 FTA in September 2008. The ASEAN–India FTA calls for the elimination of tariffs on 80% of tariff lines by 2015 and a reduction to 5% on a further 10% of tariff lines; 489 items have been excluded from the agreement, and India has signalled its intention to lower duties on sensitive items such as palm oil, tea, coffee and pepper to 40–45% by 2019.[14] India has also signed agreements with individual ASEAN members (Singapore and Thailand). In August

---

[13]Granting MFN treatment was formally part of the obligations of India and Pakistan as charter members of the WTO. Also, in December 1995, the South Asian Preferential Trade Area became operational among SAARC members. However, relations between India and Pakistan have remained strained.

[14]Tariff reductions on sensitive agricultural products were seen by some Indian commentators as an indication of how much political capital the Indian government was prepared to expend against entrenched vested interests (Nambiar, 2010). Tariff rates of 40–45% phased in over a decade hardly seem to be free trade.

2009, India signed a Comprehensive Economic Partnership Agreement with South Korea, and India is looking to reach similar agreements with Australia, China, Japan, New Zealand.[15] By 2008, 9% of India's exports went to ASEAN countries and 15% to Northeast Asian countries, while 10% of India's imports came from ASEAN and 19% from Northeast Asia, compared to less than one percent from South Asia.

As well as participating in the East Asia Summits, India promotes the Asia–Pacific Trade Agreement (APTA), a preferential trading arrangement open to all members of the UN Economic and Social Commission for Asia and the Pacific (ESCAP). In four lengthy rounds of negotiations, the list of goods on which preferential tariffs are granted to APTA signatories has been increased.[16] So far, however, APTA has had little impact on regional trade flows. Although the five APTA countries (Bangladesh, China, India, South Korea and Sri Lanka) account for over a tenth of world trade and trade among the members has been growing, only a small proportion of their total trade is undertaken at APTA preferential tariff rates.[17] The positive-list approach to integration is slow and partial, and invites selection of items where there is little expectation of trade creation at the expense of domestic producers. Although mention has been made of non-tariff barriers and

---

[15]The South Korea agreement is broadly similar to the ASEAN–India FTA, with tariffs to be abolished on 85–90% of goods, but apparently not where trade creation is most likely (e.g. by reducing Korea's high tariffs on some textiles and clothing, agricultural or fisheries items or India's high barriers to imports of vehicles, iron and steel and electrical appliances). The Agreement is expected to boost Korean direct investment in India and inflows of skilled Indian professionals into Korea, i.e. it is about promoting value chains in dynamic sectors rather than inter-industry trade specialization in traditional sectors.

[16]APTA's origins are in the Bangkok Agreement, which was ratified by Bangladesh, India, Laos, South Korea and Sri Lanka in 1975. Signatories offered preferential tariff treatment to the group on selected items, but few tariff lines were nominated and the Agreement stagnated. In 2001, China joined the group and in the 2001–2005 round of negotiations the coverage was expanded from 1,721 to 4,270 items, and the average margin of preference was widened from 22% to 27%. In November 2005, the name was changed to the Asia–Pacific Trade Agreement (APTA).

[17]Ratna (2008) reports that in the ten-month period from September 2006 to June 2007, only 3–4% of imports from APTA partners into Korea and China were eligible for preferential treatment. Even on these qualifying items, utilization rates were low, apart from imports from Bangladesh, which as a least-developed country benefits from greater margins of preference from other APTA members. Utilization rates on all APTA-eligible imports were 13% for Korea and 25% for China, but 88% of imports from Bangladesh into Korea and 58% of imports from Bangladesh into China that were eligible for APTA preferences claimed the preferential tariff rate.

trade facilitation (as well as trade in services, investment and other deep integration issues), these topics have yet to feature in APTA outcomes.

Central Asia

Central Asia was linked to East Asia for centuries by the overland Silk Road routes from Europe and the Middle East. The importance of these routes declined substantially after the opening up of ocean shipping links from Europe to East Asia in the fifteenth century. Conquest of Central Asia by Russia in the second half of the nineteenth century reoriented the region's trade towards the north. The autarchic development strategy of the Soviet Union closed down links between East Asia and Central Asia almost completely.

During the Soviet era, the Central Asian republics were part of an integrated economy, but their role in the centrally planned Soviet system was determined only in part by comparative advantage. They primarily produced natural resources — cotton, oil and gas, and minerals — which were exchanged for manufactured goods from other Soviet republics. Industrial development centred on processing activities such as cotton gins, oil refineries, steel works or other mineral-processing activities. Some Central Asian industrial production was linked to the military-industrial production complex, although information on these centrally controlled facilities is scarce.[18] A few high-profile activities were located in Central Asia to stimulate regional development, sometimes as part of a supply chain starting in Soviet client nations. The South Tajik regional complex, centred around hydroelectricity generation and an aluminium smelter, used bauxite from Guinea, and a sugar refinery near Bishkek processed Cuban cane sugar; such supply chains made no economic sense once transport was costed at market prices rather than treated as a free resource by planners.

---

[18]After the German invasion in 1941, many factories were moved far from the western Soviet Union; the aircraft industry in Tashkent is a lasting result of that operation. Later, some military production was located in Central Asia for security reasons (e.g. military instrument components factories in the Kyrgyz republic), but these were largely staffed by skilled workers from other republics, and after the dissolution of the Soviet Union their market disappeared and employees emigrated. For more details on Central Asia, see Pomfret (1995c; 2006).

Very little of this industrial infrastructure survived the transition from planning to market-based economies to become efficient production units.

After the dissolution of the Soviet Union in December 1991, the new independent states of Central Asia cautiously opened their borders with China. Physical cross-border infrastructure has been gradually improved, starting with the first railway link, which opened between Kazakhstan and China in 1990, and followed by the improvement of roads between China and Kazakhstan, the Kyrgyz Republic and Tajikistan. Air connections were also established between Central Asian hubs and China, India, South Korea, Malaysia and Thailand.

Trade links between Central Asia and East Asia are overwhelmingly with China. The volume of trade is difficult to identify precisely due to inconsistent trade data. For example, China reported exports to the Kyrgyz Republic of $9,213 million in 2008, while the Kyrgyz statistics indicated imports of $728 million from China (Mogilevsky, 2009, Table 5). Such discrepancies reflect the large amounts of unrecorded and illicit trade between Central and East Asia.

Legal trade between Central Asia and China consists primarily of exports of minerals and energy from Central Asia in return for imports of consumer goods from China. Oil, gas and iron ore are inputs, but such primary inputs are not what we usually think of when describing production networks in the "Factory Asia" setting. The manufactured goods exported from China to Central Asia are overwhelmingly finished consumer goods. The Kyrgyz Republic acts as an important entrepot for this trade by operating huge bazaars in Bishkek and Osh where imported goods are sold to customers from various Central Asian countries, primarily Uzbekistan where the retail sector is repressed.[19] While this intermediary function could be considered part of a network from producer to final consumer, it is not part of a production network.

---

[19]Although the bazaars look primitive with most sales units operating out of containers, they are huge, organized operations. Ancillary facilities include local public transport, long distance bus terminals, hotels, saunas, canteens, warehouses and parking. The Dordoi bazaar outside Bishek has 40,300 outlets, employs 54,600 people and has estimated annual sales of $4 billion (World Bank, 2009, 10).

The largest illegal trade between Central Asia and East Asia is the drug trade. In recent years, the number of laboratories in Central Asia processing opium from Afghanistan has increased dramatically, some concentrating on exports to Russia and Europe and others on export to China and East Asia. The latter are located on the border between Afghanistan and Tajikistan, and close to the Chinese border in the Taldy-Kurgan region (Kazakhstan) and the towns of Karakol and Rybache (Kyrgyz Republic). China plays a key role in the processing chain because the Chinese chemical industry is the main provider of the chemical products such as anhydride acetic required to transform opium into heroin.

Why does Central Asia play a negligible role in production networks? Formal trade barriers such as tariffs are fairly low in Central Asia, but trade costs tend to be high. In the World Bank's *Doing Business* database, for example, the Central Asian countries rank among the worst in terms of the cost in money and time of exporting or importing a standard container (Table 8.2). This may, in part, be explained by the region's landlocked status, but in some respects, such as its proximity to some of the world's fastest growing economies in recent decades (China, India and Russia), location could have been an advantage.

Poor hard and soft infrastructure for trade with East Asia contributes to limiting bilateral trade. During the 1990s, regional infrastructure and connectivity deteriorated as Central Asia went through a process of regional disintegration. The process has reversed since the turn of the century, but relations among the five countries are not warm.[20] In recent years, the large flows of Chinese consumer goods and entrepreneurial activity in the Kyrgyz bazaars suggest that the physical and bureaucratic obstacles to trade are not insuperable. The drug trade indicates that production networks can be established if there is sufficient incentive. These activities are, however, a far cry from the nature and extent of production networks in Factory Asia.

The main reason for Central Asia's lack of integration into networks such as those which flourish among the ASEAN+3 countries is

---

[20]On disintegration and reintegration, see Johannes Linn (2004; 2008). It is striking that the Secretariats of the three principal political institutions for Central Asian regionalism are all based outside the region: EurAsEc in Moscow, SCO in Beijing and ECO in Tehran.

the region's inability to offer any valuable contribution to a network. Two decades after the end of central planning, the five countries have, to varying degrees, failed to establish vibrant market-based economies. Kazakhstan, the most economically successful, has an economy dominated by energy, minerals and wheat exports; relative prices do not favour production of other tradable goods. In all Central Asian countries, establishment of the institutions appropriate to a well-functioning market economy remains as work-in-progress.[21] Throughout the region, corruption remains a major problem.

In sum, geography does not favour the integration of Central Asian countries into East Asian production networks. Nevertheless, overland transport to the Xinjiang Autonomous Region in China's Far West has much improved and air freight links could be established. The main obstacles to Central Asia becoming part of Factory Asia are the poor institutions and high cost of doing business, both of which are mortal enemies of fragmentation of production into complex value chains.

Conclusions

The geographical extent of Asian regionalism remains in a fluid state. In the twenty-first century, ASEAN's institutional relations with China have strengthened, and much of the action has centred on the reaction of Japan to the challenge of China's growing economic significance and concerns of other countries such as Korea or, in a wider circle, Australia and India about their role in regional institutional developments. This has been associated with forum competition.

In the absence of clear geographical borders, the scope for argument over the geographical extent of Asian or Asia–Pacific groupings is endless. To the north and west, Russia, Central Asia and Mongolia

---

[21] The five Central Asian countries are among the formerly centrally-planned economies with the lowest Transition Indicators in the European Bank for Reconstruction and Development's *Transition Report*. They also rank lowly in the most commonly used measures of institutions and good governance.

are geographically and culturally closely linked to neighbouring parts of China; organizations such as the Central Asian Regional Economic Cooperation (CAREC)[22] or the Shanghai Cooperation Organization (SCO) bridge these countries. To the southwest, India (as well as Pakistan and Bangladesh) are linked by history and culture to Myanmar and the rest of Southeast Asia. Southwest and Central Asia are institutionally linked in the Economic Cooperation Organization (ECO, whose members are Pakistan, Afghanistan, the Central Asian countries, Azerbaijan, Turkey and Iran). To the southeast, Papua New Guinea and Timor-Leste are contiguous with Indonesia and the three countries are neighbours of Australia, while including New Zealand in this group provides a link across Polynesia. This last link suggests that the Pacific Ocean itself may be a bridge, which is reflected in the concept and composition of APEC. The arena for fighting over influence itself becomes a source of endless manoeuvring with little net benefit.

Surprisingly absent from the debates since the APEC setbacks of 1996–1998 has been the USA. The struggle over which forum is to be central has largely turned around the struggle between China and Japan for political influence in East Asia, with the Trans-Pacific option largely ignored. India is pulling the centre of gravity westwards, while Australia seeks to maintain a Pacific dimension. However, Australia is itself split between the competing visions of the two main parties with a stronger Asian focus in 1983–1996, a reorientation towards the US in 1996–2007, and then a renewed Asian focus after 2007.

This type of international manoeuvring captures the headlines, but wastes much energy and may be harmful. The winning forum, determined by the relative power of its supporters, may not be the most appropriate for addressing regional issues. If countries reach a stalemate, then institutional development may be stymied, as illustrated by the lack of regional cooperation in South Asia or by the regional

---

[22]CAREC is a partnership of eight countries (Afghanistan, Azerbaijan, China, Kazakhstan, the Kyrgyz Republic, Mongolia, Tajikistan and Uzbekistan) and six multilateral institutions (the ADB, which hosts the secretariat, EBRD, IMF, Islamic Development Bank, UNDP and World Bank) to promote and facilitate regional cooperation in transport, trade facilitation, trade policy, and energy.

disintegration of Central Asia during the 1990s. In East Asia, the lack of regional architecture in the second half of the twentieth century proved no hindrance to stellar economic performance, and the topical question is whether the failure to develop appropriate regional institutions can still be ignored in practice. The next chapter examines the issue of whether regional integration will continue to deepen under the conditions of the early twenty-first century.

Chapter 8

How Deep is Asian Regionalism?

Bela Balassa (1961) set out a five-stage taxonomy of economic integration from simple preferential tariffs to a free trade area (preferential tariffs equal zero) to a customs union (FTA plus common external trade policy) to a common market (customs union plus free movement of capital and labour) to economic union. Although Balassa viewed this as a taxonomy from shallow to deeper economic integration, his stages have often been interpreted as a chronological sequence, capturing Western European regional integration, which broadly followed a trade-first sequence. The customs union established in the 1960s was followed by reductions in the restrictions to labour and capital movement, and finally by monetary union, at least among some European Union members.

The slow progress on intra-Asian trade liberalization combined with the establishment of the CMI encouraged some observers to identify a distinctive Asian sequence of monetary integration preceding trade integration. There is some logic to the idea that monetary integration will facilitate intra-regional trade (Dieter and Higgott, 2003), and empirical support at the global level for the proposition that a common currency is associated with larger bilateral trade (Rose, 2000). However, the empirical support for the Asian sequence remains slight (Pomfret, 2005). The CMI played a minimal role in the 2008–2009 global crisis because Asian countries' own reserves were more than adequate, i.e. governments had learned national rather than regional lessons from the 1997–1998 Asian crisis. Both the CMI and the Asian Bond Market Initiative (ABMI) are minor contributions to Asian

111

monetary integration, even with the vaunted Chiang Mai Initiative Multilateralization (CMIM) in early 2009.

More substantive steps, such as the proposal for an Asian Monetary Unit (AMU), have made no progress, and an Asian Monetary Fund (AMF) or Asian currency remain distant.[1] The key obstacle is the lack of political will. There is disagreement about which currencies should be included in an AMU and with what weights. There would be disagreement about relative voting weights in an AMF, and about who should run monetary policy in a currency union. With the multilateralization of the CMI in early 2009 came agreement on contributions and voting rights, by which equal weights for Japan and China were achieved by a fudge: the share of China plus Hong Kong is equal to that of Japan, although Hong Kong is in many respects a separate economic entity and was not party to the CMI. Even beyond the tensions between the established and rising economic powers for supremacy, it is uncertain what the weight should be of the mid-rank economic powers, led by Korea but also including the larger ASEAN economies.

In the twenty-first century, East Asian regional agreements have primarily concerned trade. Despite the proliferation of trade agreements, however, it is difficult to generalize about the agreements' content. Many of the agreements lack much serious content, and address specific, and sometimes apparently minor, issues (Pomfret, 2007). The agreements are not primarily about tariff barriers, but more often about reducing border and behind-the-border trade costs. The most purposeful regional economic integration since 2000 has centred on ASEAN; the ASEAN Economic Community project aims to unify and extend the ASEAN Free Trade Area, the ASEAN Investment Area and the ASEAN Framework Agreement on Services, and is clearly aimed at facilitating trade. At the same time as ASEAN was deepening its own regional integration, it looked for new institutional arrangements with

---

[1] Dieter (2007, 139) similarly concludes that "monetary regionalism in Asia will both be a complex endeavour and will — if at all — only be achieved in the long run." Grimes (2009) takes a slightly more upbeat position on the process, but from an international relations perspective of how the CMI, ABMI, etc., affect interaction between Japan, China and the USA rather than from a perspective of enhanced regional financial market integration or monetary coordination.

its northeast Asian trading partners as well as with India and Australia and New Zealand.

In sum, despite the stimulus of regional dissatisfaction with international monetary institutions during the 1997–1998 Asian Crisis and the CMI, regionalism in East Asia has been primarily in trade. This is consistent with the observation by Estevadeordal and Suominen (2008, 129–130) based on analysis of cooperation agreements at the global level that "states cooperate disproportionately more in the domain of trade than in other domains. This may suggest that trade has properties that render it particularly amenable to formal as well as bilateral cooperation." The distinctive feature of Asian agreements is not a novel sequencing, but the focus on trade facilitation rather than preferential trade policies.

The first section of this chapter examines evidence on the variation in trade costs across countries. Measurement of trade costs is conceptually and operationally fraught, but the most widely used indicators all point to exceptionally low trade costs in some East Asian economies. Worldwide trade costs are closely correlated with economic development, indeed, falling transaction costs are viewed by economic historians such as Douglass North as the mainspring of development. What is striking about the East Asian economies is not just the world-beating low trade costs in Singapore and Hong Kong, but that all of the ASEAN5, China and the new industrialized economies of Northeast Asia rank highly on all indicators, and much higher than their income levels would predict. The high-income countries — Japan, Australia and New Zealand — have relatively low trade costs, but in these countries there is little evidence of particularly low costs for international transactions compared to domestic transactions.

Beyond the evidence that trade facilitation is a feature of the economies at the core of East Asian regionalism, it is more difficult to identify how much further trade facilitation needs to go to promote deeper integration. Some suggestions about the potential for additional reductions in behind-the-border costs are set out in the second section of the chapter, primarily in the context of China which, since the 1970s, has experienced massive but still incomplete economic transformation. Similar deeper integration, adapted to national conditions, will be necessary in other countries if they are to benefit from participation in regional value chains. This is, of course, a choice; national policymakers can promote such change or suppress it. As mentioned in an earlier chapter, vacillation about market-opening contributed to Japan's falling behind China in Asian regional value chain formation.

Finally, this chapter briefly reviews issues related to migration. Some Asian bilateral agreements contain terms related to specific labour movements, usually of small narrowly-defined groups and strictly limited, but labour mobility has generally been absent from the agreements. In an integrated region, however, there are many reasons why labour movements are desirable — not just to take advantage of differing factor endowments, but also as specialized workers are needed temporarily at different points on the value chain.

Variations in Trade Costs

The difficulty with explanations based on trade costs and trade facilitation is that these are difficult concepts to define or to measure. Trade costs refer to all the things other than tariffs that make international trade more costly in money and time than domestic trade. They include customs, quarantine and other at-the-border costs, but the controversy is the extent to which behind-the-border costs such as poor infrastructure, corruption or inadequate financial services should be included in trade costs. The issues are analysed in greater depth in the Appendix. Here we will make use of, with little methodological debate, three of the most commonly used indicators of trade costs (Table 8.1) to assess the situation in Asia at the end of the first decade of the twenty-first century.

The World Bank's Doing Business reports contain a section on the ease of trading across borders which measures the procedural requirements for exporting and importing, placing equal weight on the number of necessary documents, the time to import and export, and the cost of importing and exporting. A striking feature is that Asia contains some of the least cost locations in which to do international trade, and some of the countries with the highest trade costs. In *Doing Business 2010*, of the 183 economies surveyed, the two where trading is easiest (Singapore and Hong Kong) and the two where trading is most difficult (Kazakhstan and Afghanistan) are both in Asia.

Table 8.1   Indicators of Trade Costs in Selected Asian Countries.

	DB Trading across Borders	GETI	cif-fob gap	
	(Rank out of 183)	(Rank out of 121)	Percent	(Rank out of 206)
Afghanistan	183		18.9	195
Australia	27	14		
Bangladesh	107	111	8.8	156
Bhutan	153		20.5	198
Brunei Darussalam	48		3.2	29
Cambodia	127	91	2.5	21
China	44	49	6.3	111
Fiji	116		6.2	109
Hong Kong	2	2	4.7	71
India	94	76	5.7	97
Indonesia	45	62	5.5	94
Iran	134		8.2	146
Japan	17	23	4.8	73
Kazakhstan	182	93	5.1	84
Korea, North			5.8	98
Korea, South	8	26	4.5	65
Kyrgyz Rep	154	101	2.3	19
Laos	168		1.6	9
Macau			4.8	74
Malaysia	35	28	4.0	46
Maldives	126		1.9	13
Mongolia	155	113	7.7	136
Myanmar			4.2	54
Nepal	161	110	12.0	181
New Zealand	26	11	4.9	78
Pakistan	78	100	7.0	125
Papua New Guinea	89		1.3	5
Philippines	68	82	5.4	91
Russia	162	109	7.9	141
Singapore	1	1	4.2	56
Sri Lanka	65	78	6.8	123
Taiwan	33	25	4.8	76
Tajikistan	179	114	2.1	17
Thailand	12	50	4.0	47
Timor-Leste	85		3.6	37
Turkmenistan			4.0	48
Uzbekistan	174		13.3	186
Vietnam	74	89	4.1	53

Source and Notes: See Tables 8.2–8.4 and Appendix.

Even apart from Singapore and Hong Kong, the long-standing ASEAN member countries and China rank fairly highly on Ease of Trading across Borders: Thailand 12th, Malaysia 35th, China 44th, Indonesia 45th, Brunei 48th and Philippines 68th. South Korea (8th) and Taiwan (33rd) also rank highly. What also characterizes all of these ten economies is that they rank higher by Ease of Trading across Borders than in the overall Ease of Doing Business (apart from Singapore which is number one in both counts — Table 8.2), suggesting that policy reform in East Asia has been particularly focussed on trade facilitation.

New Zealand (26th) and Australia (27th) also rank highly on Ease of Trading across Borders, but for both countries these are lower ranks than their overall Ease of Doing Business rank (2nd for New Zealand and 9th for Australia). Japan could also be included in this group of efficient economies, where trading across borders is fairly easy (ranked 17th), but has not been a special feature of the Ease of Doing Business (where Japan ranks 15th).

The four newest ASEAN members are characterized by more difficult trading across borders, although Vietnam (74th) is not all that far behind the Philippines. Cambodia (127th) and Laos (168th) are well down the rankings, and Myanmar is not even ranked. The candidate or potential candidate countries Timor-Leste (85th) and Papua New Guinea (89th) could be included in this group, and like Vietnam rank higher on ease of trading across borders than on ease of doing business in general.

By contrast, conditions in South and Central Asia are much less favourable to trading across borders. Sri Lanka (65th), Pakistan (78th), India (94th), Bangladesh (107th), Maldives (126th), Bhutan (153rd) and Nepal (161st) rank below the first group of East Asian countries. The formerly centrally planned economies of Central Asia and Mongolia are the least trader-friendly: the Kyrgyz Republic ranks 154th, Mongolia 155th, Uzbekistan 174th, Tajikistan 179th, Kazakhstan 182nd and Turkmenistan, the most closed of all, is unranked. This is despite the relatively business-friendly conditions in the domestic economies of the Kyrgyz Republic and Kazakhstan, reflecting lingering suspicion of international trade and poor regional infrastructure in Central Asia. Afghanistan has the worst record on Ease of Trading across Borders of all 183 countries in the *Doing Business 2010* report.

Table 8.2   World Bank *Doing Business* Indicators, 2010, Selected Asian Countries.

	Time to export (Days)	Time to import (Days)	Cost to export (US$ per container)	Cost to import (US$ per container)	Ease of trading across borders (Rank out of 183)	Ease of doing business (Rank out of 183)
Afghanistan	74	77	$3,350	$3,000	183	160
Australia	9	8	$1,060	$1,119	27	9
Bangladesh	25	29	$970	$1,375	107	119
Bhutan	38	38	$1,210	$2,140	153	126
Brunei Darussalam	28	19	$630	$708	48	96
Cambodia	22	30	$732	$872	127	145
China	21	24	$500	$545	44	89
Fiji	24	24	$654	$630	116	54
Hong Kong	6	5	$625	$583	2	3
India	17	20	$945	$960	94	133
Indonesia	21	27	$704	$660	45	122
Iran	25	38	$1,061	$1,706	134	137
Japan	10	11	$989	$1,047	17	15
Kazakhstan	89	76	$3,005	$3,055	182	63
Korea, South	8	8	$742	$742	8	19
Kyrgyz Rep.	63	72	$3,000	$3,250	154	41
Laos	50	50	$1,860	$2,040	168	167
Malaysia	18	14	$450	$450	35	23
Maldives	21	20	$1,348	$1,348	126	87
Mongolia	46	47	$2,131	$2,274	155	60
Nepal	41	35	$1,764	$1,825	161	123
New Zealand	10	9	$868	$850	26	2
Pakistan	22	18	$611	$680	78	85
Papua New Guinea	26	29	$664	$722	89	102
Philippines	16	16	$816	$819	68	144
Russia	36	36	$1,850	$1,850	162	120
Singapore	5	3	$456	$439	1	1
Sri Lanka	21	20	$715	$745	65	105
Taiwan	13	12	$720	$732	33	46
Tajikistan	82	83	$3,150	$4,550	179	152
Thailand	14	13	$625	$795	12	12
Timor-Leste	25	26	$1,010	$1,015	85	164
Uzbekistan	71	92	$3,100	$4,600	174	150
Vietnam	22	21	$756	$790	74	93

Source: World Bank *Doing Business 2010*, available at http://www.doingbusiness.org.
Note: Myanmar, North Korea and Turkmenistan are not included, reflecting lack of transparency, and they presumably have high cost of doing business.

Table 8.3   World Economic Forum *Global Enabling Trade Index* 2009, Selected Asian Countries.

	Overall GETI	Market access	Border administration	Transport and communications	Business environment
Australia	14	97	17	14	14
Bangladesh	111	57	104	108	110
Cambodia	91	27	98	109	87
China	49	103	43	38	49
Hong Kong	2	20	7	5	4
India	76	116	58	64	53
Indonesia	62	53	66	79	60
Japan	23	115	13	15	31
Kazakhstan	93	45	119	63	77
Korea, South	26	106	22	21	26
Kyrgyz Rep.	101	18	116	86	108
Malaysia	28	32	33	29	33
Mongolia	113	110	109	95	91
Nepal	110	29	113	107	117
New Zealand	11	39	5	22	11
Pakistan	100	111	63	80	102
Philippines	82	56	68	77	100
Russia	109	113	1006	56	96
Singapore	1	2	1	3	3
Sri Lanka	78	64	67	69	90
Taiwan	25	99	27	19	30
Tajikistan	114	104	118	116	70
Thailand	50	98	41	40	59
Vietnam	89	112	85	71	61

Source: World Economic Forum *Global Enabling Trade Report 2009*, available at http://www.weforum.org/en/initiatives/gcp/GlobalEnablingTradeReport/index.htm.
Notes: Rankings out of 121 economies covered.

Like the *Doing Business* reports, the World Economic Forum's *Global Enabling Trade Report* relies primarily on surveying experts, but the specific questions and the respondents differ.[2] The Global Enabling Trade Index (GETI) covers fewer countries, but among those countries the patterns are similar to those found in the *Doing Business* reports. Singapore and Hong Kong again have the world's best trade-enabling environment (Table 8.3). New Zealand (11th), Australia (14th), Japan (23rd), Taiwan (25th) and South Korea (26th) also rank highly, with

---

[2] In general, *Doing Business* relies more on private consultancy firms (see *Doing Business 2010*, 165–215), while the Global Enabling Trade Index draws more on expertise in multilateral agencies.

Malaysia (28th), China (49th), Thailand (50th), Indonesia (62nd), Philippines (82nd) and Vietnam (89th). This picture of relatively low trade costs in East Asia, and the ordering of the East Asian countries, is very similar to that based on the *Doing Business* Ease of Trading across Borders indicator. South Asia, and especially Central Asia, have on average poorer conditions for international trade.

There is a strong correlation between income levels and good institutions, including those that facilitate trade, so it is not surprising that the region's high income countries score highly on these measures. What is also striking is that the original ASEAN members, and China, score higher than would be expected on the basis of their income levels, and that in liberalizing their economies they appear to have focussed especially on trade facilitation. The newer ASEAN members (and Timor-Leste and Papua New Guinea) show some similarities but at a much lower level, i.e. with higher trade costs.

It would be desirable to have cardinal measures of trade costs rather than the indicators and rankings described so far, and to be able to trace their evolution over the 1990s and 2000s. In principle, this is possible using the cif-gap, which provides a more inclusive measure of trade costs. A few countries have appropriate import data from which the gap can be calculated over a twenty-year period, but research using the gap measure is in its infancy. The raw data, expressed as a percentage of value at the point of departure from the exporting country, from Australian import statistics are presented in Table 8.4. They are more difficult to interpret than the indicators in Tables 8.2 and 8.3. In small trade flows (e.g. Laos, Brunei, Cambodia, the Kyrgyz Republic, Maldives, Papua New Guinea or Tajikistan), individual misreported transactions may drive the results. More importantly, if the cif-fob gap is to be used to identify policy-amenable trade costs, the raw data should be adjusted to control for distance, mode of transport and commodity composition of trade.

Pomfret and Sourdin (2009) have conducted such a detailed exercise for the ASEAN countries since 1990 and found a clear downward trend of trade costs, converging on the regional best practice (Singapore). The pattern is especially clear for the ASEAN5, with more noise and volatility in the CLMV data (see also Figure 4.1). Some of this pattern is evident from the raw data in Table 8.4. In 1990, trade costs of the ASEAN5 averaged 9.7%, and ranged from 6.3% in Singapore to

Table 8.4   Trade Costs for Selected Asian Countries, 1990 and 2007 (cif-fob gap on exports to Australia).

	1990	2007	
	Ad valorem (percentage)	Ad valorem (percentage)	Rank (out of 206)
Afghanistan	7.0	18.9	195
Australia	na	na	
Bangladesh	18.2	8.8	156
Bhutan	na	20.5	198
Brunei Darussalam	7.4	3.2	29
Cambodia	9.0	2.5	21
China	9.3	6.3	111
Fiji	6.1	6.2	109
Hong Kong	6.5	4.7	71
India	11.5	5.7	97
Indonesia	9.6	5.5	94
Iran	6.7	8.2	146
Japan	7.5	4.8	73
Kazakhstan	na	5.1	84
Korea, North	7.2	5.8	98
Korea, South	7.2	4.5	65
Kyrgyz Republic	na	2.3	19
Laos	26.6	1.6	9
Macau	7.3	4.8	74
Malaysia	10.0	4.0	46
Maldives	10.9	1.9	13
Mongolia	7.5	7.7	136
Myanmar	4.7	4.2	54
Nepal	14.1	12.0	181
New Zealand	8.8	4.9	78
Pakistan	7.9	7.0	125
Papua New Guinea	0.8	1.3	5
Philippines	13.3	5.4	91
Russia	na	7.9	141
Singapore	6.3	4.2	56
Sri Lanka	10.3	6.8	123
Taiwan	7.4	4.8	76
Tajikistan	na	2.1	17
Thailand	9.1	4.0	47
Timor-Leste	na	3.6	37
Turkmenistan	na	4.0	48
Uzbekistan	na	13.3	186
Vietnam	7.1	4.1	53

Source: Pomfret and Sourdin (2008).
Notes: See the Appendix for details of the method.

13.3% in the Philippines. By 2007, Singapore, Thailand and Malaysia had converged to ad valorem trade costs of around 4% in 2007, and Indonesia and Philippines to about 5.5%. Trade costs also fell between 1990 and 2007 for the major South Asian countries, but in 2007 they were all higher than those of any of the ASEAN5: India 5.7%, Sri Lanka 6.8%, Pakistan 7.0% and Bangladesh 8.8%.[3]

Table 8.4 indicates that for the larger trade flows, where the results are more reliable, trade costs fell in the 1990s and early 2000s, despite the rising costs of oil after 1998. On average, trade costs calculated on the basis of Australian data fell from 8% in 1990 to under 5% in 2007 (Figure A1). This is a dramatic decline, but it is less than the decline in average tariff rates. In sum, the cif-fob data indicate the impact of TF among the ASEAN5 in the 1990s, highlight the continuing region-wide fall in trade costs during the 1998–2007 period despite rising fuel costs, and indicate that trade costs remain an obstacle to trade and are relatively more important than ever, given the large cuts in applied tariffs during this period.

Despite their individual conceptual weaknesses and operational difficulties, the three sources of quantitative measures of trade costs presented in Table 8.1–8.4 paint a consistent picture. Trade costs are lowest in the economies at the heart of the regional value chains that emerged in East Asia in the 1990s, and especially so in the organizing hubs of Singapore and Hong Kong. Other key players in Factory Asia, such as Thailand and Malaysia in Southeast Asia and China, South Korea and Taiwan in Northeast Asia, consistently score better on indicators of trade-friendliness than their level of development would predict and than they do on more general measures of ease of doing business. Similar comments could apply to Indonesia, Philippines and Vietnam, whose trade costs have been falling but remain higher than those of the East Asian leaders. The high-income countries of ASEAN+6 have low trade costs, but this is a corollary of higher levels of income and

---

[3]Trade costs measured by the cif-fob gap depend upon both ends of the bilateral trade flow. The percentage ad valorem trade costs cited in this chapter are based on trade between countries and Australia, and can be compared with one another because the importing country is held constant. The absolute values of the percentages would be smaller if a lower-cost importing country (e.g. the USA) were the benchmark or bigger if a higher-cost importing country (e.g. Brazil) were the benchmark. See the Appendix for further discussion of the method and data.

productivity in the economy as a whole rather than a specific focus on reducing trade costs; Japan, Australia and New Zealand could link into regional value chains, but the data suggest that they have not yet made great effort to do so. Finally, the economies of South and Central Asia lag those of East Asia and Australasia in terms of bringing down trade costs, and in consequence they are less well placed to play an active role in regional value chains.

Trade Facilitation Requires Deeper Integration

The discussion of trade facilitation so far in this book has tended to focus on at-the-border measures aimed at reducing the time and cost of crossing borders. Measures such as a Single Window, common classification of goods and customs forms, e-documents and so forth are important for most traders and critical for the profitability of regional value chains. However, just as reductions in tariffs highlighted the importance of other at-the-border costs, reducing at-the-border costs of trade brings behind-the-border costs into greater focus. These costs may be associated with the hard infrastructure of domestic transport, poor inter-modal logistics, inadequate telecommunications networks and so forth, or with the soft infrastructure of poorly designed or inconsistently administered regulations and procedures.

The interaction between trade policy and other at-the-border measures and behind-the-border costs is illustrated by China's participation in East Asian regionalization. China's pivotal role in East Asian trade followed the opening up of the economy to trade and the reform of the domestic economy. As emphasised in earlier chapters, crucial to the emergence of regional value chains involving China was not only the reduction of formal trade barriers, which had already happened in hundreds of special zones by the end of the 1980s, but also recognition that China was committed to playing by the same international trade rules as other major trading nations in East Asia; this was achieved during the lengthy WTO accession process. These changes were sufficient for the emergence of regional value chains with China playing a key role.

Nevertheless, further economic reform in China is necessary if the integration process is to be deepened by further development of regional value chains. Economic reform in China has focussed on product markets, including abandoning policy interventions in domestic markets and liberalizing trade in goods and services, to the extent that by the end of the first decade of the twenty-first century, prices of more than 95 percent of products are determined by free market forces. In contrast, factor markets remain highly distorted. Labour markets are distorted by restrictions on mobility, especially from rural to urban labour markets, and by under-developed social welfare systems.[4] The education system, which was successful in rapidly increasing literacy rates during the Maoist era, is poorly attuned to the needs of a middle-income market-based economy, although this is changing rapidly in the twenty-first century.[5] The domestic financial system remains repressed, with regulated interest rates and state influences on credit allocation.[6] Externally, capital account controls are more restrictive on outflows than on inflows, and the currency has probably been undervalued since at least the mid-1990s. The price of key energy products, such as oil, gas and electricity, are also regulated by the state, e.g. when world oil prices peaked at nearly $150 per barrel in 2008, domestic prices were only around $80. China's environmental laws and regulations have not been well-enforced. According to Huang (2010), the above cost distortions amounted to RMB 2,138 billion in 2008, or 7.2 percent of GDP. Artificially low input costs increase profits, raise investment returns and

---

[4]Since the mid-1990s, China has been replacing enterprise-based social security provision by a wider system of pensions, medical insurance and unemployment support with the intention of improving the operation of labour markets. In a study of China's coal industry between 2000 and 2005, Shi and Grafton (2010) find that these reforms contributed to increased technical efficiency. Restrictions on labour migration have been gradually relaxed since the 1990s, but the *hukou* (household registration) system means that unregistered migrants to cities (estimated to number around 140 million people) are denied access to many social services; reforms of the registration system announced in December 2009 apply only to small and medium-sized cities, while residency status in the most sought-after destinations remains tightly controlled (e.g. Shanghai's points system to grant residency to well-qualified migrants excludes over 99% of actual migrants).

[5]Analysing the growth and increased sophistication of Chinese exports with 1995–2005 data disaggregated by commodity and location, Wang and Wei (2008) identify improvements in human capital and policies towards R&D and skill-intensive activities as more crucial than simple exploitation of abundant unskilled labour.

[6]China's financial system is overly dependent on banks, especially the large state-owned commercial banks, and the central bank maintains floors for lending rates and ceilings for deposit rates. Compared with other Asian economies, China's nominal growth potential is among the highest in Asia, but long-term government bond yields are among the lowest, suggesting that China's capital is too cheap.

improve international competitiveness, but depress household income; labour compensation dropped from 52 percent of GDP in 1997 to only 40 percent in 2007. China's large external sector imbalance is a product of incomplete economic reform. The best way to reduce the external imbalance and head off complaints by Asian neighbours of an unequal playing field is to finish the task of economic reform by liberalizing the factor markets.[7] All of these reforms, being actively discussed within China, cover traditionally domestic matters, but in the early twenty-first century they also have implications for regionalization of the East Asian economy.

Not only is deeper integration confusingly intertwined with traditionally domestic economic policy issues, but the increasing complexity of regional value chains makes it difficult to identify exactly which policies interact with regionalization. The Japanese car companies' operations in Thailand are not limited to unskilled-labour-intensive activities. In 2003, Toyota opened a Technical Centre, for research and development, design and testing, in Thailand, one of only two in East Asia outside Japan (the other is in Tianjin). Honda took a similar step in 2006. These steps reflect the accumulation of human capital in Thailand since the Japanese carmakers established an assembly plant there in the late 1980s, i.e. education policies or encouragement of learning-by-doing at the workplace can increase regionalization and change RVC patterns. Policymakers wishing to build on this insight, however, face difficult choices between the extent to which they promote general purpose skills and the extent to which they foster specific skills that might lead to the creation of a niche advantage in value chains but which may also become outdated due to technological change.[8]

---

[7] Huang (2010) advocates that reforms should include the abolition of the Household Registration System, better enforcement of employers' social welfare contribution, the introduction of market-based interest rates, an increase in exchange rate flexibility, liberalization of land and energy markets, and rigorous implementation of environmental protection policies.

[8] The dilemma can be illustrated from the experience of Central Asia. After the dissolution of the Soviet Union and replacement of central planning by market-based economies, the former Soviet republics expected to find niches in the global division of labour because they had highly trained workforces. However, many skilled workers found that the skills they had accumulated in specialized technical programs and applied with obsolete equipment in the centrally planned economy were useless in best-practice workplaces. The only beneficiaries from Soviet-era education were those with particular skills such as computer scientists or linguists or those with general purpose university training who could adapt to the new economic environment (Anderson and Pomfret, 2002).

The creation and expansion of regional value chains is not only responsive to policy-driven regionalism. Taiwan has played little part in the proliferation of RTAs, and for China an important advantage of the ASEAN+3 and EAS fora has been the exclusion of Taiwan.[9] Nevertheless, Taiwan plays a key role in computer RVCs (Dent, 2008, 61–63) because Taiwanese producers have created niches where they are the global leader, and the policy environment is sufficiently RVC-friendly that the big brand names in computers prefer to source through Taiwan regardless of its place in formal regional architecture.

On the other hand, governments seeking to participate in Asian regionalism may be thwarted by powerful domestic interest groups that limit their capacity to deliver on market-opening promises. The clearest examples, already mentioned earlier in Chapter 6, concern agriculture, which has had a low profile in Asian trade agreements. The rice trade is especially controversial because East Asia contains the world's first and second largest rice exporters (Thailand and Vietnam) and two of the world's most protected domestic rice markets (Japan and Korea). The potential gains from trade, and the costs of not having agreements, were highlighted by the sudden and large increase in the price of rice on the world market in 2007–2008, which were especially threatening to major rice importers such as Indonesia and the Philippines.[10] More corrosive for Asian regionalism has been the reluctance of Japan and Korea to open up their markets to agricultural imports. Such reluctance has inhibited the ability of Japan and Korea to conclude far-reaching trade agreements with ASEAN because Thailand, in particular, has pushed for the inclusion of rice in any agreement. Whether India, Australia and New Zealand will be able to deliver on far-reaching agreements to promote deep integration with Southeast Asia will also depend upon

---

[9]Taiwan's RTAs are limited to the 24 small developing countries, mostly in Latin America or Africa, with which it maintains formal diplomatic relations. Taiwan is a member of APEC (since 1991) and the WTO (since 2002) because those organizations are based on "economies," or customs units, rather than nation states.

[10]The world rice price, which had been around $200 per ton in 2003, gradually rose to $300 by the start of 2007 and in the first half of 2008 surged from $400 to a peak of $1,000. In late 2007 and early 2008, both India (the third largest exporter) and Vietnam imposed export restrictions in order to moderate domestic price increases, raising food security concerns in rice-importing countries.

their willingness to open domestic markets to inter-industry trade (and especially farm imports) as well as intra-industry trade.

Migration

Migration has long been a part of the East Asian economic landscape, but intra-regional labour migration driven by economic motives began to increase rapidly in the 1990s. From the 1970s until the energy price collapse of the mid-1980s, the main outflow of labour from East Asia had been to the Middle East. Intra-region immigration, in the decades before the mid-1990s, was dominated by Singapore and Hong Kong, plus increased migration to Australia towards the end of this period. In the 1990s, however, Japan, South Korea, Taiwan, Malaysia and Thailand all began to receive migrants from the labour-abundant countries of East Asia, i.e. Cambodia, China, Indonesia, Laos, Myanmar, the Philippines and Vietnam.

The intra-regional labour migration clearly reflected the economic dynamism of the receiving countries. Immigration in turn contributed to that dynamism as domestic workers moved up the skill ladder and immigrants filled the least-skilled jobs. According to Chris Manning (2002, 382), "increased international labour migration was an important dimension of structural change and globalisation in East Asia from the mid-1980s." Globalization meant that, although most migrants were employed in construction, agriculture, labour-intensive manufacturing and service sectors, migration was more complex than a simple flow of unskilled workers from poor countries to countries moving up the quality ladder.[11]

Numerically, low-skilled migrants moving to take low-wage jobs in the non-traded sectors of the higher-income countries has been the largest component of regional migration. In earlier decades, Hong Kong and Singapore were important destinations, most visibly for maids and other service-sector workers. By the mid-2000s, Malaysia and Thailand had by far the largest stocks of foreign workers in East Asia, over a million and a half in each country, compared to under a

---

[11]Graeme Hugo (2005) and Premachandra Athukorala (2006) review the evidence on Asian migration, although they emphasise the poor quality of data as well as definitional issues.

million in all other receiving countries. The Philippines, Myanmar and Indonesia had the largest numbers of nationals working elsewhere in East Asia. These patterns reflect greater regionalization in Southeast Asia than in Northeast Asia, although nationalist resistance to immigration may play a part in Japan, South Korea and Taiwan whose high income levels and larger economies might be expected to provide a magnet for poor migrants.

With thickening regional value chains, there is an increasing role for short-term migration by skilled workers. Transnational corporations employ expatriate managers and technical staff in foreign operations. Even when regional value chains involve arms-length transactions among independent producers, the coordination might require footloose managers to maintain quality or cost control, i.e. a regional rather than a national market for people with the skills needed to make value chains profitable. Technicians or people with specific skills may be needed to travel, perhaps on short notice, to troubleshoot or to complete a particular short-term task.[12] The conditions for such fixed-term migration can be changed by administrative decisions or by sub-national governments, and thus be difficult to monitor.[13]

Since the turn of the century, temporary migration for education has been growing rapidly, with fast-changing patterns. In this market, Australia and New Zealand have played a central role, in part due to the rise of English as the common language of international discourse in Asia and a strong preference for education in English. The competitiveness of Australian schools, colleges and universities was boosted by the weak Australian dollar in the early 2000s, and education was commonly thought to have become Australia's third largest export after iron ore and coal.[14] By the end of the decade, several East Asian countries

---

[12] Top-rated operators of large building cranes, for example, fulfill limited-term assignments in foreign countries upon demand. This is a global labour market, but when Asian contractors have a big job requiring such a crane, they will first look to national or regional crane operators.

[13] For example, in July 2009, the city of Shanghai allowed six categories of foreign workers to apply for visas of up to five years instead of the previous single year. Workers qualifying for extended residence visas included the managing director, vice managing director or chief financial officer of a new and high-tech enterprise or foreign-invested product exporting enterprise. Report posted at http://www.globaltradealert.org/ on 9 February 2010 (accessed 15 February 2010).

[14] Australia's international competitive position was also helped by increasing education costs in the USA, plus highly publicized instances of violence against Asian students and tighter US visa

had strengthened their domestic education sectors, including increased opportunities to study in English and some internationally competitive universities (e.g. the Hong Kong University of Science and Technology or the Singapore Management University). The increasingly shared curricula and status of English are contributing to reducing national differences, especially among younger members of the elites and professional classes of Asia.

The phenomenon of intra-region migration is almost entirely market-driven. National policies limit migration, and there have been successful reverse-brain-drain policies in, for example, Taiwan and South Korea. There is, however, no regional framework for migration and it had little mention in the regional agreements that proliferated after 2000.[15]

Conclusions

Among economists, the depth of regional integration has historically been framed in terms of the Balassa sequence with product market integration preceding factor market integration and deeper integration involving common policies in areas such as competition or regulatory policy capped by full economic union with unified monetary and fiscal policies.[16] This taxonomy has, however, limited usefulness in the context of East Asian regionalism in the twenty-first century. Obstacles

---

requirements after 2001. It is difficult to measure the full value of education exports because this should include all expenditures by students and not just fees. Many Australian universities and colleges invested in offshore facilities in Asia, in part to channel students into their home campuses for more advanced study.

[15]The APEC Business Travel Card Scheme facilitates temporary visa arrangements and customs clearance, but its take-up by APEC members remains limited (see Chapter 3). An ASEAN Plan of Action on Immigration Matters was adopted at the 2002 summit, but actual cooperation is weak. Terms in RTAs dealing with migration refer to specific groups of skilled workers, e.g. the 2007 Japan–Philippines Economic Partnership Agreement allowed 400 nurses and 600 carers from the Philippines to work in Japan over the next two years subject to certain conditions and the Japan–Thailand Agreement allowed Thai cooks, healthcare workers and entertainers to work in Japan up to a fixed quota.

[16]This is the sense in which Lawrence (1996), who popularized the concept of deeper integration, analysed the process in RTAs such as the EU, NAFTA and the CER which in the mid-1990s had proceeded beyond trade.

to trade in goods and, to a lesser extent, trade in services have tumbled and flows of capital and labour have grown, but these changes have generally occurred within a non-discriminatory policy environment, rather than the discriminatory regionalism associated with the Balassa sequence. East Asian regionalism also involves the evolution of a web of regulatory regimes, both public and private, tying the region together.

Jayasuriya (2009a; 2009b) argues that emerging regulatory regionalism is evident in economic fields (as in the Executives' Meeting of East Asia–Pacific Central Banks) as well as in other fields where national policies must take account of regional or global implications and risks.[17] Terrorism, for example, has led to increased contacts between police and security officers from different countries which, in turn, has led them to modify their own procedures to take account of the desirability of international cooperation; this is completely different from traditionally defined national security concerns which were addressed by treaties between states. Regional health disasters, such as the severe acute respiratory syndrome (SARS) outbreak in 2002–2003, highlight the value of coordinated responses by national health services and border guards. Cross-border environmental problems, such as the haze following forest burning on Kalimantan (Borneo) which affects not only other provinces of Indonesia but also Malaysia, Brunei and Singapore, demand international coordination at a sub-regional level.[18]

---

[17]As a new form of regional governance, he highlights the creation of the Regional Assistance Mission to Solomon Islands (RAMSI). In response to a break-down of law and order and request for international aid by the Governor-General of the Solomon Islands, police and troops from Australia, New Zealand, and other Pacific nations began arriving in July 2003. Following a disputed general election in April 2006, RAMSI forces were strengthened by further Australian and New Zealand soldiers and police. The Participating Police Force comprises police officers from 15 Pacific nations: Australia, New Zealand, Papua New Guinea, Fiji, Cook Islands, Vanuatu, Nauru, Kiribati, Marshall Islands, Palau, Federated States of Micronesia, Niue, Tonga, Samoa, and Tuvalu.

[18]Slash-and-burn agriculture has a long history in the region, but the haze problem reached a new level in 1997/8 when the haze cloud caused by the fires covered around five million square kilometres for up to seven months, affecting some 70 million people of which 40,000 had to be hospitalized (Jones, 2006). The economic losses to Malaysia and Singapore from lost tourism revenues, airport shutdowns and so on were large (Dent, 2008, 230–231). Haze problems have recurred, especially in the months March–May and August–October, since 1998 despite attempts to address the problem nationally by Indonesia or within regional fora such as ASEAN.

Even national policies in areas such as labour standards may benefit from agreement on best practice.[19]

Between market-driven regionalization and issue-specific regulatory regionalism, the various bilateral and plurilateral agreements of the 2000s have sought to remove policy-responsive grit from the wheels of regional commerce. Although vision statements have been a component of East Asian regionalism, the inter-governmental negotiating reality has been more prosaic: a network of agreements whittling away obstacles in an incremental way. Such an approach has, however, been well-suited to strengthening the regional value chains and still has plenty of scope for further deepening of regional integration.

---

[19] Jayasuriya (2009a, 343; 2009b, 107) cites the example of Cambodia. Inclusion of labour standards in the US–Cambodia bilateral textile trade agreement led to a partnership between the Cambodian government and the International Labour Organization (ILO) in which companies exporting textiles must register with the inspection program of the ILO's Better Factories Programme. Such registration protects partners in regional value chains involving Cambodian textile firms from trade restrictions being imposed on the finished product in the name of inadequate labour standards.

Chapter 9

Conclusions

The map of regional agreements in East Asia has been transformed from an almost empty space to one that is so cluttered that it has been compared to a noodle bowl. Although the 1997 financial and exchange rate crisis was the catalyst for regional initiatives in the monetary area, these initiatives have had minor impact. When significant regionalism finally arrived in East Asia after 2000, it centred on trade and was a response to the regionalization that accelerated in the 1990s. The regionalization was based on the flourishing of regional value chains, and the process of production fragmentation will continue to drive Asian trade.

As economy after economy adopted outward-oriented development strategies in the second half of the twentieth century, East Asian economies grew rapidly on the back of exports of labour-intensive manufactured goods sold to the high-income countries. Even before they joined the WTO (or its predecessor, GATT), East Asian exporters were beneficiaries of the global trading system that operated under GATT rules, and they were the strongest exponents of non-discrimination in their own trade policies. The only significant regional trading arrangement in Asia was ASEAN, whose origins lay in security (an association of non-Communist countries when war raged in Communist Southeast Asia) and whose practical economic content was minimal.

When intra-regional trade began to grow in the 1990s, stimulated first by Japan's off-shoring after the 1985–1987 yen appreciation and later by China's integration into production networks, the policy responses were national. Countries drastically cut their MFN tariffs, and applied tariffs were even lower. APEC provided a useful forum in the

131

mid-1990s for policymakers to announce unilateral tariff cuts, which could be better sold at home when other APEC countries also cut their tariffs. Low applied tariffs were the result of duty exemptions for equipment, components, processing, etc.[1] When, however, the USA tried to push more aggressively for trade liberalization by APEC members in the EVSL initiative, it was rebuffed; Asian countries were only willing to reduce those tariffs that they wanted to cut, and not to be told what trade barriers they had to liberalize.

A catalyst for Asian regionalism was the perceived failure of the multilateral institutions, primarily the IMF, and APEC to respond appropriately to the 1997–1998 Asian Crisis. Japan took the lead, and was joined by China, Korea and the ASEAN countries, in pursuing regional approaches to international monetary arrangements. This culminated in the 2000 Chiang Mai Initiative, and despite much talk in the following decade the money-led regionalism proved to be a dead-end. When the next financial crisis threatened Asian growth in 2008–2009, governments looked to their own defences in the form of massive foreign exchange reserves rather than to regional solutions.

The East Asian regionalism that flourished from about the turn of the century was trade-led. The ASEAN Free Trade Area finally became a serious arrangement as the exemptions were whittled away; before 2000, take-up rates of preferences were very low because only goods with low MFN tariffs were included in AFTA, but from the end of the 1990s margins of preference became significant as goods with higher MFN tariffs were included, and take-up rates increased. The ASEAN agreement with China, and subsequent negotiations with Korea and Japan were primarily about trade. The dozens of bilateral trade agreements negotiated after 2000 were diverse, but trade-centred.

East Asian regionalism is not traditional regionalism as in the Balassa sequence of preferential tariffs, free trade area, customs union,

---

[1]China's average tariff, for example, is difficult to measure. In the 1990s, published legal tariffs were much higher than applied tariffs, but there were many exemptions, e.g. for goods produced in special zones of which there were hundreds by the early 1990s (Pomfret, 1991). The ratio of import duties to total imports, which measures the average tariff collected, was about 3% during the 1990s. When China joined the WTO in 2001, its bound tariff rates were generally set higher than current applied rates, which is a source of uncertainty because applied tariffs could be increased at any time without breaking China's legal obligations (Baldwin, 2006).

common market, economic and monetary union. Although some of the trade agreements are called FTAs, none are FTAs in the classic definition of internal free trade. Most of the agreements, starting from the Japan–Singapore New Economic Partnership Agreement, are given explicitly new or specific titles and several claim to be "new age" agreements. Preferential tariffs, the bottom step on Balassa's ladder, or indeed any kind of preferential trading arrangement, have a very low profile in the Asian agreements, with the possible exception of AFTA post-2000. Implications of this are that, apart from AFTA, take-up rates are not a meaningful guide to the impact of the agreements and rules of origin are of less significance than in other parts of the world where RTAs involve serious margins of preferential treatment.[2]

The trade agreements that proliferated after 2000 focused on trade facilitation, rather than traditional trade policies. In this sense, East Asian regionalism is deep integration because it addresses issues of domestic administration and regulation that are beyond the scope of the first three stages of Balassa's taxonomy, which emphasise the removal of tariffs on intra-regional trade and a coordinated trade policy towards countries outside the region. Tariffs that might impinge on regional value chains had already tumbled in East Asia during the 1990s, and these reductions were mostly non-discriminatory, reducing trade barriers equally on imports from all trading partners with MFN status. Symptomatic of the limited relevance of tariffs in Asian regionalism was the lead taken by Singapore, an almost free-trade economy, whose would-be partners in trade agreements could expect no benefits from preferential tariffs.

Openness and an essentially non-discriminatory nature are a distinctive feature of the new regionalism in Asia. For example, although trade facilitation measures within ASEAN are agreed at a regional level or among a subset of members, improved documentation, port logistics and so forth reduce costs of trade with all partners; a Thai–Malaysian bilateral agreement to reduce border costs, e.g. by simplifying customs

---

[2] Pomfret, Kaufmann and Findlay (2010) discuss the utilization of preferential tariffs, with evidence from FTAs involving Australia.

forms or having a one-stop process, is likely to benefit all traders cross-ing the Malaysian or Thai border. The impact differs fundamentally from a preferential tariff cut which transfers rent, previously realized as tariff revenue, to preferred trading partners, while damaging the export competitiveness of non-preferred trading partners.[3] The current wave of East Asian regionalism with its plethora of bilateral and plurilateral agreements is not creating an EU or NAFTA style of RTA with clear-cut external borders. It is creating a less well-defined area of trader-friendly conditions, so far centred on ASEAN and China but with malleable outer limits. Ironically, although APEC as an economic institution has been eclipsed since the late 1990s, the spirit of APEC — especially the concept of open regionalism — remains at the heart of Asian regional-ism in the early twentieth century.

In contrast to this view of the nature of Asian regionalism, some commentators focus on the contradiction between Asian agreements and a preconceived notion of regionalism. For example, Heydon and Woolcock (2009) argue that the proliferation of agreements in East Asia is the antithesis of regionalism insofar as the agreements enhance hub-and-spoke patterns, and this is manifested in the establishment of Japan and China as the two hubs while the importance of ASEAN as a regional arrangement is eroded. This is primarily because they see the issues in these agreements in traditional (European) terms of tariffs and rules of origin and non-tariff barriers, such as TBT/SPS and public procurement services, with a nod to "American" concerns such as intellectual property rights, the environment and core labour standards. These issues can be found in the various Asian agreements, but the primary purpose of the majority of the agreements is trade facilitation.

Thus, the AFTA/AEC or the ASEAN–China FTA are less about preferential tariff reductions to promote bilateral trade, than about

---

[3]Philippa Dee argues that, unlike tariff cuts which are resisted by groups who will lose rents as a result of the cuts, trade facilitation is about cutting trade barriers that add to costs and whose removal will yield benefits without hurting any group; see Dee *et al.* (2008) and references to her work therein. This is true for imports for which there are no competing domestic producers, but import-competing producers will benefit from trade costs that raise the costs of imports relative to the costs of domestic products. It may, however, be politically harder to oppose trade facilitation measures that reduce transactions costs than to oppose tariff cuts that reduce government revenue.

facilitating trade so that the signatories can participate in regional value chains, i.e. creating multilateral networks among interested countries rather than bilateral spokes. From this perspective, there is no incentive to be discriminatory. The essence of global value chains is to locate activities in their most productive place and to source all supplies from the best supplier in terms of price and quality and reliability. Moreover, given that the final destination of many goods produced in Factory Asia is still the high-income countries in the rest of the world, there is little point in alienating those countries' governments by introducing trade policies that explicitly discriminate against their goods. Thus, there is an essential continuity from the staunch multilateralism of Asia's leading exporters in the second half of the twentieth century and from the open regionalism of APEC to the Asian regionalism of the first decade of the twenty-first century. Open regionalism is not an oxymoron if regionalism is not defined restrictively to only include preferential trade liberalization. Asian regionalism includes any countries which want to reduce trade costs in order to become part of regional value chains.

In sum, there has been considerable activity aimed at reducing trade costs in East Asia. Some of this is in a broad Asia–Pacific context, but most determinedly it has centred on ASEAN since the mid-1990s and subsequently included China, and, to a lesser extent, Japan and Korea.[4] This has coincided with increased regionalization of East Asian trade and the growing importance of regional value chains. The needs of participants in these value chains have driven unilateral, bilateral and regional moves to reduce trade costs.[5]

---

[4]South Korea's role consists almost entirely of its bilateral relations with China. Before 1992, recorded trade and investment flows were zero, although unofficial links occurred through intermediaries in Hong Kong. After normalization of economic relations began in 1992, bilateral trade and investment flows increased rapidly. In 2008, 22% of Korean exports went to China, double the share of the next destination (11% to the USA), and China was the top destination for Korean foreign direct investment; at $26 billion in 2008, Korea was the third largest source of FDI in China after Hong Kong and Japan. The commodity composition of bilateral trade is dominated by electronics, and is mostly covered by the 1996 WTO Information Technology Agreement, so there is little pressure for a bilateral trade agreement (Nicolas, 2009).

[5]Another Asian feature is the legal fuzziness of some of the trade facilitation measures and willingness to tolerate multi-speed compliance, which is reminiscent of the role of township and village enterprises in China's development or of well-connected diasporas in international trade in Southeast Asia. However, tolerance has its limits and it is salutary to remember that some of the world's potential flashpoints for major wars lie in Northeast Asia.

The resilience and desirability of these networks was tested in 2008–2009 by the sharp decline in global trade following the financial crises and recessions in the USA, UK and other European economies. There was no serious financial crisis in Asia, certainly nothing as severe as 1997–1998, so the term 'global financial crisis' is a misnomer, but the outward-oriented Asian economies were hit by the fall in global demand, especially as in the final months of 2008 and early part of 2009, world trade fell by more than global output. Some observers saw this as a consequence of fragmentation of production, and economies that were heavily involved in global value chains had little scope for independent action when final demand dropped.[6] There were also concerns that governments might turn to protectionism to mitigate the recession in their economy, but among WTO members this temptation was largely avoided.[7] By the end of 2009, most of the Asian economies had recovered, suggesting that both their development model and the structure of regional trade rested on firm foundations.[8]

---

[6]Trade is measured by gross value whereas GDP is the sum of value-added, so there is double-counting in trade flows which is avoided in GDP estimates and, over time, fragmentation increases the measured trade/output ratio. In the short-run, however, if the share of imported inputs in output and in exports is constant and there is no change in relative prices, then trade will change by the same proportion as GDP. The drop in world trade in 2008 was largely due to a relative price effect as oil prices fell by over half; as energy accounted for about a tenth of global trade, this change alone resulted in a drop in world trade of over five percentage points.

[7]The Global Trade Alert (Evenett, 2009) reports many examples of restrictive trade barriers being introduced in 2008–2009, with Russia as the worst offender, but both the Global Trade Alert and WTO reports found that the worst concerns about the protectionist threat had not yet materialised by the end of 2009. Mikic (2009) argues that strengthened monitoring mechanisms made WTO members aware that their actions would be in the public domain and under scrutiny. The Trade Policies Review Mechanism, which had been introduced in 1988, became a permanent feature of the new WTO in 1995, when the mandate was broadened to cover services trade and intellectual property; reviews are conducted by the Trade Policy Review Body and a report prepared by economists in the WTO Secretariat's Trade Policy Review Division. From January 2009, the WTO Secretariat used its surveillance mandate to expand its monitoring of trade flows and the use of trade-related measures by member governments. Mikic concludes that "shaming" was effective in making countries consider other options to protectionism

[8]The fall in demand in the North Atlantic economies and the subsequent stimulus packages were not neutral across sectors. Public spending focussed on infrastructure, education and other social services, increasing the price of non-traded goods and services relative to that of traded goods. The drop in private sector demand was especially severe for goods affected by capital shortage or where spending could be delayed, which explains why Japan (and Germany) were especially hard-hit as the demand for their cars and expensive equipment plummeted.

The width of Asian regionalism is likely to be determined by the geo-graphical range of the regional value chains, which is partly endogenous (i.e. dependent on public policies) and partly exogenous (e.g. mountains and distance may exclude isolated locations such as Tajikistan or Bhutan). Geography is, however, not always destiny; in several sub-regions, some governments are striving to be more RVC-friendly while others show no interest. Among ASEAN's newest members, the CLMV countries, Vietnam is taking steps in this direction (and, as shown in Chapter 8, may have already achieved better trade facilitation outcomes than the Philippines), but Myanmar is not. Timor-Leste and Papua New Guinea could become part of East Asian regionalism via affiliation to ASEAN, but Timor-Leste seems more serious about regional economic integration than Papua New Guinea. Even more obviously, in Northeast Asia, South Korea participates actively in RVCs, while North Korea is totally absent. In a wider circle, Australia, New Zealand and India have, through EAS membership, indicated interest in participating in regional integration, but practical trade facilitation measures are still needed, especially by India, if they are to become significantly integrated with East Asia.

The formal architecture is also tied up with political struggles for power or influence in the region. Thus, whether the primary institution will be ESCAP or the ADB or whether the grouping will be ASEAN+3 or the EAS (ASEAN+6) or a Trans-Pacific partnership including the USA will depend upon politics as well as economics. The USA continues to provide crucial security to many participants and hence cannot be ignored, but within East Asia the key interaction in the coming years will be between China and Japan. In the first decade of the twenty-first century, China was the driver of regional integration through its market opening and willingness to negotiate a wide-ranging agreement with ASEAN, while Japan appeared to be concluding more limited agreements and marshalling a wider grouping, the EAS, primarily in order to dilute Chinese influence; this is not a stable situation.

The depth of regional integration will reflect the underlying cause of post-2000 trade agreements. Governments will trade sovereignty in return for facilitating the location of value chain activities in their jurisdiction, but they will not give up sovereignty over areas less critical to that location decision. Thus, the Asian trade agreements are often referred to as free trade or economic partnership agreements, but never as customs unions or common markets, because governments retain control over regulating imports of sensitive items and generally do not want to allow free immigration or to give up the possibility of regulating capital flows or land ownership, and so forth.[9] Governments may unilaterally adopt convertibility on current account and even capital account, but will not give up independent monetary policy — or at least the possibility of making their own choice between a fixed exchange rate and monetary policy independence.[10] East Asian regionalism is unlikely to encompass meaningful monetary integration in the near future.

These are arguments based on economics, and the theme of this book is that economics has been the driving force behind both the absence of regionalism before 2000 and its emergence after 2000. Unwillingness to engage in areas of migration or macroeconomic policy reflects ongoing distrust among national governments. This is not static, and within ASEAN there has been a sea-change in Southeast Asian politics since the association was established in 1967, but the crucial great power relationship between China and Japan remains fragile and its future unpredictable.

---

[9]A customs union involves a common external trade policy, which not only cedes sovereignty over trade policy but will affect fiscal policy too. In the European customs union formed under the 1957 Treaty of Rome, the common external tariff meant that a disproportionate share of tariff revenue would be collected by the Netherlands because many German imports entered the customs union through the port of Rotterdam. This could be dealt with by a formula for revenue redistribution, but that would be subject to endless renegotiation as trade flows changed, or by a common budget into which all tariff revenues would be placed, with spending from that budget agreed upon by the six customs union members. The European customs union members took the second approach, creating a source of revenue for the European Commission to run common polices for agriculture, regional development and whatever else the members as a group decide upon.

[10]Very small countries are an exception, e.g. Brunei is in a currency union with Singapore in which the exchange rate policy is run by Singapore.

Appendix

Measuring Trade Costs and Trade Facilitation

This Appendix discusses the definition and measurement of trade costs and describes properties of the cif-fob measure of trade costs that is referred to at several points in the text.[1]

As traditional trade barriers have fallen, attention has focussed on other costs of international trade. Trade facilitation (TF) was one of the four new issues raised at the WTO Singapore Ministerial meeting in 1996, and is now explicitly included in the Doha Development Round of multilateral trade negotiations.[2] In the 2001 Shanghai Accord, APEC members committed to reduce their trade costs by five percent between 2002 and 2006, and in 2007 they agreed on a further five percent cut between 2007 and 2010 (Chapter 4). The bilateral trade agreements which have proliferated since the turn of the century often contain trade facilitation measures (Chapter 6). National policymakers and international negotiators focus on specific measures that self-evidently reduce trade costs; WTO Articles provide guidelines, and regional groups, such as the EU, ASEAN or APEC, try to coordinate trade facilitation among their members.[3] The characteristic of these approaches is to set rules, proscribe certain procedures, advocate

---

[1] The Appendix is based on a joint research with Patricia Sourdin, and draws heavily on Pomfret and Sourdin (2010). We are grateful to the editors of the *Journal of International Commerce, Economics and Policy* for permission to reproduce material from that article.

[2] Trade facilitation issues are addressed in GATT Articles X (transparency), VIII (fees and formalities) and V (goods in transit), but these are statements of principles rather than binding commitments. At the December 2005 Hong Kong WTO Ministerial meetings, an agreement was reached to move towards text-based negotiations on TF proposals.

[3] In regional trade agreements, trade facilitation has featured most notably in the EU's single market program and establishment of Schengenland.

best practices and so forth. They have been primarily the concern of policymakers, lawyers and officials of multilateral organizations such as the World Customs Organization, rather than being subject to economic analysis and quantification.[4]

Measurement of trade costs is important. Agreements on targets, such as APEC goals of reducing trade costs by five percent, are meaningless without benchmarks. Changing procedures or customs forms may facilitate trade, but we have no idea of the size of their impact or of their relative importance. Trade facilitation is difficult to define because the obstacles to trade are heterogeneous, which makes it hard to measure trade costs and hence difficult to determine the relative significance of different elements of trade facilitation or to test hypotheses about why trade costs vary across countries or across commodities. Empirical work on trade costs by economists came out of studies on the border effect and on the impact of trade cost components on trade flows, which highlighted the size of trade costs and the variation across countries, but direct measurement of trade costs remains in its infancy.

Defining Trade Costs: Theoretical and Historical Perspectives

In multilateral trade negotiations on TF, the focus is on procedures, emphasizing principles of nondiscrimination, transparency, and simplicity in customs or transit procedures. A TF definition frequently used by the OECD and WTO is:

> ... the simplification and harmonization of international trade procedures, including the activities, practices and formalities involved in collecting, presenting, communicating and processing data and other information required for the movement of goods in international trade.[5]

---

[4] Radelet and Sachs (1998) highlighted the role of geography and of shipping costs in explaining cross-country differences in manufactured export expansion and economic growth. Obstfeld and Rogoff (2001) identified trade costs as the key to resolving six major problems in macroeconomic theory. These two contributions were, however, more influential among development and macro economists than among trade economists, who were slow to respond to the challenge of quantifying and explaining trade costs, as a necessary step towards contributing to TF policy debates.

[5] This definition is in the factsheet of the Doha Development Database maintained by the WTO at http://tcbdb.wto.org/. The same definition is used, *inter alia*, in "The Costs and Benefits of Trade Facilitation," *OECD Policy Brief*, October 2005, and by the ASEAN Secretariat.

This definition of the scope of trade facilitation refers to administrative processes at the border which are the focus of trade negotiations in the WTO and in various regional trading arrangements (Dee, Findlay and Pomfret, 2008).

Interest in measuring trade costs was stimulated by Anderson and van Wincoop (2004). Combining direct and indirect measures from a variety of sources, they estimated ad valorem trade costs in high-income countries to be around 170% — a dramatic number when tariffs average under 10%. Anderson and van Wincoop adopted a very broad definition, measuring all the costs from when a good leaves the producer to when it is purchased by the final consumer. In the trade facilitation context, a more appropriate measure would include only the costs of international trade, ignoring transport and retail costs which would be incurred in a domestic transaction.

For economists, TF is about reducing trade costs, and they have generally sought a definition of trade costs that captures the differential costs of international as opposed to domestic trade, excluding trade policy as reflected in legislated tariff rates. The at-the-border focus of the OECD/WTO definition is too narrow insofar as many international trade transactions involve money and time costs before and after the border. A fundamental obstacle to reaching a universally agreed definition of trade costs and TF is that the distinction between the costs of domestic and international trade is not clear-cut in practice. Nevertheless, the fact that such costs exist independent of traditional trade barriers (tariffs and NTBs) or transport costs was highlighted by research on US–Canada bilateral trade in the 1990s that found a large border effect despite contiguity, free trade and cultural similarities (McCallum, 1995; Engel and Rogers, 1996).[6]

Trade costs create a wedge between the price received by the seller and the price paid by the buyer. The bigger the wedge, the larger the foregone gains from trade and the more that actual trade will fall short of the level that would occur with minimal trade costs. The gap between the price paid by the buyer and the price received by the seller means

---

[6]Gorodnichenko and Tesar (2009) cast doubt on the method of Engel and Rogers, but McCallum's results are robust (see Krugman and Obstfeld, 2009, 19–21).

that there are buyers who would have been willing to buy more at a lower price and sellers who would have been willing to supply more at a higher price, but these potentially mutually beneficial trades are excluded by the magnitude of trade costs.[7] The welfare effect of a given shortfall of trade depends upon the elasticities of demand and supply, whose size is largely determined by the extent to which substitutes exist for the goods affected by high trade costs. Evans (2003), applying a gravity model to a cross-section of OECD countries, estimated the causal composition of the border effect to be high elasticity of substitution 20%, trade barriers (as in traditional trade policy analysis) 34%, and transaction costs associated with crossing borders (trade costs) 46%; the last is the biggest source of the border effect. In sum, the border effect exists and there is some evidence that trade costs are a significant cause, but this literature provides no measure of the size of trade costs.

Trade costs also influence the pattern of trade. Markusen and Venables (2007) develop a multicountry-multicommodity trade model in which the degree of specialization in an economy is determined by the interaction of trade costs and comparative advantage based on relative factor endowments. High trade costs inhibit a country from taking advantage of potential gains from specialization and trade in order to promote economic development. When Markusen and Venables allow for multi-stage production, low trade costs permit the fragmentation of the production process which is globally beneficial, although some countries may experience reduced trade and welfare. In this setting, trade expands at both the extensive margin (i.e. more goods are traded) and the intensive margin (i.e. more of each good is traded). In broad terms, this model captures the East Asian regionalization described in Chapter 4.

---

[7]The bigger the wedge between the price received by the foreign supplier and the price paid by the importer, the lower the elasticity of supply; this can explain the "missing trade" found by Trefler (1995) and perhaps explain the border effect. Obstfeld and Rogoff (2001) claimed that introducing trade costs into macroeconomic models would go far toward explaining some of the main puzzles that international macroeconomists had struggled with over the previous quarter century. As well as the home bias in trade puzzle, trade costs can explain the Feldstein-Horioka saving-investment puzzle, the French-Poterba equity home bias puzzle, and the Backus-Kehoe-Kydland consumption correlations puzzle.

A feature of the unprecedented global economic boom since 1945 has been that world trade grew faster than global output.[8] Paul Krugman (1995) pointed out that the question "Why has world trade grown?" remains surprisingly disputed; journalistic discussion tends to view technology-led declines in transportation costs (containerization, jet aircraft, reduced cost of specialized ships, and so forth) as the driving force, while many economists argue that policy-led trade liberalization spurred the growth of world trade.[9] Baier and Bergstrand (2001) try to disentangle the impact of income growth and the effects of transport-cost reductions, tariff liberalization, and income convergence on the growth of world trade among OECD countries between the late 1950s and the late 1980s. Their empirical results suggest that income growth explains about two-thirds, tariff-rate reductions about a quarter, and declining transport-costs about eight percent of the average world trade growth of their sample. In subsequent research, the same authors have found that trade flows have increased after economic integration agreements, and as a result of the EU in particular, to a much greater extent than predicted by estimates of the impact of the tariff cuts using general equilibrium models.[10] This may be interpreted as evidence that the non-tariff aspects of regional integration, including TF measures, are of greater importance than the preferential tariff cuts, but as the authors emphasise this type of empirical decomposition must be treated with caution.

---

[8] Part of this may be a statistical artefact because trade flows are measured by gross values rather than by value-added, as for other GDP components. Fragmentation will increase reported trade flows as components move backwards and forwards across borders, but this may overstate the magnitude of the growth of trade relative to the growth of world GDP. Yi (2008) provides a more sophisticated model of the magnification effect of trade costs and other trade barriers on the level of international trade when multi-stage production is possible.

[9] Economists have also sought historical perspectives on the relative importance of tariff policy, trade costs and other explanations for the pace of globalization in the period 1870–1914. Jacks, Meissner and Novy (2006; 2008; 2009) argue that international trade costs dropped much faster during the first wave of globalisation up to World War I than during the second wave after World War II, and that for the same countries the average level of trade costs increased by 10% in the 20 years after the end of World War I. They measure trade costs by the ratio of domestic to international deliveries.

[10] According to Baier, Bergstrand, Egger and McLaughlin (2008), the EU more than doubled members' trade after 15 years, while membership of EFTA only increased members' trade by 35% over a similar time horizon. Jeffrey Bergstrand (2008) provides a non-technical review of this work.

Whatever the relative contribution of causes of economic growth in the second half of the twentieth century, transport costs did decline. Hummels (2007) reviews the evidence on maritime and air transport costs from a variety of sources. He concludes that ad valorem maritime shipping costs did not change much because technological advances like containerization were offset by cost increases of fuel, labour, etc., while air transport costs fell substantially. This led to continuous shifts in the proportion of freight transported by sea and by air, and an increase in the average speed of delivery.

Partial and Indirect Measures of Trade Costs

The cost of individual components of trade costs, such as customs procedures, or of trading along a particular route can be measured. The Time Release Study methodology developed by the World Customs Organisation (WCO) or the Time/Cost Transport Route methodology of the United Nations Economic and Social Commission for Asia and the Pacific (UNESCAP) are examples.[11] Such microeconomic measures provide valuable information about costs at individual border crossing points or along specific transport corridors, but they cannot be generalised to compare aggregate trade costs across countries. Similarly, measures of trade costs based on shippers' published freights are better described as transport costs, and only partially capture the economically meaningful concept of trade costs.[12] What is needed for policy-relevant economic analysis of trade costs are aggregate measures comparable to average tariffs on manufactured goods or the producer support estimates used in agricultural trade negotiations.

Survey-based methods are often used to compare trade costs or perceived lack of trade facilitation across countries. The *Global*

---

[11] These methodologies are described at http://www.wcoomd.org/home_wco_topics_pfo verviewboxes_tools_and_instruments_pftoolstimerelease.htm and http://www.unescap.org/ TTDW/index.asp?MenuName=RouteStudiesWelcome respectively. See also the UNESCAP-ADB *Trade Facilitation Handbook* (Asian Development Bank, Manila, 2009).

[12] Shipping rates, primarily from Maersk Line, the world's largest container shipping company, have been used by Prabir De to estimate trade costs for Asian countries; see De (2008) and chapters by De in Brooks and Hummels (2009).

Competitiveness Report published annually by the World Economic Forum since 1979 measures the set of institutions, policies, and factors that set the sustainable current and medium-term levels of economic prosperity; the questions include one on the quality of port infrastructure which has frequently been used by TF researchers (see below). Since 2008, the World Economic Forum has published *The Global Enabling Trade Report* in collaboration with international trade experts and leaders from the logistics and transport industry; the Global Enabling Trade Index (GETI) is intended to capture the full range of issues that contribute to impeding trade, ranking nations according to factors that facilitate the free flow of goods across national borders and to destination.[13] Indexes of economic freedom are published by the Fraser Institute and the Heritage Foundation, but they focus more on closeness to laissez faire conditions than on trade costs per se.[14] Since its first publication in 2004, the World Bank's annual *Doing Business* report is often cited.[15] The overall ranking of the Ease of Doing Business is a simple average of the rankings in ten component areas: starting a business, construction permits, employment laws, property registration, obtaining credit, investment protection, taxation, trading across borders, contract enforcement, and closing a business.

The *Doing Business* component most relevant to trade facilitation, the "Trading Across Borders" segment, reports time and cost taken to import and export. It should be noted, however, that the time in days and cost in US dollars (as cited in Table 8.2) does not refer to actual time and cost. The "Trading across Borders" indicator compiles

---

[13]The GETI is available at http://www.weforum.org/en/initiatives/gcp/GlobalEnabling TradeReport/index.htm See also the World Economic Forum *Global Competitiveness Report* available at http://www.weforum.org/en/initiatives/gcp/Global%20Competitiveness% 20Report/index.htm.

[14]Fraser Institute *Economic Freedom of the World*, available at http://www.freetheworld.com/ release.html, Heritage Foundation *Index of Economic Freedom* available at http://www.heritage. org/index/.

[15]Available at http://www.doingbusiness.org/ The reports refer to conditions around June of the previous year. The 2010 survey contains about 8,900 indicators administered to almost 6,700 respondents consisting of local experts in law, business, accounting, as well as private and public officials. The World Bank and its partner institutions consulted about 700–900 respondents for most indicator sets (e.g. 817 for the "Trading across Borders" indicator).

the time and cost necessary for the completion of every procedural requirement for exporting and importing a hypothetical standardized cargo of goods by ocean transport, from the contractual agreement between the two parties to the delivery of goods and payment by letter of credit.[16] Respondents are asked to estimate time and cost based on the standardized transaction not on their actual experience.

Surveys capture practitioners' experience as well as perceptions of non-measurable indicators of trade facilitation such as corruption, management practices or regulatory perceptions, usually with only a short time-lag. On the other hand, survey responses may be subjective and non-representative, especially if a premium is placed on speed of collection and dissemination. At best, the surveys described in the previous paragraphs are proxies for trade costs, usually reported as rankings. They can provide a useful reality check in that any credible measure of trade costs should not be too out of line with practitioners' perceptions, but survey questions do not correspond to appropriate definitions of trade costs and the responses do not provide overall measures of trade costs.

Gravity Studies

The empirical literature on the determination of bilateral trade flows has been overwhelmingly based on the gravity model. The gravity model was used by economic modellers from the 1960s, but largely ignored by trade economists before the 1990s on the grounds that despite its predictive success the model had weak theoretical foundations. The revival of interest was driven by a series of studies which highlighted the impact of borders (McCallum, 1995), trade agreements (Frankel,

---

[16]The benchmark is for export and import by a private domestically-owned business with 60 employees located in the economy's largest business city of a dry-cargo 20-foot container full of goods weighing ten tons, valued at $20,000 and having no special needs (refrigeration, sanitary inspection, hazardous materials, etc.). For exporting goods, procedures range from packing the goods at the factory to their departure from the port of exit. For importing goods, procedures range from the vessel's arrival at the port of entry to the cargo's delivery at the factory warehouse.

1997) and a common currency (Rose, 2000) on bilateral trade flows. These studies had the common form of assuming that the basic gravity model relating bilateral trade to the size of the two economies and the distance between them determines trade flows, while a dummy captures the impact of the variable of interest. Despite the influence of these studies' results, many economists were uneasy about the lack of theoretical foundations for this approach, an issue addressed in Anderson and van Wincoop (2003) for cross-country analyses and by Baldwin and Taglioni (2006) for panel data.

The more recent gravity model literature, following Anderson and van Wincoop (2003), has accepted that bilateral trade flows depend not only on distance and mass but also on country-specific trade resistance terms, e.g. if a country has policies or institutions inimical to trade, its bilateral trade flows will be smaller or if it grants preferential access to goods from one trading partner that could affect trade with all partners. The econometric response has been to use country-fixed effects in cross-sectional models, and Baldwin and Taglioni (2006) castigate failure to do so as the gold medal error in gravity-based studies. Baldwin and Taglioni make the point that, unlike in Newtonian physics where gravitational pull between i and j is determined by mass and distance multiplied by a constant term, g:

$$gravity_{ij} = g \left(\frac{mass_i \cdot mass_j}{distance_{ij}} \right), \qquad (A1)$$

in international trade, the relationship between mass, distance and trade is a 'gravitational un-constant.' The un-constant depends on the degree of trade resistance, which is similar to the border effect:

$$trade_{ij} = TR \left(\frac{GDP_i \cdot GDP_j}{distance_{ij}} \right) \qquad (A2)$$

where TR is a variable which depends upon characteristics of each economy, such as the height of multilateral and preferential trade barriers, and upon shared features such as a common language, contiguity, membership in a free trade area or a common currency.[17] Baldwin and Taglioni (2006) sometimes refer to the 'gravitational un-constant' as trade costs, but it is not a useful, single quantifiable measure of trade costs.

Work in the gravity vein has focused on the paradox that the coefficient on the distance variable has not responded in a predicted manner to improvements in transport technology or to increases in transport costs due to higher fuel costs. Bilateral trade decreases with distance, but the popular belief that this relationship has continuously diminished in recent decades (the Death of Distance hypothesis) does not appear to be supported by the evidence. In a meta-analysis of 103 papers containing 1,467 estimates of distance effects, Disdier and Head (2008) conclude that the estimated negative impact of distance on trade rose around the middle of the twentieth century and has remained persistently high since then. Even more strikingly, Berthelon and Freund (2008) estimated that the elasticity of trade to distance increased by about ten percent between 1985 and 2005, which they ascribed mainly to changes in the commodity composition of trade.

Aside from the debate over the direction of change of the distance coefficient over time, there has been increasing evidence that distance only explains a small part of cross-country variations in trade costs, even allowing for differences in the commodity composition of bilateral trade flows. The literature was stimulated by the finding by Limao and Venables (2001) of a large variation in the cost of shipping a standard container from Baltimore to different countries. Some of the variation is physically determined (by distance and because landlocked countries have higher transport costs), but Limao and Venables argued that much

---

[17] Bergstrand, Eggers and Larch (2007) modify the Anderson and van Wincoop formulation to allow for asymmetric trade resistance terms. Empirical studies may use any or all of importing country-fixed effects, exporting country-fixed effects and, with panel data, time-fixed effects, as well as time-country interaction terms because in a panel framework relative prices are time-varying. In practice, the gravity terms are good at explaining a large proportion of bilateral trade, but gravity models are less convincing at decomposing the unexplained part (the gravitational un-constant); coefficients on dummies are sensitive to the specification, e.g. Stack (2009, 774) using a dummy for EU membership finds that the "dummy coefficient declines in magnitude and becomes insignificant as an increasing degree of heterogeneity is allowed in the model."

more is due to differences in infrastructure, which they measured by an index based on kilometers of road, paved road and railway per square kilometer and telephone main lines per capita. Clark, Dollar and Micco (2004) came up with similar results for the costs of shipping a container from Latin American countries to the USA, and emphasized the importance of port efficiency. Their principal measure of port efficiency is a survey data drawn from the Global Competitiveness Report published by the World Economic Forum.[18]

Many papers have studied the impact of other individual components of trade costs. Nordas, Pinali and Gross (2006) adopted a broader view of infrastructure, although they still found that, of all the indicators of the infrastructure that they used, port efficiency appeared to have the largest impact on trade. They also found sector-specific variations, with timeliness and access to telecommunications relatively more important for export competitiveness in the clothing and automotive sectors respectively. Devlin and Yee (2005) document the wide variation in logistics costs among the Middle Eastern and North African countries and how they can influence shipping costs; inefficient trucking services, for example, lead to longer stand time on the dockside and costly inventory accumulation, as well as reducing export volumes so that there are infrequent shipping services. The World Bank Logistics Performance Index, which was first produced in 2007 and which provides proxy measures for cross-country variations in logistic quality (Arvis *et al.*, 2007), will facilitate future global cross-country studies of the impact of logistics. The Digital Divide between developed and developing countries and the impact of internet adoption on trade appear to have become more pronounced since the mid-1990s; Freund and Weinhold (2004) found that internet use had no impact on world trade in 1995, but after 1997 it had an increasing impact.

---

[18]Wilson, Mann and Otsuki (2003) and Wilmsmeier, Hoffmann and Sanchez (2006) use the same source, and Sanchez *et al.* (2003) use Latin American survey data. One problem with using survey data is the "halo effect." If respondents are generally impressed by the efficiency of Singapore, then they may give high marks to Singapore on every question asked, even if on some specific questions Singaporean efficiency is not at the highest level. Bloningen and Wilson (2008) show that survey data overstate the importance of port efficiency because respondents include other country-fixed effects. However, the usefulness of Bloningen and Wilson's measures of port efficiency is limited because they cover a smaller number of ports and countries.

A number of World Bank studies break down trade costs into various components and estimate their impact on trade with a gravity model. Wilson, Mann and Otsuki (2003) use four broad TF indicators, and find that port efficiency has the largest positive effect on trade flows, regulatory barriers deter trade, and customs environment and e-business usage are statistically significant but less important. Simulating a scenario in which Asia–Pacific countries with below average port efficiency improve to half the APEC average, they estimate that intra-APEC trade would increase by $254 billion a year. In a similar study, Wilson, Mann and Otsuki (2005) estimate that TF could produce a $377 billion increase in global trade in manufactured goods.

This literature has enhanced our understanding of variations in trade costs, which clearly depend upon more than distance and the commodity composition of bilateral trade. However, isolating port efficiency, logistics and so forth only provides a partial explanation, and, because the importance of each measure may vary from country to country, any one of these indicators is a poor guide to overall TF across countries. Many studies suggest that a deep determinant of trade costs is institutional quality (e.g. Anderson and Marcouiller, 2002; Pomfret and Sourdin, 2008), which may be proxied by indicators such as the World Bank's *Cost of Doing Business* surveys, Transparency International's *Corruption Perception Index*, the Heritage Foundation's *Economic Freedom Index*, and so forth. These indicators tend to be correlated and give similar results, but they are, at best, indicators rather than measures of trade costs and can provide no more than an ordinal ranking across countries.

Although the literature described in this and the previous section has been valuable in highlighting the importance of trade costs, it is less useful in providing measures of trade costs. The various gravity model exercises estimate the impact of components of trade costs on trade, rather than measuring the size of trade costs. In the first major attempt to measure trade costs in aggregate, Anderson and van Wincoop (2004) brought together a mixture of direct and indirect evidence to construct estimates of the cost of getting a good from the point of production to a final consumer in another country, but their definition is much broader than the normal emphasis on the difference between the cost of international and domestic trade, and their measure is a hybrid in which some elements are very rough estimates. In a similar vein, Jacks, Meissner and Novy (2009) construct a measure of the multilateral resistance terms, TR in equation (A2), which provides a guide to changes in trade costs over time, but this too is a broad measure of trade costs, which includes domestic trade costs in the importing country.[19] Microeconomic measures such as WCO trade release studies are more precise and firmly based, but focusing on a single element of trade costs (in the WCO case, the costs of clearing customs) they are partial. What is required for more rigorous analysis of the impact of trade costs and to assess policy targets such as the APEC goal of a 5% reduction in trade costs is an accepted aggregate measure of trade costs conceptualized as the difference between the cost of domestic and international transactions.

An Aggregate Measure of Trade Costs: The cif-fob Gap

The difference between the cost of international and domestic trade has an operational counterpart in the gap between the free-on-board (fob) value of a traded good upon arrival at the point of export and the cost-insurance-freight (cif) value of the same good when it enters the importing country. The fob value approximates the cost of the producer delivering a good to a domestic wholesaler, while the cif value is roughly equivalent to the cost of obtaining a domestic good from the factory door or farm gate. The difference between the fob and cif value can be interpreted as the difference between the costs of domestic and international trade.

The cif/fob price gap is an economically meaningful measure of the wedge between the cost of producing and moving a good to the

---

[19]The measure, which compares intra-national trade flows to bilateral trade flows in order to capture the cost of bilateral trade relative to costs of domestic trade, is described more fully in Novy (2008) and Chen and Novy (2009). Novy (2008, 2) says that it "can be interpreted as a 'gravity residual' that compares actual trade flows to those predicted in the absence of all trade frictions." The numbers are large, e.g. Novy (2008) reports trade costs on US–Mexico bilateral trade falling from 96% in 1970 to 33% in 2000 and on US–Canada trade falling from 50% to 25% over the same period. The meaning of 25% in this context is that if a good is worth $10 at the factory gate, and domestic trade costs are 55% (as estimated by Anderson and van Wincoop, 2004), then the price to the consumer after the good crosses the border will be $19.40 (=1.25 × $15.50).

exporter's port and the price paid by the importer upon the good's arrival in the destination country. Some of the cif/fob price gap is exogenously determined by geography and the commodity composition of trade (e.g. low value/weight commodities have higher ad valorem transport costs); but the cif/fob measure captures more than narrowly defined transport costs, because features such as poor port infrastructure or other factors that increase dwell times at the port of exit or entry will widen the cif-fob gap. Moreover, freight rates themselves are not independent of the policy environment, being higher when there is less competition due to cartel agreements among shipping companies or in the absence of inter-governmental open skies agreements.[20] Thus, it is not surprising that there are large variations across countries in the cif-fob gap which are only in part explained by exogenous factors such as geography or commodity characteristics, and that the cif-fob gap can be reduced by TF policies.[21]

Radelet and Sachs (1998) used the cif-fob gap in their pioneering study of the geographical determinants of trade and development.[22] Its use was, however, limited by serious inconsistencies in the trade data collected by exporters and importers. The volume of any import of a good by country i from country j is identical to country j's export of the good to country i, and the cif import value of that trade flow must exceed fob export values because they include

---

[20] Formal cartels (shipping conferences) no longer exist, but uncompetitive practices remain; see the annual UNCTAD Review of Maritime Transport and Hummels, Lugovskyy and Skiba (2009). Competition in air transport services is analysed by Micco and Serebrisky (2006), Geloso Grosso (2008), Piermartini and Rousova (2008) and Geloso Grosso and Shepherd (2009).

[21] Even geography and commodity characteristics may not be completely exogenous. Absence of a natural deep sea harbour in Riau Province of Indonesia was overcome by reducing the cost of using Singapore as the province's harbour, whereas Malaysia has built new ports in neighbouring Johor state; the differing policy responses of Indonesia and Malaysia to a similar geographical challenge affect their trade costs. When producers shift from sea to air transport, this is often followed by innovations to reduce the traded goods' weight, i.e. relevant characteristics of a good in which an exporter has a comparative advantage can be endogenous to the choice of mode of transport.

[22] For a sample of 92 developing countries, Radelet and Sachs (1998) found that an extra 1,000 miles of sea distance tends to increase the cif/fob ratio by about 0.6 percent and that landlocked countries pay about 5.6 percent more for shipping than a coastal economy. Their results indicate that overland transport costs tend to be considerably higher than sea freight costs, so that for a given distance from major markets countries with a higher proportion of transit by land tend to have higher overall shipping costs.

transport, insurance and other costs. However, reported trade flows by importing and exporting countries never match, even among countries with high reporting standards such as the OECD countries, and the sign of the cif-fob gap is often negative.[23] The difference between the mirror statistics can be very large across poorly monitored borders or where incentives to smuggle exist.[24] In aggregate, according to national trade data, the world's countries import more than they export, which is impossible (unless Martians are buying from Earth). Hummels and Lugovskyy (2006) have demonstrated that the discrepancies between matched partner trade statistics (so-called mirror statistics) are so large and inconsistent that they are unusable for the study of trade costs.[25]

Thus, any study of trade costs using the cif-fob gap must be based on data collected at a common source where the volume of each good reported in the cif and fob totals is identical. In recent years, the cif-fob measure of trade costs has seen a revival of popularity as an increasing number of national statistical offices report consistent cif and fob data for their countries' imports. Datasets for Australia, New Zealand, the USA and some Latin American countries are described in Hummels (2007, 152–153).[26] The detailed Australian data have been used by Pomfret and Sourdin (2008; 2009) to analyze the differential speed of TF in East Asian and other trading countries.

Apart from the limited number of countries collecting appropriate data, a limitation of this approach is that it is not well-suited to identifying components of trade costs, which might be desirable for trade negotiations. Moreover, measuring trade costs by the cif-fob gap

---

[23]Stack (2009) found that in her OECD trade data, about half the bilateral flows had reported export values exceeding the corresponding reported import values.

[24]To give one example, China reported exports to the Kyrgyz Republic of $9,213 million in 2008, while the Kyrgyz statistics indicated imports of $728 million from China. In principle, cif import value should exceed fob export values, but China's reported exports were more than twelve times as large as Kyrgyz reported imports (Mogilevsky, 2009, Table 5).

[25]The discord between the ease with which fob and cif values of bilateral trade could be used by researchers who assumed them to be matching and the shortcomings of using mirror statistics led the IMF to discontinue presenting fob and cif data in easily matchable form in the *Direction of Trade Statistics* data series.

[26]A large OECD project assembling these data on maritime trade is described in Korinek and Sourdin (2008).

does not allow a simple concordance between reduced trade costs and trade facilitation insofar as some elements of trade facilitation cannot be measured in ad valorem terms even in principle and are not picked up by the cif-fob gap. A reduction in technical barriers to trade (TBTs), for example, may increase the quantity of trade without affecting the cif-fob gap; the approach in the WTO under the TBT Agreement is on a case-by-case basis to identify harmful TBTs rather than to derive aggregate measures of the size of TBTs.[27] The current approach to TF in WTO negotiations is to reach an agreement on procedures rather than to set quantitative targets.[28]

As with all of the measures discussed in this Appendix, the cif-fob gap captures only the financial side of trade costs, not the time costs of international trade, which are critical for goods such as perishables or fashion items. Although time is not explicitly addressed, it affects the cif-fob gap indirectly and may bias some of the results and interpretations. Some goods are more time-sensitive than others, and the time dimension is closely connected to the choice of mode, especially air versus sea transport, which has implications for estimating trade costs from data disaggregated by commodity and mode. The time premium may not be constant; when demand is volatile, air may be preferred because it permits a faster response to price changes (Hummels and Schaur, 2009). Time may also interact with other variables related to cost, e.g. the time advantage of air is more pronounced over longer distances.[29] In sum, although time is ignored

---

[27] The TBT Agreement is part of the Uruguay Round single undertaking and hence mandatory for WTO members. The approach is to inventory barriers and assess their impact on trade; between 1995 and October 2009 over 10,000 technical barriers to trade were notified to the WTO of which 248 were raised at the TBT Committee as having specific trade concerns, and a single one proceeded to the dispute resolution mechanism (a 2003 Peruvian complaint about the EU description of sardines).

[28] The TF proposals in the Doha Round, as set out by the Negotiating Group on Trade Facilitation in June 2009 (WTO document TN/TF/W/43/Rev.19), include twelve families of measures, most of which are procedural rather than quantifiable (e.g. advance rulings, availability of information, appeal procedures). Helble, Shepherd and Wilson (2009), using various measures of transparency in a gravity model of trade among APEC members, provide evidence of the importance of transparency.

[29] To the extent that transport costs are related to weight rather than value, they are closer to a specific than an ad valorem charge, and hence trade costs are declining with respect to unit

in constructing the trade costs measure, it cannot be ignored in its analysis and interpretation.

Choice of Mode, Time and Competition

The mode of transport is an important decision variable for traders and it is related to trade costs. In his survey article, Hummels (2007) points to the falling air freight costs and more constant sea freight costs in the second half of the twentieth century as drivers of a large shift in mode.[30] The shift to air will occur first for more time-sensitive items and for high value/weight items. The changing mode composition has perverse implications for average trade costs; falling air freight costs could lead to an increase in average trade costs both by air and by sea as the lightest sea freight items become the heaviest air freight items, and measured transport costs increase, although the higher payment is for faster service and quality-adjusted costs have fallen.

In an earlier unpublished but influential paper, Hummels (2001) applied a model of the choice of mode (air versus sea) to disaggregated US trade data to estimate the importance of time as a trade barrier and its impact on bilateral trade. Using variation across exporters and commodities in the relative price/speed trade-off for air and ocean shipping, Hummels (2001) estimates willingness-to-pay for time savings: each day saved in shipping time is worth 0.8 percent of the value of manufactured goods.[31] His estimates of the magnitude of time costs

value. If the charge is by ton-kilometre, then for a given value the preference for air is likely to be increasing with distance.

[30] Between 1965 and 2004, the share of air in the total value of US imports increased from 8% to 32% and in US exports from 12% to 53%. Worldwide average revenue per ton-kilometre air-freighted (in constant 2000 US dollars) fell from $3.87 in 1955 to under $0.30 in 2004; the biggest decline was in 1955–1972, before rising oil prices led to a flattening of the decline during the 1970s, but since the late 1980s air transport costs by this measure more than halved (Hummels, 2007, 133 and 138).

[31] Djankov, Freund and Pham (2010) estimated that a one-day delay reduces trade by one percent and is equivalent to adding 70 kilometres to distance. Evans and Harrigan (2005), Harrigan and Deng (2008), Berthelon and Freund (2008), Egger (2008), Moreira, Volpe and Blyde (2008), and Li and Wilson (2009) contribute to the literature on time and provide references to other work.

indicate that each additional day spent in transport reduces the probability that the US will source imports from a country by one to one and a half percent. He concludes that relative declines over time in air shipping prices have made time-savings less expensive, explaining both aggregate trade growth and compositional effects such as the growth in vertical specialization.

Detailed analyses of the choice of transport mode are rare. Martinez-Zarzoso and Nowak-Lehmann (2007) provide a detailed analysis of maritime and road transport costs for Spanish exports to Poland and to Turkey. For both markets, road and sea are competing modes, but the determinants of transport costs are not the same for the two modes. Efficiency and service quality are crucial determinants of maritime transport costs, while for road transport geographical distance is more important. This last result is, however, likely to be specific to Europe where roads are good and border crossing facilities relatively simple. In other regions, the number of border crossings at which delays or official and unofficial costs may be high is a deterrent to road transport.

The degree of competition also influences trade costs and the choice of mode. Maritime or air transport costs may also be influenced by how many shipping lines or airlines serve the bilateral route and by how much monopoly power they have. Micco and Serebrisky (2006) find that the existence of an Open Skies Agreement reduces air transport costs to the USA by 9% and increases the share of imports arriving by air by 7%; these results hold for US trade with high and upper-middle income countries, but an Open Skies Agreement with a lower-middle or low income partner is not associated with lower costs. In the study of maritime transport costs of South American countries by Clark, Dollar and Micco (2004) the measures of market power are not statistically significant. However, Hummels, Lugovskyy and Skiba (2009) show that one sixth of importer/exporter pairs are served by a single liner service, and over half are served by three or less, and they also present evidence of shipping companies charging higher rates on goods with inelastic demand, which is consistent with the exercise of market power.

An important link between falling trade costs, the increased importance of time and the relevance of competition is the rise of international value chains.[32] Evans and Harrigan (2005) analyse these connections from the perspective of US retailers in the apparel industry. The growth of lean retailing, with just-in-time deliveries, allows retailers to respond faster to changes in demand in a fashion-conscious industry, as well as reducing the need to hold costly inventories. Improved communications, barcodes, electronic data interchange, and modern distribution centres and logistics are all part of the enabling conditions for this development. Evans and Harrigan (2005) also highlight the relationship to distance, as US retailers have shifted to nearby locations (Mexico and the Caribbean, rather than Asia) in their search for more reliable timely delivery. Time-sensitive importers will avoid the possibility of hold-up by monopoly shippers, but competition may be endogenous as larger trade volumes increase competition.

Trade facilitation involves reducing both the financial and the time costs of international trade. With the ever-increasing fragmentation of international production reducing the length and variance of time taken to trade will become increasingly important and a major challenge for researchers in this area. Pioneering estimates, such as by Hummels (2001), estimate that each day saved in shipping time is worth 0.8 percent of the value of manufactured goods or that of Djankov, Freund and Pham (2010) that each additional day that a good is delayed before shipping reduces trade by at least one percent are widely cited, but we have little idea how robust they are. Apart from the inherent difficulties of measuring the cost of time, calculating the trade costs in terms of time is commodity-specific and related to the choice of mode of transport.[33]

Estimates of the cif-fob Gap

With the increased availability of high quality disaggregated trade data which allows the matching of identical import and export quantities

---

[32]This was highlighted by Feenstra (1998) who broke down the costs of designing and assembling a Barbie doll for sale in the USA. Despite textbook examples of trading cloth for food, intermediate goods have accounted for a larger share of merchandise trade than finished goods for many years.
[33]This is not just a matter of some modes of transport being inherently faster than others. For a landlocked country, air-freighting may be desirable because it avoids delays in transit and at a third country's port which are difficult to control; cost of delay, risk of pilfering, propensity for corruption, etc., are all commodity-specific.

and separation by mode of transport, the cif-fob gap has become an increasingly popular measure of trade costs. Usable cif-fob data are now available for the USA, Australia, New Zealand, Brazil, Chile, and other Latin American countries.[34] Much of the empirical work has used the US data, which are available at detailed disaggregation levels (10-digit HS) and for different ports. Analysing the choice of mode is, however, difficult with US data because the alternatives include not just sea and air but also rail or road, perhaps even from a Canadian or Mexican port.[35] Thus, many US studies consider only maritime shipping, although the analysis should address the prior decision about which imports enter the USA by sea rather than by air or by land.

Hummels (2007) highlighted the size of the cif-fob gap, which was 7–11% of import value in New Zealand between 1963 and 1997 and 4–8% in the USA between 1974 and 2004, i.e. much higher than the average ad valorem tariffs by the end of the period covered. The relative constancy of these measures in a period when we might expect transport and other trade costs to have fallen may be in part due to composition bias related to changes in mode of transport as the relative cost of air freight fell. Between 1965 and 2004, the share of air in the total value of US imports increased from 8% to 32% and in US exports from 12% to 53% (Hummels, 2007). At the margin, goods with the highest value to weight ratio shift from sea to air, and the change in composition could lead to average trade costs associated with maritime trade increasing even if costs for every individual shipment have fallen, while average costs associated with airborne trade might also increase because the average weight/value of air freight has risen; average trade costs by both modes of transport might increase and overall average trade costs therefore increase, even though the costs for any shipment by air or by sea have fallen.

The choice of mode is an issue for all countries' trade data, but less so for Australia or New Zealand, where land is not an option.

---

[34]See Hummels (2007) and Pomfret and Sourdin (2010). Based on a large project at the OECD, Korinek and Sourdin (2008) describe the data on maritime trade costs. Studies using Latin American data include Martínez-Zarzosoa and Suárez-Burguet (2005), Wilmsmeier, Hoffmann and Sanchez (2006) and Moreira, Volpe and Blyde (2008).

[35]Hummels (2007) emphasises the difficulty of measuring costs of land transport (the mode used by over a fifth of international trade) and how they interact with costs of sea and air transport, which may be substitutes to varying degrees.

Pomfret and Sourdin (2008; 2009) have analysed the Australian trade statistics, which provide matched cif and fob HS 6-digit data for years since 1990, i.e. a fairly fine aggregation level distinguishing over 5,000 "commodities."[36] Average trade costs, measured by the cif-fob gap, fell substantially from 8.0% in 1990 to 4.9% in 2007. In 2007, they were higher than the average applied tariff. The cif-fob gap varies substantially across trading partners, and, although distance and commodity characteristics are significant determinants of trade costs, a large unexplained variation remains after these have been controlled for. Preliminary results using a measure of corruption (the Transparency International Corruption Perceptions Index) suggest that poor institutions increase trade costs, but that the pattern is commodity-specific and the results are stronger for air transport. This is consistent with the hypothesis that time-sensitive goods are more responsive to high trade costs, and also implies that the choice of mode is endogenous.[37]

Controlling for distance and commodity characteristics and separating by mode of transport, Australian trade costs fell substantially over the period 1990–2007, but not equally for all trading partners. Trade costs of ASEAN countries fell faster than global trade costs in the 1990s, when those countries introduced concerted trade facilitation steps such as standardized customs forms and single windows for border clearance; the pattern within ASEAN was of convergence to the group's best practice, Singapore (Pomfret and Sourdin, 2009).[38]

Pomfret and Sourdin (2010) estimate the cif-fob gap measure of trade costs using customs data from Australia, Brazil, Chile and the USA

---

[36]After deleting parcel post, re-imports, destinations such as Australian forces overseas or ships supplies, and the miscellaneous (HS99) category, the 1990–2007 dataset contained 2,097,969 observations.

[37]Anderson and Marcouiller (2002) argue that corruption adds a security cost to trade costs. The relationship may be more complex if corruption imposes uncertainty and possible delays, so that traders concerned about time select a mode of transport that avoids hold-ups. Nordas *et al.* (2006) find that corruption-associated delays reduce the level of trade in a set of time-sensitive goods. Sequeira and Djankov (2008) report evidence of traders paying a premium to use routes that avoid corruption-ridden ports in southern Africa.

[38]The differential fall in trade costs is not observable after the turn of the century, presumably because many other countries introduced policy changes to reduce trade costs.

Table A1   Average Trade Costs (cif-fob gap), Australian, Brazilian, Chilean and US Imports, 1990–2008.

Year	Chile All	Chile Air	Chile Sea	Brazil All	Brazil Air	Brazil Sea	USA All	USA Air	USA Sea	Australia All	Australia Air	Australia Sea
1990	0.093	0.087	0.096	0.087	0.068	0.100	0.050	0.040	0.053	0.080	0.066	0.086
1991	0.101	0.089	0.107	0.092	0.071	0.105	0.049	0.039	0.052	0.076	0.058	0.084
1992	0.096	0.083	0.101	0.084	0.064	0.097	0.045	0.037	0.048	0.075	0.062	0.080
1993	0.093	0.080	0.096	0.081	0.073	0.089	0.045	0.036	0.049	0.073	0.061	0.077
1994	0.088	0.083	0.091	0.074	0.074	0.079	0.045	0.034	0.049	0.070	0.058	0.075
1995	0.086	0.082	0.089	0.083	0.104	0.082	0.044	0.032	0.050	0.067	0.056	0.072
1996	0.081	0.082	0.082	0.065	0.069	0.066	0.040	0.029	0.045	0.066	0.053	0.071
1997	0.080	0.081	0.081	0.061	0.067	0.063	0.039	0.029	0.045	0.066	0.054	0.071
1998	0.083	0.072	0.084	0.059	0.059	0.062	0.042	0.028	0.049	0.064	0.047	0.072
1999	0.084	0.067	0.084	0.054	0.056	0.055	0.043	0.028	0.052	0.056	0.041	0.063
2000	0.081	0.065	0.083	0.055	0.053	0.057	0.043	0.027	0.053	0.057	0.040	0.064
2001	0.085	0.065	0.085	0.057	0.052	0.059	0.043	0.025	0.052	0.057	0.040	0.064
2002	0.082	0.065	0.080	0.053	0.055	0.052	0.042	0.029	0.049	0.051	0.038	0.056
2003	0.078	0.066	0.074	0.053	0.056	0.051	0.046	0.028	0.055	0.051	0.037	0.057
2004	0.082	0.065	0.084	0.058	0.058	0.057	0.048	0.029	0.056	0.055	0.040	0.062
2005	0.075	0.064	0.075	0.055	0.054	0.055	0.046	0.028	0.054	0.055	0.039	0.061
2006	0.071	0.063	0.068	0.049	0.055	0.047	0.043	0.026	0.049	0.051	0.037	0.057
2007	0.073	0.066	0.072	0.050	0.059	0.048	0.040	0.026	0.046	0.049	0.036	0.054
2008	0.078	0.087	0.076	0.053	0.065	0.051	0.038	0.026	0.043	0.049	0.036	0.053

Notes: Ad valorem trade costs $= \Sigma cif/\Sigma fob - 1$; the means are import-weighted, and hence biased downwards because goods or trading partners with higher trade costs will be under-represented.

for 1990 to 2008.[39] They present the raw measures for each country, both in aggregate (Table A1) and broken down by trading partner (Table A2). The first indicates the level of trade costs in each of the four importing countries, while the second provides a comparative picture of trade costs associated with exports from all countries in the world. They then report estimates of trade costs which abstract from the impact of exporter and commodity characteristics (Table A3).

---

[39]The Brazilian and Chilean data were obtained from ALADI (Asociación Latinoamericana de Integración/Associação Latino-Americana de Integração), at a cost of USD 1,710 for both countries for the period 1990–2007. The US data were obtained from the US Census Bureau at a cost of USD 150 per year. The Australian data are available from the Australian Bureau of Statistics; we are grateful to the University of Adelaide for paying for the 1990–2007 data (AUD 4,135) and subscribing to annual updates (AUD 1,175 per annum). New Zealand data are freely available online from Statistics New Zealand, but do not distinguish by mode, and are not reported here.

Table A2   Average Trade Costs by Country 2008.

(a) Number of observations

Ad valorem trade costs	Australia	Brazil	Chile	USA
Less than 2 percent	11	20	4	23
2–3.9	28	41	5	60
4–5.9	78	48	27	66
6–7.9	25	36	36	41
8–9.9	22	20	22	15
10–11.9	15	5	14	2
12–13.9	10	6	6	3
14–15.9	2	1	4	2
16–17.9	3	7	2	0
18–19.9	3	3	5	3
20.0 percent or more	7	19	29	10
Total	204	206	154	225

(b) Selected trading partners

Argentina	0.120	16	0.045	6	0.096	13	0.062	15
Australia	x		0.179	16	0.116	14	0.037	8
Brazil	0.098	15	x		0.072	7	0.058	13
Canada	0.083	14	0.097	15	0.086	10	0.022	4
Chile	0.048	5	0.036	2	x		0.098	16
China	0.058	11	0.085	14	0.091	11	0.056	12
France	0.034	2	0.041	5	0.055	2	0.022	4
Germany	0.040	4	0.036	2	0.056	3	0.023	6
Indonesia	0.053	9	0.071	13	0.242	16	0.058	13
Italy	0.051	6	0.047	7	0.063	6	0.039	10
Japan	0.053	8	0.052	9	0.094	12	0.030	7
Korea	0.052	7	0.062	11	0.081	9	0.037	8
Mexico	0.061	12	0.049	8	0.051	1	0.018	1
Russia	0.066	13	0.063	12	0.157	15	0.043	11
Singapore	0.037	3	0.034	1	0.056	3	0.019	2
UK	0.026	1	0.038	4	0.058	5	0.020	3
USA	0.056	10	0.054	10	0.074	8	x	15

Notes: The second column under each country ranks the 16 trading partners' trade costs.

Table A1 presents the raw cif-fob measures of trade costs. In all four countries, trade costs declined substantially between 1990 and 2008, although the pattern varies (Figure A1). The USA starts with the lowest trade costs, 5.0% in 1990, and they decline to 3.8% in 2008. Australia and Brazil have the largest declines in trade costs, and the magnitudes are very similar; from 8.0% to 4.9% for Australia and from 8.7% to 5.3% for Brazil. Chile starts with the highest trade costs, 9.3%, and they fall

Table A3   Ad valorem Trade Costs, Adjusted for Exporter-commodity Effects, 1990–2008.

year	Chile sea	Chile air	Brazil sea	Brazil air	USA sea	USA air	Australia sea	Australia air
1990	0.092	0.172	0.038	0.153	0.054	0.078	0.076	0.159
1991	0.094	0.169	0.078	0.139	0.052	0.078	0.073	0.157
1992	0.091	0.162	0.083	0.159	0.050	0.078	0.069	0.152
1993	0.089	0.163	0.083	0.159	0.051	0.077	0.068	0.144
1994	0.085	0.167	0.075	0.155	0.051	0.076	0.066	0.139
1995	0.079	0.165	0.070	0.151	0.049	0.076	0.063	0.135
1996	0.072	0.159	0.067	0.156	0.046	0.070	0.062	0.131
1997	0.067	0.161	0.062	0.148	0.044	0.068	0.062	0.135
1998	0.067	0.165	0.061	0.149	0.044	0.068	0.060	0.131
1999	0.061	0.166	0.057	0.147	0.046	0.065	0.054	0.105
2000	0.065	0.164	0.048	0.143	0.048	0.065	0.053	0.108
2001	0.069	0.159	0.051	0.145	0.046	0.064	0.051	0.112
2002	0.064	0.157	0.052	0.145	0.045	0.067	0.046	0.113
2003	0.057	0.152	0.045	0.146	0.047	0.070	0.045	0.113
2004	0.058	0.147	0.040	0.150	0.047	0.069	0.049	0.114
2005	0.059	0.145	0.042	0.152	0.046	0.068	0.051	0.113
2006	0.055	0.147	0.043	0.149	0.044	0.066	0.047	0.105
2007	0.054	0.147	0.038	0.145	0.041	0.072	0.044	0.103
2008	0.055	0.185	0.036	0.146	0.039	0.074	0.044	0.106

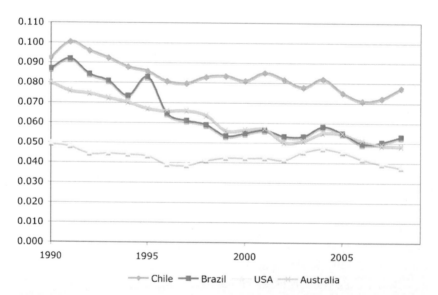

Fig. A1   Average Trade Costs (cif-fob gap), Australian, Brazilian, Chilean and US Imports, 1990–2008.

to 7.8%. Disaggregating by the two main reported modes of transport, the decline in trade costs in the USA and Australia was led by falling trade costs associated with airborne trade, while in Brazil and Chile the trade costs associated with air hardly changed and the aggregate decline in trade costs was due to lower costs associated with maritime trade.

The numbers in Table A1 present a plausible picture of the trade costs associated with the four countries' imports over the period studied, and permit interesting comparisons. Some caveats are, however, in order. Although the definitions of cif and fob are universal, measurement by the national customs services may not be uniform in detail. The coverage of the four datasets differs insofar as land transport is not included in the US numbers and there may be differences in coverage of parcel post or of some destinations (e.g. military or diplomatic missions overseas or international organisations). The presumption is that these variations are small, given that the vast majority of observations are imports from commonly recognised trading partners arriving by sea or air.

The data from each importing country can be used to measure trade costs for all other countries of the world. For each of the four datasets, the importing country's contribution to trade costs and the measurement practices of the importing country are constant, so measures of the trade costs of each trading partner do not encounter the possible biases described in the previous paragraph. Table A2 summarizes the trade costs associated with exporting in 2008.

Table A2(a) highlights the cross-country variation in trade costs. The range of trade costs is large, although the extreme observations tend to be countries with small trade flows where misreporting of individual transactions may be a problem.[40] The size of trade costs does not depend simply on geographical variables such as distance or landlockedness.[41] Pomfret and Sourdin (2008) show that distance and

---

[40]To address the small-trading-nation problem, Table A2(b) identifies some of the largest trading nations for analysis, while in Table A3 the unit of observation is the commodity so small trading nations with few commodity exports are appropriately underweighted.

[41]In both the US and Chilean data, double-landlocked Uzbekistan has the lowest trade costs, while in the Chilean data the highest trade costs, 258%, are associated with Uzbekistan's neighbour the Kyrgyz Republic.

commodity characteristics explain part, but far from all, of the variation in trade costs in the Australian data.[42]

The rankings of high and low trade cost countries are similar in each dataset. Table A2(b) reports the cif-fob gaps associated with imports from the four data-source countries and 13 other countries (other G8 countries, two large Latin American and four large Asian trading nations) in 2008. As shown in Table A1, the trade costs are generally lower on exports to the USA and higher on exports to Chile. There are some obvious differences in the rankings associated with geography, e.g. Canadian and Mexican exports to the USA have lower trade costs than Canadian and Mexican exports to the South American countries or Australia. Some other anomalies are likely associated with differing commodity composition, e.g. the difference between trade costs associated with Chilean exports to the USA and to Australia or Brazil. Nevertheless, there are consistent patterns: Singapore and the UK are among the partners with the lowest trade costs using any of the four countries' data, and Russia, China and Indonesia are among those with the highest. The rankings from the four countries' import data are positively correlated, and the rank correlation is strong.[43] The conclusion is that any of the four countries' import data provide a reasonably consistent measure of their trading partners' trade costs, although there is need to be careful in allowing for specifics of geography such as contiguity or of commodity composition.

Trade costs vary for different bilateral trade flows. The above measures indicate substantial differences across the four importing countries

---

[42] Using the 2007 Australian data, the simple correlation between ad valorem trade costs and distance is -0.001. The negative sign disappears with other specifications, e.g. if a simple regression is run in logarithms or with a squared distance term, but the coefficient is always less than 0.1. For the 556,468 observations identified by consistent measures of weight (i.e. metric tons, kilograms, grams or metric carats), the correlation between weight and costs is 0.0013. In sum, ad valorem trade costs are positively related to distance and to weight, but in the Australian data both are weak correlations.

[43] The Spearman rank correlations for the 13 non-data countries (with t-statistics in parentheses) are Australia–Brazil 0.66 (2.94), Australia–Chile 0.57 (2.32), Australia–USA 0.47 (2.20), Brazil–Chile 0.62 (2.61), Brazil–USA 0.44 (1.63), and Chile–USA 0.83 (4.89). All are statistically significant at the 5% level except for Brazil–USA, which is significant at the 10% level. Note that although the choice of countries to include in these calculations was subjective, it includes relatively efficient traders; most sub-Saharan countries, for example, have high trade costs with all four countries.

in aggregate and by mode and over time, as well as large variations in the trade costs of exporting countries across the world. Some of the variance is due to geographical factors (distance, landlockedness, ice-free natural harbours, etc.) and some follows from a country's comparative advantage (e.g. the ad valorem trade costs associated with Chilean exports of copper will be higher than trade costs for Brazilian exports of swimsuits).

To abstract from geography and commodity characteristics, Pomfret and Sourdin (2010) use a fixed effects model to analyse trade costs using disaggregated import data from Australia, Brazil, Chile and the USA for 1990 to 2008. The dependent variable is $(\text{cif}_{i,j,k} - \text{fob}_{i,j,k})/\text{fob}_{i,j,k}$ for imports by country i of a commodity k (i.e. goods in a HS 6-digit category) from a trading partner j. Since each dataset identifies about 200 trading partners, with over 5,000 commodities and 19 years, there could be 20 million observations. The actual sample sizes are as follows:

- Australia 2,222,614 observations, of which sea 1,161,364 and air 1,061,250;
- Brazil 1,527,272 observations, of which sea 719,943, air 682,820, road 98,238, post 22,968, train 1,767, fixed installation 70, river 1,433 and lake 33;
- Chile 1,384,431 observations, of which sea 615,973, air 572,475, road 193,877, post 1,399, train 533, fixed installation 81, river 54 and lake 39;
- USA 2,997,418 observations, of which sea 1,476,011 and air 1,521,407.

Thus, the number of commodity-country observations varies from 1.4 to 3.0 million.[44]

---

[44]There are many empty cells. In the Australian dataset, for example, one small Pacific island only trades four out of the over 5,000 possible commodities. The number of observations for each of the four countries is more similar than the value of trade; in 2008, merchandise imports into the USA were $2,170 billion (13.2% of the world total), compared to $200 billion (1.2%) into Australia, $182 billion (1.1%) into Brazil and 62 billion (0.4%) into Chile. Larger aggregate trade is likely to reduce the incidence of observations based on a small number of transactions, and hence the influence of an individual misreported transaction.

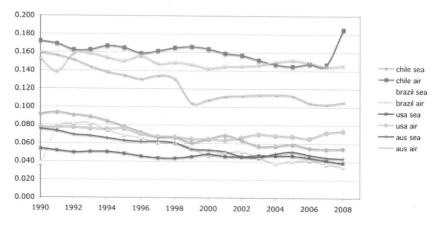

Fig. A2   Adjusted ad valorem Trade Costs, various modes, Australian, Brazilian, Chilean and US Imports, 1990–2008.

The results of the regressions with exporting country and commodity fixed effects are reported in Table A3. The main difference between Tables A1 and A3 is that, once allowance is made for exporter-commodity fixed effects, trade costs are higher by air than by sea (Figure A2). Goods with high value to bulk are shipped by air and the raw ad valorem trade costs are lower for these goods because their value is high. However, once allowance is made for commodity characteristics, air freight is more costly than maritime freight. It costs more to ship a ton of merchandise by air than by sea, but relative to the value of the goods the costs of air-freighting a ton of diamonds is much lower than the cost of shipping a ton of coal by sea.

The ranking of the four countries' trade costs by both the unadjusted ad valorem rates in Table A1 and the adjusted measures in Table A3 is similar. Chile has the highest trade costs by sea or air, and the USA generally has the lowest trade costs. The exception is the striking drop in Brazil's adjusted maritime trade costs between 2002 and 2008, when they fell below those of both Australia and the USA. In general, trade costs associated with maritime trade are more similar across the four countries than trade costs associated with air transport. Anecdotal evidence suggests that reducing trade costs associated with air freight has much to do with associated services and logistics, which can be rapidly upgraded, as perhaps reflected in the Australian data of the 1990s.

Conclusions

The border effect is real, and international trade involves larger costs than domestic trade. Trade costs depend on many things of which, apart from distance-related transport costs, port efficiency and regulatory burdens appear to be most important. However, the evidence on such decompositions is not conclusive. Deriving conclusions from gravity models depends upon whether the heterogeneous determinants of the gravity un-constant have been properly specified prior to measuring the treatment effect. Microeconomic or synthetic measures of trade costs suggest that they are high, e.g. compared to the level of tariffs in high income countries, but such measures are difficult to produce on a consistent aggregate basis that can be compared across countries.

The best aggregate measure of trade costs is the cif-fob gap. The data needed to construct cif-fob measures are only available for imports into a small number of countries, and the existing literature draws primarily on US or Australian data.[45] The US data are the most detailed and cover the largest value of imports, but are compromised by the prevalence of overland transport and its implication for the choice of mode of transport. The evidence from the Australian data is that trade costs vary substantially across countries, depending in part on distance from trading partners and on the commodity composition of their trade. However, even after controlling for distance and commodity composition, large cross-country variations remain, some of which are policy-determined and are amenable to reduction by trade facilitation measures. The best quantitative evidence of successful trade facilitation is from the ASEAN countries in the 1990s (Figure 4.1).

---

[45] In the previous section of this Appendix, we report on data from the USA, Australia, Brazil and Chile to assess the extent to which cif-fob gap measure of trade costs are idiosyncratic with respect to the reporting (importing) country. Although there are differences related to contiguity or differing import bundles, the overall patterns appear to be similar. The conclusion is that findings about trade costs based on US or Australian cif-fob data are likely to be reasonably robust.

References

ADB (2008). *Emerging Asian Regionalism: A Partnership for Shared Prosperity*. (Asian Development Bank, Manila).

Afrasiabi, K (2000). Three part series on ECO: (1) The Economic Cooperation Organization aims to Bolster Regional Trade Opportunities, 14th September 2000, (2) ECO Strives to Improve Transportation and Communication Networks, 1st November 2000, (3) Economic Cooperation Organization Presses Energy Initiative, 5th December 2000 — posted at http://www.eurasianet.org

Aggarwal, V and C Morrison (eds.) (1998). *Asia–Pacific Crossroads: Regime Creation and the Future of APEC*. New York: St. Martin's Press.

Amiti, M and J Romalis (2006). Will the Doha Round lead to Preference Erosion? *IMF Working Paper 06/10*, January.

Anderson, J and D Marcouiller (2002). Insecurity and the pattern of trade: An empirical investigation. *Review of Economics and Statistics*, 84, 342–352.

Anderson, J and E van Wincoop (2003). Gravity with gravitas: A solution to the border puzzle. *American Economic Review* 93(1), 170–192.

Anderson, J and E van Wincoop (2004). Trade costs. *Journal of Economic Literature* 42, 691–751.

Anderson, K and R Pomfret (2002). Relative living standards in new market economies: Evidence from central Asian household surveys. *Journal of Comparative Economics* 30(4), 683–708.

Ando, M (2010). Impacts of Japanese FTAs/EPAs: Preliminary Post Evaluation. In *Free Trade Agreements in the Asia Pacific*. C Findlay and S Urata (eds.), pp. 259–299. Singapore: World Scientific Publishing Co.

Ando, M, A Estevadeordal and CV Martincus (2009). Complements or Substitutes? Preferential and Multilateral Trade Liberalization at the Sectoral Level, paper prepared for an Asian Development Bank Project on "Quantifying the Costs and Benefits of Regional Economic Integration in Asia," March.

Ando, M and F Kimura (2005). The Formation of International Production and Distribution Networks in East Asia. In *International Trade in East Asia*. T Ito and A Rose (eds.), pp. 177–213. Chicago, IL: University of Chicago Press.

APEC Policy Support Unit (2009). *Trade Creation in the APEC Region: Measurement of the Magnitude of and Changes in Intra-regional Trade since APEC's Inception*, unpublished report, APEC Policy Support Unit, Singapore.

Ariff, M and G Tan (1992). ASEAN–Pacific trade relations. *ASEAN Economic Bulletin* 8, 258–283.

Arndt, S and H Kierzkowski (eds.) (2001). *Fragmentation: New Production Patterns in the World Economy*. Oxford, UK: Oxford University Press.

Arvis, J-F, MA Mustra, J Panzer, L Ojala and T Naula (2007). *Connecting to Compete: Trade Logistics in the Global Economy* — short version with the same title is in Robert Lawrence, Jennifer Blanke, Sean Doherty and Margareta Drzeniak Hanouz (eds.). *The Global Enabling Trade Report 2008* (World Economic Forum, 2008), 53–65.

Athukorala, P-C (2006). International labour migration in East Asia: Trends, patterns and policy issues. *Asian–Pacific Economic Literature* 20(1), 18–39.

Athukorala, P-C (2009). The rise of China and East Asian export performance: Is the crowding-out fear warranted? *The World Economy*, 32, 234–266.

Athukorala, P-C and J Menon (1996). Foreign Direct Investment in ASEAN: Can AFTA make a difference? In *AFTA in the Changing International Economy*, J Tan (ed.). Singapore: Institute for Southeast Asian Studies.

Baier, S and J Bergstrand (2001). The growth of world trade: Tariffs, transport costs, and income similarity. *Journal of International Economics* 53(1), 1–27.

Baier, S, J Bergstrand, P Egger and P McLaughlin (2008). Do economic integration agreements actually work? Issues in understanding the causes and consequences of the growth of regionalism. *The World Economy* 31(4), 461–497.

Balassa, B (1961). *The Theory of Economic Integration*. Homewood, IL: Richard D. Irwin.

Baldwin, R (2006). Managing the Noodle Bowl: The fragility of East Asian regionalism, *CEPR Discussion Paper No. 5561* (Centre for Economic Policy Research, London).

Baldwin, R and D Taglioni (2006). Gravity for Dummies and Dummies for Gravity Equations. *NBER Working Paper No. 12,516*, September.

Bergsten, CF (2009). APEC 20-20-20-2.0, Keynote Address to the 2009 APEC Study Centres Consortium Conference on *APEC at 20: Looking ahead to the next decade*, Singapore, 13–14 July.

Bergstrand, J (2008). How much has European Economic Integration actually increased Members' Trade? Posted on EUVox, 6 September — available at http://www.voxeu.org/index.php?q=node/1623.

Bergstrand, J, P Eggers and M Larch (2007). Gravity *Redux*: Structural estimation of gravity equations with asymmetric bilateral trade costs. Unpublished MS.

Berthelon, M and C Freund (2008). On the conservation of distance in international trade. *Journal of International Economics* 75, 310–20.

Bhagwati, J (2008). *Termites in the Trading System: How Preferential Agreements Undermine Free Trade*. Oxford, UK: Oxford University Press.

Bird, G and R Rajan (2002). The Evolving Asian Financial Architecture, *Essays in International Economics No. 226* (International Economics Section, Princeton University NJ), February.

Bloningen, B and W Wilson (2008). Port efficiency and trade flows. *Review of International Economics* 16(1), 21–36.

Borrus, M, D Ernst and S Haggard (eds.) (2000). *International Production Networks in Asia: Rivalry Or Riches*. London: Routledge.

Bowles, P (2002). Asia's post-crisis regionalism: Bringing the state back in, keeping the (United) States out. *Review of International Political Economy* 9(2), 230–256.

Brooks, D and D Hummels (eds.) (2009). *Infrastructure's Role in Lowering Asia's Trade Costs: Building for Trade*. Cheltenham, UK: Edward Elgar.

Cavoli, T (2007). Capital mobility, sterilization and interest rate determination in east Asia. *Journal of Economic Integration* 22(1), 210–230.

Cavoli, T and R Rajan (2009). *Exchange Rate Regimes and Macroeconomic Management in Asia*. Hong Kong: Hong Kong University Press.

Chen, N and D Novy (2009). International Trade Integration: A disaggregated approach, *CESifo Working Paper No. 2595*.

Clark, X, D Dollar and A Micco (2004). Port efficiency, maritime transport costs, and bilateral trade. *Journal of Development Economics* 75, 417–450.

Corbett, J and E Fitriani (2008). Australian Perspectives on the Road Map towards East Asian Economic Integration, *APEC Economies newsletter* 12(5), June (available at http://www.crawford.anu.edu.au).

Corden, WM (2007). The Asian crisis: A perspective after ten years. *Asian–Pacific Economic Literature* 21(2), 1–12.

De, P (2008). Empirical Estimates of Trade Costs for Asia. In *Infrastructure and Trade in Asia* D Brooks and J Menon (eds.), pp. 71–112. Cheltenham, UK: Edward Elgar.

Dean, J and M Lovely (2008). Trade Growth, Production Fragmentation, and China's Environment, *NBER Working Paper 13,860*.

Dee, P (2007). East Asian economic integration and its impact on future growth. *The World Economy* 30(3), 405–423.

Dee, P, C Findlay and R Pomfret (2008). Trade Facilitation: What, why, how, where and when? In *Infrastructure and Trade in Asia*. DH Brooks and J Menon (eds.), 28–53. Cheltenham, UK: Edward Elgar.

Dent, C (2008). *East Asian Regionalism*. London: Routledge.

DeRosa, D and J Gilbert (2005). Predicting Trade Expansion under FTAs and Multilateral Agreements, *Working Paper 5–13*, Peterson Institute for International Economics, Washington DC.

Devlin, J and P Yee (2005). Trade logistics in developing countries: The case of the Middle East and North Africa. *The World Economy* 28(3), 435–456.

Dieter, H (ed.) (2007). *The Evolution of Regionalism in Asia: Economic and Security Issues*. London: Routledge.

Dieter, H and R Higgott (2003). Exploring alternative theories of economic regionalism: From trade to finance in Asian co-operation? *Review of International Political Economy* 10(3), 430–454.

Disdier, A-C and K Head (2008). The puzzling persistence of the distance effect on bilateral trade. *Review of Economics and Statistics* 90(1), 37–48.

Djankov, S, C Freund and C Pham (2010). Trading on time. *Review of Economics and Statistics* 92, 166–173.

Drysdale, P (2009). Japan in the Spotlight in the Lead-up to APEC, *East Asia Forum*, posted 11 October — available at http://www.eastasiaforum.org/2009/10/11/japan-in-the-spotlight-in-the-lead-up-to-apec/.

Drysdale, P, A Elek and H Soesastro (1998). Open Regionalism: The nature of Asia Pacific integration. In *Europe, East Asia and APEC: A shared global agenda?* P Drysdale and D Vines (eds.). Cambridge University Press.

Egger, P (2008). On the role of distance for bilateral trade. *The World Economy* 31, 653–662.

Eichengreen, B (2004). Real and Pseudo Preconditions for an Asian Monetary Union, paper presented at the Asian Development Bank High-Level Conference on Asia's Economic Cooperation and Integration, Manila, 1–2 July.

Engel, C and J Rogers (1996). How wide is the border? *American Economic Review* 86, 1112–1125.

Estevadeordal, A and K Suominen (2008). Sequencing regional trade integration and cooperation agreements. *The World Economy* 31(1), 112–140.

Evans, C (2003). The economic significance of national border effects. *American Economic Review* 93, 1291–1312.

Evans, C and J Harrigan (2005). Distance, time and specialisation: Lean retailing in general equilibrium. *American Economic Review* 95, 292–313.

Evenett, S (ed.) (2009). *The Unrelenting Pressure of Protectionism: The 3rd GTA Report — A Focus on the Asia–Pacific Region* (Centre for Economic Policy Research: London UK).

Feenstra, R (1998). Integration of trade and disintegration of production in the global economy. *Journal of Economic Perspectives* 12(4), 31–50.

Feenstra, R and A Taylor (2008). *International Economics*. New York: Worth.

Feridhanusetyawan, T (2005). Preferential Trade Agreements in the Asia–Pacific Region, *IMF Working Paper 05/149*.

Flood, R and A Rose (2005). Financial integration: A new methodology and an Illustration. *Journal of the European Economic Association* 3(6), 1349–1359.

Francois, J, B Hoekman and M Manchin (2005). Preference Erosion and Multilateral Trade Liberalization. *World Bank Policy Research Working Paper WPS3730*, September.

Francois, J and G Wignaraja (2008). Economic implications of Asian integration. *Global Economy Journal* 8(3), 1–46.

Frankel, J (1997). *Regional Trading Blocs in the World Economic System* (Institute for International Economics, Washington DC).

Frankel, J and M Kahler (1993). *Regionalism and Rivalry: Japan and the United States in Pacific Asia*. Chicago: University of Chicago Press.

Freund, C and D Weinhold (2004). On the effect of the internet on international trade. *Journal of International Economics* 62, 171–189.

Fröbel, F, J Heinrichs and O Kreye (1980). *The New International Division of Labour*. Cambridge, UK: Cambridge University Press.

Fujita, M and N Hamaguchi (2008). Regional Integration in East Asia: Perspectives of spatial and neoclassical economics. In *Economic Integration in East Asia: Perspectives from Spatial and Neoclassical Economics*. M Fujta, S Kumagai and K Nishikimi (eds.), pp. 13–42. Cheltenham, UK: Edward Elgar.

Garnaut, R (2000). APEC Ideas and Reality: history and prospects. In *Asia Pacific Economic Cooperation (APEC): Challenges and tasks for the twenty-first century*. I Yamazawa (ed.), pp. 1–18. London: Routledge.

Gaulier, G, F Lemoine and D Ünal-Kesenci (2006). China's Emergence and the Reorganisation of Trade Flows in Asia, *CEPII Working Paper No. 2006–05*, Centre d'Etudes Prospectives et d'Informations Internationales, Paris — revised version published in *China Economic Review* 18, 2007, 209–243.

Geloso Grosso, M (2008). Liberalizing Air Cargo Services in APEC, *GEM (Groupe d'Economie Mondiale) Working Paper* — available at http://gem.sciences-po.fr/content/publications/pdf/GelosoGrosso_Air%20cargo_122008.pdf.

Geloso Grosso, M and B Shepherd (2009). Liberalizing Air Cargo Services in APEC, *GEM (Groupe d'Economie Mondiale) Working Paper* — available at http://www.gem.sciences-po.fr/content/publications/pdf/GelosoGrosso_Shepherd_Liberalising_aircargo_services_in%20APEC102009.pdf.

Ghosh, S and S Yamarik (2004). Are regional trading arrangements trade creating? An application of extreme bounds analysis. *Journal of International Economics* 63(2), 369–395.

Gokan, T (2008). Location Choices of Japanese MNEs in East Asia. In *Economic Integration in East Asia: Perspectives from Spatial and Neoclassical Economics.* M Fujita, S Kumagai and K Nishikimi (eds.), pp. 249–275. Cheltenham, UK: Edward Elgar.

Gorodnichenko, Y and L Tesar (2009). Border effect or country effect? Seattle may not be so far from Vancouver after all. *American Economic Journal: Macroeconomics* 1, 219–241.

Goto, J and K Hamada (1994). Economic Preconditions for Asian Regional Integration. In *Macroeconomic Linkage: Savings, Exchange Rates, and Capital Flows.* T Ito and A Krueger (eds.), pp. 359–385. Chicago, IL: University of Chicago Press.

Grimes, W (2009). *Currency and Contest in East Asia: The Great Power Politics of Financial Regionalism.* Ithaca, NY: Cornell University Press.

Gruenwald, P and M Hori (2008). Intraregional Trade Key to Asia's Export Boom, *IMF Survey*, March, 45 — summary of chapter 4 of International Monetary Fund, *Asia and Pacific Regional Outlook*, October 2007.

Haddad, M (2007). Trade integration in East Asia: The role of China and production networks, *World Bank Policy Research Working Paper 4160*, Washington, DC.

Hamanaka, S (2009). Re-considering Asian Financial Regionalism in the 1990s. *ADB Working Paper Series on Regional Economic Cooperation No. 26* (Asian Development Bank, Manila) http://www.aric.adb.org/res.php?sec=Papers.

Harrigan, J and H Deng (2008). China's Local Comparative Advantage. *National Bureau of Economic Research Working Paper 13, 963*.

Harris, R and P Robertson (2009). Dynamic gains and market access insurance: Another look at the Australia–US free trade agreement. *Australian Economic Review* 42(4), 435–452.

Hatch, W and K Yamamura (1996). *Asia in Japan's Embrace: Building a Regional Production Alliance.* Cambridge, UK: Cambridge University Press.

Hedi Bchir, M and M Fouquin (2006). Economic Integration in Asia: Bilateral Free Trade Agreements versus Asian Single Market, *CEPII Working Papers No. 2006-15*, Paris, October.

Helble, M, B Shepherd and J Wilson (2009). Transparency and regional integration in the Asia Pacific. *The World Economy*, 32(3), 479–508.

Henderson, J, P Dicken, M Hess, N Coe and H Wai-Chung Yeung (2002). Global production networks and the analysis of economic development. *Review of International Political Economy* 9(3), 436–464.

Henning, CR (2002). East Asian Financial Cooperation, *IIE Policy Analyses in International Economics 68*, Institute for International Economics, Washington DC, October.

Hertel, T, T Walmsley and K Itakura (2001). Dynamic effects of the "new age" free trade agreement between Japan and Singapore. *Journal of Economic Integration* 16(4), 446–484.

Hew, D (ed.) (2007). *Brick by Brick: The Building of an ASEAN Economic Community.* Singapore: Institute of Southeast Asian Studies.

Heydon, K and S Woolcock (2009). *The Rise of Bilateralism: Comparing American, European and Asian Approaches to Preferential Trade Agreements.* Tokyo: United Nations University Press.

Hiratsuka, D (ed.) (2007). *East Asia's de facto Economic Integration.* Basingstoke, UK: Palgrave Macmillan.

Huang, Y (2010). Fixing China's Current Account Surplus. *East Asian Bureau of Economic Research (EABER) Newsletter*, January.

Hugo, G (2005). *Migration in the Asia–Pacific.* Global Commission on International Labour Migration: Geneva.

Hummels, D (2001). Time as a Trade Barrier. *GTAP Working Paper No. 1152*, Center for Global Trade Analysis, Purdue University — available at: https://www.gtap.agecon.purdue.edu/resources/res_display.asp?RecordID=1152.

Hummels, D (2007). Transportation costs and international trade in the second era of globalization. *Journal of Economic Perspectives* 21(3), 131–154.

Hummels, D and V Lugovskyy (2006). Are matched partner trade statistics a usable measure of transport costs? *Review of International Economics* 14(1), 69–86.

Hummels, D, V Lugovskyy and A Skiba (2009). The trade reducing effects of market power in international shipping. *Journal of Development Economics*, 89, 84–97.

Hummels, D and G Schaur (2009). Hedging Price Volatility using Fast Transport. *National Bureau of Economic Research Working Paper*, 15, 154.

Imada, P (1993). Production and trade effects of the ASEAN free trade area. *The Developing Economies* 31, 3–23.

Jacks, D, C Meissner and D Novy (2006). Trade Costs in the First Wave of Globalization, *NBER Working Paper 12,602* (National Bureau of Economic Research, Cambridge MA).

Jacks, D, C Meissner and D Novy (2008). Trade Costs, 1870–2000. *American Economic Review, 98(2), Papers & Proceedings*, 529–534.

Jacks, D, C Meissner and D Novy (2009). Trade Booms, Trade Busts, and Trade Costs. *National Bureau of Economic Research Working Paper 15267.*

Jayasuriya, K (2009a). Regulatory regionalism in the Asia–Pacific: Drivers, instruments and actors. *Australian Journal of International Affairs* 63(3), 335–347.

Jayasuriya, K (2009b). The emergence of regulatory regionalism. *Global Asia* 4(4), 102–107.

Jones, D (2006). ASEAN and transboundary haze pollution in Southeast Asia. *Asia–Europe Journal* 4(3), 431–446.

Kawai, M and G Wignaraja (2007). ASEAN+3 or ASEAN+6: Which Way Forward? *ADB Institute Discussion Paper No. 77*, September.

Kawai, M and G Wignaraja (2009). The Asian "Noodle Bowl": Is it serious for business? *ADB Institute Working Paper No. 136*, April-shorter version available online at EUVox as "Tangled up in Trade? The "Noodle Bowl" of Free Trade Agreements in East Asia" — posted at http://www.voxeu.org/index.php?q=node/3979 on 15 September 2009.

Kim, HY (2008). Location Choices of Korean MNEs in East Asia: Escaping the nutcracker. In *Economic Integration in East Asia: Perspectives from Spatial and Neoclassical Economics*. M Fujita, S Kumagai and K Nishikimi (eds.), pp. 203–248. Cheltenham, UK: Edward Elgar.

Kim, S and J-W Lee (2008). Real and Financial Integration in East Asia, *ADB Working Paper Series on Regional Economic Cooperation No. 17* (Asian Development Bank, Manila) http://www.aric.adb.org/res.php?sec=Papers.

Kimura, F, Y Takahashi and K Hayakawa (2007). Fragmentation and parts and components trade: Comparison between East Asia and Europe. *North American Journal of Economics and Finance* 18(1), 23–40.

Kirkman, K (1989). Graduation in the generalized system of preferences: The projected impact on remaining beneficiaries in the United States scheme. *World Development* 17(10), 1597–1600.

Korinek, J and P Sourdin (2008). Maritime Transport Costs and Trade: New data and new evidence, paper presented at the International Economic Association Congress, Istanbul — circulated as OECD working paper TAD/TC/WP(2009)7.

Krugman, P (1995). Growing world trade: Causes and consequences. *Brookings Papers on Economic Activity* (1), 327–377.

Krugman, P and M Obstfeld (2009). *International Economics: Theory and Policy*, 8th ed. Boston, MA: Pearson Addison Wesley.

Kwei, E (2006). Chinese Trade Bilateralism: Politics still in command. In *Bilateral Trade Agreements in the Asia-Pacific: Origins, evolution, and implications*, V Aggarwal and S Urata (eds.), pp. 117–139. Routledge.

Lawrence, R (1996). *Regionalism, Multilateralism and Deeper Integration*: Washington, DC: The Brookings Institution.

Lee, H-H, CM Koo and E Park (2008). Are exports of China, Japan and Korea diverted in the major regional trade blocs; Why and whither? *The World Economy*, 31, 841–860.

Lee, J-W (2008). Patterns and Determinants of Cross-Border Financial Asset Holdings in East Asia, *ADB Working Paper Series on Regional Economic Integration 13* (Asian Development Bank: Manila).

Lee, J-W, I Park and K Shin (2008). Proliferating regional trade arrangements; Why and whither? *The World Economy*, 31, 1525–1557.

Li, Y and J Wilson (2009). Time as a determinant of comparative advantage, *World Bank Policy Research Working Paper No. 5128*.

Lim, CY (2009). *Southeast Asia: The long road ahead*. 3rd. ed. Singapore: World Scientific.

Limao, N and A Venables (2001). Infrastructure, geographical disadvantage and transport costs. *World Bank Economic Review* 15, 451–479.

Lincoln, E (2004). *East Asian Economic Regionalism*. Washington, DC: Brookings Institution Press.

Linden, G, K Kraemer and J Dedrick (2007). Who captures value in a global innovation system? The case of Apple's ipod, Personal Computing Industry Center Working Paper, University of California, Irvine.

Linn, J (2004). *Economic (Dis)Integration Matters: The Soviet Collapse Revisited*, unpublished paper (Brookings Institution, Washington DC).

Linn, J (2008). Regional Cooperation in Central Asia: Another Step Forward with CAREC, unpublished paper (Brookings Institution, Washington DC) — available at http://www.brookings.edu/opinions/2008/1210_carec_linn.aspx.

Lorenz, D (1991). Regionalization versus regionalism: Problems of change in the world economy. *Intereconomics* 26, 3–10.

Madhur, S (2002). Costs and Benefits of a Common Currency for ASEAN, *ERD Working Paper No. 12*, Asian Development Bank, Manila, May.

Manchin, M and A Pelkmans-Balaoing (2008). Clothes without an emperor: Analysis of the preferential tariffs in ASEAN. *Journal of Asian Economics* 19, 213–223.

Manning, C (2002). Structural change, economic crisis and international labour migration. *The World Economy* 25(3), 359–385.

Manupipatpong, W (2002). The ASEAN Surveillance Process and the East Asian Monetary Fund. *ASEAN Economic Bulletin* 19(1), April, 111–122.

Markusen, J and A Venables (2007). Interacting factor endowments and trade costs: A multi-country, multi-good approach to trade theory. *Journal of International Economics* 73, 333–354.

Martinez-Zarzoso, I and F Nowak-Lehmann (2007). Is distance a good proxy for transport costs? The case of competing transport modes. *Journal of International Trade and Economic Development* 16(3), 411–434.

Martínez-Zarzosoa, I and C Suárez-Burguet (2005). Transport costs and trade: Empirical evidence for Latin American imports from the European Union. *Journal of International Trade and Economic Development* 14, 353–371.

Mathews, J and D-S Cho (2000). *Tiger Technology: The Creation of a Semiconductor Industry in East Asia*. Cambridge, UK: Cambridge University Press.

McCallum, J (1995). National borders matter: Canada–US regional trade patterns. *American Economic Review* 85, 615–623.

McKinnon, R (2004). The East Asian dollar standard. *China Economic Review* 15, 325–330.

McKinnon, R and G Schnabl (2003). Synchronized Business Cycles in East Asia: Fluctuations in the Yen/Dollar Exchange Rate and China's Stabilizing Role. *The World Economy*, 1067–88 — also published as a chapter in Ronald McKinnon, *Exchange Rates under the East Asian Dollar Standard: Living with conflicted virtue* (MIT Press, Cambridge MA).

McLean, I (1995). Trans-Tasman Trade Relations: Decline and rise. In *Australia's Trade Policies*. R Pomfret, pp. 171–189. Melbourne: Oxford University Press.

Medeiros, E and MT Fravel (2003). China's new diplomacy. *Foreign Affairs* 82(6), 22–35.

Menon, J (1996). The dynamics of intra-industry trade in ASEAN. *Asian Economic Journal* 10(1), 105–115.

Menon, J (2007). Bilateral trade agreements. *Asian-Pacific Economic Literature* 21(2), 29–47.

Micco, A and T Serebrisky (2006). Competition regimes and air transport costs: The effects of open skies agreements. *Journal of International Economics* 70, 25–51.

Mikic, M (2009). Crisis-Era State Measures and Asia-Pacific Economies. In *The Unrelenting Pressure of Protectionism: The 3rd. GTA Report — A Focus on the Asia-Pacific*

Region. S Evenett (ed.), pp. 33–47. London, UK: Centre for Economic Policy Research.

Mogilevsky, R (2009). Trends in Foreign Trade of CAREC Countries, unpublished paper prepared at the CAREC Institute, Almaty.

Moreira, MM, C Volpe and J Blyde (2008). *Unclogging the Arteries: The Impact of Transport Costs on Latin American and Caribbean Trade*. Washington DC: Inter-American Development Bank.

Munakata, N (2006). *Transforming East Asia: The Evolution of Regional Economic Integration*. Tokyo: Research Institute of Economy, Trade and Industry and Washington DC: Brookings Institution Press.

Murase, T (2002). *A Zone of Asian Monetary Stability*. Canberra, Australia: Asia Pacific Press.

Naiki, Y (2009). TBT Provisions in Japan's RTAs: Some prospects for greater convergence of TBT policies, paper presented at a OECD Workshop and Policy Dialogue on Technical Barriers to Trade, Paris, 5–6 October.

Nambiar, S (2010). India and ASEAN: An FTA and Beyond, posted in the *East Asia Forum* at http://www.eastasiaforum.org/2010/01/21/india-and-asean-an-fta-and-beyond/.

Naya, S (2004). Japan in emerging east Asian regionalism. *East Asian Economic Perspectives* 15(2), 1–16.

Nezu, R (2009). Comprehensive Economic Partnership in East Asia, *Fujitsu Research Institute Column.* http://jp.fujitsu.com/group/fri/en/column/message/2009/2009-9-9.html.

Ng, F and A Yeats (2003). Major Trade Trends in East Asia: What are their implications for regional cooperation and growth? *World Bank Policy Research Working Paper 3084*, June.

Nicolas, F (2009). The changing economic relations between China and Korea: Patterns, trends and policy implications. *The Journal of the Korean Economy* 10(3), 341–365.

Nordas, HK, E Pinali and M Geloso Gross (2006). Logistics and Time as a Trade Barrier, *OECD Trade Policy Working Paper No. 35*, Organization for Economic Cooperation and Development, Paris.

Novy, D (2008). Gravity Redux: Measuring trade costs with panel data. *Warwick Economic Research Papers No. 861*, University of Warwick UK.

Obstfeld, M and K Rogoff (2001). The Six Major Puzzles in International Macroeconomics: Is there a common cause? In *NBER Macroeconomics Annual 2000*. B Bernanke and K Rogoff (eds.), pp. 339–390. Cambridge, MA: MIT Press.

Ochiai, R, P Dee and C Findlay (2010). Services in Free Trade Agreements. In *Free Trade Agreements in the Asia Pacific*. C Findlay and S Urata (eds.), pp. 29–80. Singapore: World Scientific Publishing.

Ogawa, E (2001). A regional monetary fund and the IMF. *The Journal of the Korean Economy* 2(2), 229–248.

Oh, J and C Harvie (2001). Exchange rate coordination in East Asia. *The Journal of the Korean Economy* 2(2), 249–296.

Pacific Economic Cooperation Council (2005). *The Evolution of PECC: The First 25 Years*. Singapore: Pacific Economic Cooperation Council.

Parsley, D and S-J Wei (2001). Explaining the Border Effect: The role of exchange rate variability, shipping costs, and geography. *Journal of International Economics* 55, 87–105.

Perroni, C and J Whalley (2000). The New Regionalism: Trade liberalization or insurance? *Canadian Journal of Economics* 33(1), 1–24.

Petri, P (1993). The East Asian Trading Bloc: An Analytical History. In *Regionalism and Rivalry*. J Frankel and M Kahler (eds.), pp. 21–52. Chicago: University of Chicago Press.

Petri, P (2006). Is East Asia becoming more interdependent? *Journal of Asian Economics* 17(3), 381–394.

Piermartini, R and L Rousova (2008). Liberalisation of Air Transport Services and Passenger Traffic, *World Trade Organization Staff Working Paper ERSD-2008-06* — http://www.wto.org/english/res_e/reser_e/ersd200806_e.pdf.

Plummer, M (2007). Best practices in regional trading agreements: An application to Asia. *The World Economy* 30(12), 1771–1796.

Plummer, M (2009). *ASEAN Economic Integration: Trade, Foreign Direct Investment, and Finance*. Singapore: World Scientific.

Plummer, M and CS Yue (2009). *Realizing the ASEAN Economic Community: A comprehensive assessment*. Singapore: Institute of Southeast Asian Studies.

Pomfret, R (1991). *Investing in China 1979–89; Ten Years of the Open Door Policy*. Hemel Hempstead, UK: Harvester Wheatsheaf and Ames: Iowa State University Press.

Pomfret, R (1994). The localisation of economic growth in East Asia. *Australian Economic Review*, 107, 20–28.

Pomfret, R (1995a). Strategic Trade and Industrial Policy as an Approach to Locational Competitiveness: What Lessons from Asia? In *Locational Competition in the World Economy*. H Siebert (ed.), pp. 205–226. Tübingen, Germany: JCB Mohr.

Pomfret, R (1995b). Regional economic co-operation in Northeast Asia: The Tumen river project. *Pacific Economic Papers* 249, 6.1–6.22.

Pomfret, R (1995c). *The Economies of Central Asia*. Princeton, NJ: Princeton University Press.

Pomfret, R (1996a). Sub-Regional Economic Zones. In *Regional Integration and the Asia Pacific*. B Bora and C Findlay (eds.), pp. 207–222. Melbourne: Oxford University Press.

Pomfret, R (1996b). *Asian Economies in Transition: Reforming Centrally Planned Economies*. Cheltenham, UK: Edward Elgar.

Pomfret, R (1997/1998). The Tumen river area development programme. *Boundary and Security Bulletin* 5(4), 80–88.

Pomfret, R (1999). *Central Asia Turns South? Trade Relations in Transition*. London: The Royal Institute of International Affairs and Washington DC: The Brookings Institution.

Pomfret, R (2001). *The Economics of Regional Trading Arrangements*. Oxford, UK: Oxford University Press.

Pomfret, R (2003). Currency unions in East Asia: Lessons from Europe. *Asia-Pacific Journal of Economics and Business* 7(1), 4–17.

Pomfret, R (2005). Sequencing trade and monetary integration: Issues and application to Asia. *Journal of Asian Economics* 16(1), 105–124.

Pomfret, R (2006). *The Central Asian Economies since Independence.* Princeton, NJ: Princeton University Press.

Pomfret, R (2007). Is regionalism an increasing feature of the world economy? *The World Economy* 30(6), 923–947.

Pomfret, R (2008). *Lecture Notes on International Trade Theory and Policy.* Singapore: World Scientific Publishing Company.

Pomfret, R (2009). Regionalism in the Asia-Pacific region: How wide, how deep? *Journal of the Korean Economy* 10(3), 1–22.

Pomfret, R (2010): Regional Value Chains and Asian Regionalism. In *Light the Lamp: Papers on World Trade and Investment in Memory of Bijit Bora.* C Findlay, M Pangestu and D Parsons (eds.), Singapore: World Scientific.

Pomfret, R, U Kaufmann and C Findlay (2010). Are Preferential Tariffs Utilized? Evidence from Australian Imports, 2000–2009, *University of Adelaide School of Economics Working Paper.*

Pomfret, R and P Sourdin (2008). Why Do Trade Costs Vary? *University of Adelaide School of Economics Working Paper 2008–08.*

Pomfret, R and P Sourdin (2009). Have Asian trade agreements reduced trade costs? *Journal of Asian Economics* 20(3), 255–256.

Pomfret, R and P Sourdin (2010). Trade Facilitation and the Measurement of Trade Costs. *Journal of International Commerce, Economics and Policy (JICEP).*

Porter, M (1985). *Competitive Advantage: Creating and Sustaining Superior Performance.* London: Macmillan.

Porter, M (1990). *The Competitive Advantage of Nations.* London: Macmillan.

Pula, G and T Peltonen (2009). Has Emerging Asia Decoupled? An analysis of production and trade linkages using the Asian International Input-Output Table, *ECB Working Paper 993* (European Central Bank, Frankfurt).

Radelet, S and J Sachs (1998). Shipping Costs, Manufactured Exports, and Economic Growth, paper presented at the American Economics Association annual meeting, available at http://www.earthinstitute.columbia.edu/about/director/pubs/shipcost.pdf.

Rajan, R (ed.) (2006). Asian regionalism: A symposium. *The North American Journal of Economics and Finance* 17, 231–302.

Rajan, R, R Sen and RY Siregar (2001). *Singapore and Free Trade Agreements: Economic Relations with Japan and the United State.* Singapore: ISEAS Publications.

Ratna, RS (2008). APTA Market Access: Results from the Third Round, paper presented at the APTA seminar organized by ESCAP in Bishkek, 5 November.

Rose, A (2000). One money, one market: Estimating the effects of common currencies on trade. *Economic Policy* 30, 9–48.

Sanchez, R, J Hoffmann, A Micco, G Pizzolitto, M Sgut and G Wilmsmeier (2003). Port efficiency and international trade: Port efficiency as a determinant of maritime transport costs. *Maritime Economics and Logistics* 5, 199–218.

Scollay, R (1996). Australia–New Zealand Closer Economic Relations Agreement. In *Regional Integration and the Asia Pacific.* B Bora and C Findlay (eds.), pp. 184–196. Melbourne: Oxford University Press.

Sen, R (2004). *Free Trade Agreements in Southeast Asia*. Singapore: Institute of Southeast Asian Studies.

Sequeira, S and S Djankov (2008). On the Waterfront: An empirical study of corruption in ports — http://www.doingbusiness.org/documents/Corruption_in_Ports.pdf.

Severino, R (2009). Regional Institutions in Southeast Asia: The First Movers and their Challenges, paper prepared for the Asian Development Bank project *Institutions for Regionalism: Enhancing Economic Cooperation and Integration in Asia and the Pacific*, presented at a workshop in Jakarta on 9–10 June 2009.

Shepherd, B and J Wilson (2008). Trade Facilitation in Southeast Asia: Measuring progress and assessing priorities, *World Bank Policy Research Working Paper No. 4615* — published in *Journal of Asian Economics* 20(4), September 2009, 367–383.

Shi, X and R Grafton (2010). Efficiency impacts of the Chinese industrial transition: a quantitative evaluation of reforms in the coal industry. *Economic Change and Restructuring* 43(1), 1–19.

Sohn, BH (2002). Regionalization of trade and investment in East Asia and prospects for further regional integration. *Journal of the Asia Pacific Economy* 7(2), 160–181.

Stack, M (2009). Regional integration and trade: Controlling for varying degrees of heterogeneity in the gravity model. *The World Economy* 32, 772–789.

Sturgeon, T (2001). How do we define value chains and production networks? *IDS Bulletin* 32(3), 9–18.

Takahashi, K and S Urata (2010). On the Use of Free Trade Agreements by Japanese Firms. In *Free Trade Agreements in the Asia Pacific*. C Findlay and S Urata (eds.), pp. 241–257. Singapore: World Scientific Publishing Co.

Trefler, D (1995). The case of the missing trade and other mysteries. *American Economic Review* 85(6), 1029–1046.

Tumbarello, P (2007). Are Regional Trade Agreements in Asia Stumbling or Building Blocks? Some implications for the Mekong-3 countries, *IMF Working Paper 07/53*.

UNESCAP-ADB (2009). *Trade Facilitation Handbook* (Asian Development Bank, Manila).

Urata, S and M Okabe (2010). The Impacts of Free Trade Agreements on Trade Flows: An application of the gravity model approach. In *Free Trade Agreements in the Asia Pacific*. C Findlay and S Urata (eds.), pp. 195–239. Singapore: World Scientific Publishing Co.

Urata, S and J Sasuya (2010). Analysis of the Restrictions on Foreign Direct Investment in Free Trade Agreements. In *Free Trade Agreements in the Asia Pacific*. C Findlay and S Urata (eds.), pp. 81–130. Singapore: World Scientific Publishing Co.

Vogel, E (1989). *One Step Ahead in China: Guangdong Under Reform*. Cambridge, MA: Harvard University Press.

Wang, Z and S-J Wei (2008). What accounts for the Rising Sophistication of China's Exports? *NBER Working Paper 13,771* (National Bureau of Economic Research: Cambridge MA).

Wang, Y (2004). Financial cooperation and integration in East Asia. *Journal of Asian Economics* 15, 939–955.

Whalley, J (2008). Recent regional arrangements: Why so many, Why so much variance in form, Why coming so fast, and Where are they headed? *The World Economy* 31, 517–532.

Wilmsmeier, G, J Hoffmann and R Sanchez (2006). The Impact of Port Characteristics on International Maritime Transport Costs. In *Port Economics: Research in Transportation Economics*, Vol. 16. K Cullinane and W Talley (eds.), pp. 117–140. Oxford: JAI Press/Elsevier.

Wilson, J, C Mann and T Otsuki (2003). Trade facilitation and economic development: A new approach to quantifying the impact. *World Bank Economic Review* 17, 367–389.

Wilson, J, C Mann and T Otsuki (2005). Assessing the potential benefit of trade facilitation: A global perspective. *The World Economy* 28(6), 841–871.

World Bank (1993). *The East Asian Miracle: Economic growth and public policy.* Washington DC: World Bank.

World Bank (2009). Bazaars and Trade Integration in CAREC Countries, report posted by the CAREC Institute at http://www.carecinstitute.org/uploads/events/2009/10th-TPCC/10thTPCC-Bazaars-Trade-Integration-Paper.pdf.

Xing, Y (2007). Foreign direct investment and China's bilateral intra-industry trade with Japan and the US. *Journal of Asian Economics* 18(4), 685–700.

Yi, K-M (2008). Can Multi-stage Production explain the Home Bias in Trade? *Working Paper 08–12/R*, Research Department, Federal Reserve Bank of Philadelphia.

Zhang, J, A van Witteloostuijn and C Zhou (2005). Chinese bilateral intra-industry trade: A panel data study for 50 countries in the 1992–2001 Period. *Review of World Economics (Weltwirtschaftliches Archiv)* 141(3), 510–540.

Index